John Milne
Born 1850

'No man ever reveals his true self to others: only by his conduct and public utterances can he be understood in part. Careful assessment of both must be made before a judgement of his character is attempted since friends tell of his charity and his enemies seek to destroy by distortion of fact.'

JOHN MILNE

The words and works of John Milne are referred to extensively in this book, and the reader is invited to make a personal decision as to the value of this man's life.

Endpapers: Hakodate in the 1870s

JOHN MILNE
FATHER OF MODERN SEISMOLOGY

JOHN MILNE:
FATHER OF
MODERN SEISMOLOGY

A.L. HERBERT-GUSTAR
&
P.A. NOTT

 Paul Norbury Publications Limited
Tenterden, Kent.

JOHN MILNE: FATHER OF MODERN SEISMOLOGY

PAUL NORBURY PUBLICATIONS LTD.
Caxton House, High Street, Tenterden, Kent, England.

First published 1980

© A.L. Herbert-Gustar & P.A. Nott 1980

ISBN 0 904 404 34 X

The Publishers are indebted to the Japan Foundation, Tokyo, for their generous support in the making of this book.

This book has been set in 10 on 11 point Bembo

Printed by Bookmag of Inverness and bound by James Joyce & Duffin Ltd. of Edinburgh

For Peggy & Hilary

Contents

List of Illustrations

★Courtesy Science Museum, London

Between pages 104 and 105

A superb collection of over 400 slides taken by Milne, mostly in Japan and a great number hand-coloured, has miraculously survived the years. A small selection has been made to highlight Life in Meiji Japan (Ch. 6)

Detailed notes on these pictures can be found on page 197ff.

Acknowledgements

The authors wish to express their sincere thanks to the great number of organisations and individuals — far too numerous to mention each by name — from many countries who have helped in the preparation of this biography by providing information and the loan of material, giving permission to quote from copyright works, and for all the encouragement and constructive criticism received.

Nevertheless, the cooperation of the Japanese Embassy, London, and the Japan Foundation; University of Tokyo; Hokkaido authorities and Milne's nephew — Professor Shindo Akashi — has been particularly appreciated. In Britain the support given by the Royal Society; the British Association; the Science Museum, London; the International Seismological Centre; professional institutions, and the national, university and local library services has been invaluable. Colleagues at the Isle of Wight College of Arts and Technology have offered much support and tolerance during the lengthy project. Friends and associates of Milne here and abroad have also helped to ensure the reliability of this biography through their anecdotes and memories.

Where photographs have been loaned their source is stated. When reference to Milne's published work has been made the title of the book or paper together with its publisher is given in the text.

For both his advice and for writing the Foreword the authors are especially grateful to Dr John Wartnaby, a well-known authority on the history of seismology and author of several earlier works on Milne (see bibliography). His book, *John Milne — Seismologist Extraordinary*, now in preparation will deal comprehensively with Milne's contribution to seismology.

Introduction

The name of John Milne first came to my notice when, as a young man recently appointed to the curatorial staff of the Science Museum, I received from the British Association a letter generously offering to the Museum the original Milne-Shaw seismograph and the Milne Library. This dates back to 1952; both items were, of course, accepted gratefully and added to our Geophysics Collection. This Collection includes more historically important seismological material than any other museum in the world. As far as the work of John Milne is concerned, we have examples of the early Gray-Milne seismograph, the Milne horizontal instrument, the first type capable of recording earthquakes occurring in any part of the world, one of his twin-boom instruments, the lamp post seismograph from his Shide observatory as well as his small portable seismometer and an example of the Milne-MacDonald vibration recorder. Obviously John Milne had been a prolific worker and had left his mark in no uncertain manner on the new science of seismology which had forged ahead so strongly in the latter half of the nineteenth century. Who then was this man whose impact on the science had been so great?

This was for me the beginning of some fascinating historical research made as time allowed in the busy and absorbing life of a curator in a great national museum. The Milne Library was a useful though by no means adequate source for this research. It was, after all, only the remnants of Milne's books and papers which had survived the disastrous fire at his home in Japan plus works added later by Professor Turner, Miss Bellamy and their successors working on behalf of the British Association. Biographical details of Milne seemed adequate at the time — the present work demonstrates that, in fact, we were acquainted only with the tip of an iceberg. Almost all his scientific papers, both as regards seismology and his many earlier interests, were readily available but they formed an unclassified, often unrelated and indigestible mass of formidable proportions. The task of sorting this into some sort of meaningful system and assessing the importance and historical significance of these papers seemed at first to be overwhelming. Some 20 years later, with two higher degrees as incidental rewards, not only was this job complete but the much larger mass of all the remaining nineteenth-century work contributed by other investigators had also been researched. This allowed Milne's own contributions to be placed in their proper historical perspective.

It was in 1973 that I first had the pleasure of meeting Leslie

Herbert-Gustar and Patrick Nott. It was their intention at the time to make detailed studies of the lives of prominent scientists and technologists who had been in some way associated with the Isle of Wight. They elected to start with John Milne and subsequently found his life to be of such absorbing interest that they have proceeded no further with their original project. The work assembled here is a fitting monument to their enthusiasm, diligence and patient research into every aspect of John Milne's life. The biographical details available when they started would scarcely have filled half a dozen pages in this format so the extent of their achievement will be immediately apparent to the reader.

The authors have provided us with a sensitive and sympathetic biography which includes an imaginative approach to the backcloth of life in Victorian England and the conditions prevailing in the formative Meiji period marking the very beginnings of Japan's industrial might of today. I found the first and eighth chapters especially informative because of the wealth of new material which the authors have uncovered and recorded there. Appendix I reveals a facet of Milne's activities of which I knew very little. But those coming to the adventurous life of John Milne for the first time will surely be gripped by the work in its entirety. For me, the authors have provided the flesh and blood to complement completely my earlier work on his scientific achievements and have thereby brought to fruition a rounded and well-integrated picture of the Father of Modern Seismology. I trust that you, the reader, will as a result come to share my admiration for this fascinating Victorian pioneer.

JOHN WARTNABY
Science Museum, London

Dr John Wartnaby is Keeper of the Department of Earth and Space Sciences.

Preface

Earthquakes are something that many have never experienced, yet there are few who do not find them strangely fascinating to contemplate. The movement of the earth's crust, the tremendous energy involved, the devastation which can be caused, the insignificance of man against this power of nature — all stimulate this interest, this desire to know more about the forces of nature under our feet. *John Milne: Father of Modern Seismology* is the story of the man who put the study of earthquakes on a firm scientific foundation and did much to lessen the loss of life and destruction caused by these erratic movements.

But Milne was more than just a cold scientist. He was a man bounding with energy and contagious enthusiasm and above all he loved adventure. As a schoolboy in the mid-1860s he took a holiday on his own in Ireland without parental consent. After studying geology and mining in England and on the continent of Europe, he made important expeditions to Iceland and Newfoundland, and also went to the Middle East in search of the 'true' position of Mount Sinai.

Later, when appointed Professor of Mining and Geology at the Imperial College of Engineering in Tokyo, he went overland to Japan, crossing Europe, Siberia, Mongolia and China during winter, travelling by camel, sleigh and tarantass, on foot and in river boats, a journey of extreme hardship and danger which few westerners had dared attempt at that time. On his first night in Japan he experienced an earthquake and from then on decided to study this alarming phenomenon in depth. It was soon to become his life's work and one which helped to satisfy his adventurous spirit.

This book, the first full biography of this remarkable man, is not just a summary of his scientific achievements as these are well documented elsewhere in his writings. It is a story which reveals much of his personal character and the immense drive and dedication by which he overcame almost insurmountable obstacles in his pursuit of knowledge. No experience in the field of seismology is required by the reader to follow the quotations taken from Milne's own works.

Milne possessed an exceptional personality and a lively wit. Travelling to nearly every corner of the world he became friend of princes and poor alike. He fell in love with and married Toné, a beautiful Japanese girl. Before they left Japan to live in England, the Professor's important work in the country led to an audience with the Emperor Meiji who decorated him with the Order of the Rising

Sun, a high distinction rarely awarded to a foreigner.

Milne published millions of words on earthquakes and also stories which we would now call science fiction. Under a pen name, 'Mark Kershaw', he wrote *Colonial Facts and Fictions*, an amusing travelogue which sold well at the beginning of the twentieth century.

John Milne was one of the last great Victorian pioneers and the purpose of this biography is to present a picture of the interesting life of this forgotten man who the authors believe, should be accorded his rightful place in the history of science.

1

Early Days

A cold wind, increasing in strength as dusk approached, came
sweeping down from the Pennines to scourge a Lancastrian
countryside already in the grip of winter. Hard-driven before its
onslaught, massive dark clouds, heavy with the threat of snow,
struggled ineffectively to release their precipitous burden. On the
lowlands the already fading light drew out reluctant stockmen to
tend the famished cattle which, huddled together for warmth in
whatever shelter could be found from the icy blast, were mournfully
bellowing their discontent.

Hastening onwards, the now near-gale fell at last upon the port of
Liverpool standing squarely in its path, dislodging loose slates from
roofs and inciting the street-litter into a crazy, gyrating dance. Its
chill fingers penetrated the clothing of those few pedestrians
scurrying about their business in the city who bemoaned the need
which compelled them to be out in such foul weather. In the dock
area, massive work-horses struggled desperately to keep their
footing on the icy cobblestones, scarcely heeding the curses of the
waggoners as they hauled their heavy loads to and from the gloomy
warehouses crowded along the Merseyside wharves. Shrieking
through the taut rigging of ships berthed alongside or at anchor in
the estuary, the wind whipped up the sullen river before howling on
over the Wirral peninsula and out into the storm-tossed sea beyond.
Although it was only 30 December 1850, in the crowded, noisy
ale-houses of the dingy streets by the river, sailors and landsmen
were already toasting a hoped-for prosperity in the coming year.

But a short distance away from these riverside activities, in a
warm, cosily-furnished bedroom of a quiet house in the Mount
Vernon, Edge Hill district of Liverpool, the turmoil outside went
unheeded. Here a proud father gazed fondly upon his young wife as
she nursed their sturdy son, born that day. A sudden flurry of hail
against the windows whose heavy curtains had been drawn to keep
out draughts could not distract the man as he gently took the
sleeping child to place it in a cot beside the bed. Although necessity
had demanded that he should make a business trip to the city at this
time of the year, John Milne was very much in love with his
beautiful wife and despite her advanced pregnancy had persuaded

her to accompany him from Rochdale to his mother's home so that they could be together when the baby was born. A successful wool-stapler, he had met and married Emma, a daughter of James Twycross of Wokingham, a man whose own financial interest in the flourishing textile industry had been partly responsible for bringing the two young people together in the first instance.

As was the widely held custom of the period, the boy was named after his father. Young John, who was to be an only child, did not remain long in the place of his birth for barely three weeks later the family returned to their home in Rochdale where he was to spend most of his early childhood, living first at 147 Drake Street, and later at 'Tunshill House' in comfortable if not luxurious circumstances.

The Rochdale area had been the home of the Milnes for generations. According to one story which seems to be well-founded, the ancestors had come originally from Aberdeen, where, in the fifteenth century for some reason now lost in the mists of time, a party of Irish monks had tried to murder two of the brothers. Escaping from these villains by the skin of their teeth, the two men fled southwards across the border into England. From the records of the Duchy Court they appear to have settled in the township of Butterworth during the reign of Queen Elizabeth I, married locally, and as generation succeeded generation, gradually spread until there were Milnes in Burnage, Hades, Ladyhouse and Milnrow. It was into this latter branch of the family, which had given its name to the surrounding district, that young John Milne was born.

In those days Rochdale was a typical mill town of some 30,000 inhabitants with perhaps an equal number in the surrounding villages for which it served as a market centre. It had two principal industries, woollen manufacture — particularly that of flannel — and the spinning and weaving of cotton goods. Although most of the textile centres of Lancashire and Yorkshire had been, during the 'Hungry Forties' among the most deprived areas of Britain, by the 1850s both the status and wages of the mill workers in Rochdale had improved sharply and it had been among the first areas to recover from the years of depression which had brought wage reductions and heavy unemployment to the town. Now once again it was beginning to ride on a peak of prosperity and the Milnes had few financial worries. Not for them the necessity of membership of the Rochdale Society of Equitable Pioneers, the now rapidly spreading cooperative movement which had had its origins in Toad Lane.

The wool-dealer and his family lived quietly and the boy's early upbringing was unremarkable enough. Years later he would sometimes recall childhood memories of 147 Drake Street, and tell of being dressed in fine clothes to be paraded along the quiet thoroughfares by his mother, ostensibly, he thought, for the admiration and envy of neighbours. Stamped on his memory, too, was the sight of her titivating before a large looking-glass on her dressing-table in the back bedroom of the house. Often she would wear a large hat with ostrich feathers which, like her velvet petticoat, she prized greatly as both were considered highly fashionable at the time.

Milne could remember that two objects in this room had fascinated him. There was a skylight in the high ceiling through which he could watch the changing patterns of passing clouds, but close at hand was a curtained piece of furniture he had been forbidden to touch. Young John could not have been much more than two years old when curiosity about the latter finally got the better of him. As was usual in the afternoons he had been prepared for the daily perambulation in the park and his mother was occupied in applying the final touches to her own toilet prior to setting out. While her attention was thus diverted the youngster crept behind the curtains. Once inside he discovered an enamelled knob which looked something like the now old-fashioned bell-pull. Chubby fingers grasped this firmly and it was twisted and turned. To his terror he was immediately soaked to the skin by a deluge of icy water — he had found the shower-bath! On that day, Milne would add wryly, he was not taken out. Doubtless some psychiatrists would be interested to learn that for many years afterwards he always hesitated before using bell-pulls either in rooms or at front doors, but whether this was due to the fear of unexpected reactions or to half-forgotten memories of the punishment meted out by his frustrated mother is a matter for speculation. His satirical description of a strange shower-bath he is supposed to have encountered in Australia many years later could well have had its origin in this childhood prank.

John grew to be a bright little lad who, like so many youngsters, was forever asking questions. With his father away so often on business it must have been with a sigh of relief that Mrs Milne eventually was able to take her son to his first morning at the little school in Milkstone Road run by Miss Fisher. Unfortunately, the records of what must have been a typical dame school of the period do not seem to have survived but it is known that it was from this lady that the boy received his first prize, a book entitled *The Guide to Knowledge*, which, he once said, awakened an interest in the world around and doubtless helped to develop those fine powers of observation that stood him in such good stead in later years. Eventually, having absorbed all she could teach, John was sent as a private pupil to the Rector of Knutsford in Cheshire. Then, in the autumn of 1864, at the age of thirteen and a half, he entered the Liverpool Collegiate Institute, which in that year changed its name to the Liverpool College. In the Middle School of this establishment he had the distinct advantage of being tutored by the principal, Dr Howson, an excellent and inspiring teacher who subsequently became Dean of Chester.

John's latent spirit of adventure now began to manifest itself. He was still in his early teens and, as evidenced by his school reports, was a naturally hard worker who gained many prizes. One was a sum of money amounting to only a few shillings but sufficient to be invested in a ticket for a trip to the Cumberland lakes. Vastly impressed by their splendour, a desire for further exploration overcame his better judgement and instead of returning at once he crossed to Ireland. There he tramped southwards from Dublin through the land of Thomas Moore, existing mainly on apples and what he could earn by playing the piano at wayside inns.

All his life Milne was to regard Rochdale as his 'native' town. He was fond of telling stories of the people who lived in both Drake and Yorkshire Streets and of describing the various characters he had met during school holidays around the market place and in Old Skye's shop. He remembered with affection, too, 'Rushbearing' and 'Old Ben' the great shires which pulled the carrier's wagon from the 'Red Lion' to Tunshill. Memories of the streets and shops left a lasting impression. As a child he was frequently taken to Pollitt's, the barber, to have his hair curled. During his last visit to the town some fifty years later he again entered the shop. On this occasion he was thought to be the manager of a nigger-minstrel troop then playing at the local theatre and was asked for complimentary tickets. Having made it clear with some asperity that he was not the man in question he received a deep cut when he was being shaved and wondered if the annoyed barber had not believed him! Although Milne was to spend many years abroad, whenever it was possible he would return to the town to meet relatives and enjoy strolls around the scenes of his childhood. Despite the fact that little of his life was actually lived there he was proud to consider himself a 'Rochdalian'.

The family moved to the London area, living at various addresses in the Hounslow and Richmond boroughs. Here, too, whenever the opportunity presented itself John continued his wanderings. There was first a journey to France and this was followed by a longer expedition when, having purchased from his uncle, Walter Grindrod, an outrigger canoe named *Ranger*, he paddled along the rivers and canals of southern England. It was in this craft that his uncle and two companions had travelled from Rochdale to London Bridge in 1868, a journey lasting three weeks which resulted in an amusing book, *The Waterway to London*. Built of pine, this boat was 16 feet overall and had a beam of 2 feet.

> She carried under her deck, fore and aft, a mast, yard and sail, and various waterproof bags containing tea, coffee, chocolate, sugar, salt, pepper and other stores, including a formidable piece of bacon; the large and small spoon, with the knife and

fork, were wrapped in a dishcloth. The kettle, saucepan, teapot and gridiron were also stored away.

In this craft and accompanied only by his dog, young Milne spent halcyon days until arrival at Littlehampton on the Sussex coast. There, in a heavy sea, the canoe overturned and the frightening moments which followed abruptly ended that particular escapade in which he barely escaped being drowned.

In his seventeenth year John became a student in the Department of Applied Sciences at King's College, University of London. His studies included mathematics, mechanics, geology, mineralogy, the manufacturing arts, geometric drawing, surveying and divinity, together with practical instruction in the workshops. The gradings on his annual reports were usually 'very good' although one commentary for chemistry was 'very good but rather careless', but in workshop activities he never attained better than 'fair'. In most repects Milne was a model student. By the end of the first year he received prizes for mineralogy and divinity together with certificates of approval for mathematics and the manufacturing arts; at the end of the second, further prizes were gained, this time for physics, manufacturing arts and mineralogy and yet more certificates of approval in mathematics, drawing, geometrical drawing, chemistry and geology. He was also awarded an A.K.C. (Associate of King's College) for his studies in divinity. The principal of the college at that time was Dr Barry, later to become Bishop of Sydney. His liberal-minded theology inspired a progressive outlook among the students; Milne, in particular, benefited greatly from his association with this astute man.

John's main interests were now centred around geology and mineralogy, particularly the latter, and in July of 1871, accompanied by a friend, W.L. Watts, he sailed in a Danish steamer to Iceland. The object of this journey was described somewhat ostentatiously by the pair as 'The exploration of the Unknown Interior of the Great Glacier, Vatna Jokul'.

Milne casually informed his mother by post from Liverpool that letters and money could reach him at the Post Office in Reykjavik which both surprised and shocked her as she had not been told previously of the intended expedition. (The statement often made in biographical sketches that 'he visited Iceland as a schoolboy' is incorrect since he was now twenty-one years old. The confusion which has arisen is probably through the similarity of the words 'Iceland' and 'Ireland'.)

The highlight of the intrepid pair's outward journey was in meeting a large, grey-bearded, dreamy-eyed man who was constantly writing poetry which he insisted on reading to his fellow passengers. This was the poet and social reformer, William Morris, then on his way to study the scene of the Icelandic sagas of which he afterwards became the 'Homer'. Young Milne retained the memory of this encounter all his life and often quoted stanzas which Morris had composed during the voyage, adding, 'He was always making poetry — as if men who were seasick wanted to hear poetry!'

Milne and Watts spent a strenuous time among the snows of the Vatna Jokul, a large district in the south-east corner of the island. Later in the year John lectured on their experiences to the Engineering Society at King's College. He spoke first of the less pleasant aspects of the expedition, telling of the many difficulties they had encountered; the rushing, icy rivers which had to be waded; the wet marshes traversed; the dreary solitude of ice, snow and lava; the deathlike stillness which brooded over all; the intense cold when they were under canvas and particularly during the two nights they were forced to sleep on the snow in the open. To live in a perpetual state of wetness was the rule, he said, and to be dry the exception. Of the hospitality of the Icelanders he was caustic and referred with some distaste to what he considered were their dirty habits. In his account of the geology and mineralogy of that part of the country he drew attention to the undeveloped wealth of sulphur deposits. His fascinating talk ended with vivid descriptions of geysers and the great volcano, Mount Hecla.

Having made copious notes during the expedition, in the summer of 1872 while living at Richmond he re-wrote the Icelandic part of the journey in narrative form. An extract from this unpublished work is included in an appendix which discusses his ability to tell an interesting story.

Milne obtained a coveted Royal Exhibition Scholarship and continued his studies at the Royal School of Mines in Jermyn Street, London. He worked hard and long and fully deserved the praise given him by Sir Andrew Ramsey, who at that time was the Director-General of the United Kingdom Geological Survey. In a personal letter to Milne he expressed high satisfaction at the way in which his young student had distinguished himself. Some practical experience in the mining districts of Lancashire and Cornwall was obtained and was followed by a course at the famous mining school of Freiburg in Saxony during which time he was able to travel fairly extensively about western Europe. Milne was fortunate in that he had had the advantage of an excellent education and training from some of the ablest teachers available. With his tremendous capacity for work he had become competent in mining techniques and was, in addition, an able geologist. His studies now at an end, the time had come for him to seek paid employment.

At the age of twenty-two, he was not tall, being rather less than five feet six inches in height but was already a thick-set man without an ounce of surplus fat to mar a physical fitness of which he was proud. He had not at this stage grown the moustache which was later to adorn his features and looked far younger than he actually was. Like all young men he speculated upon what fortune held in store for him.

2

The Explorer

It was not long before an opportunity of interesting work came Milne's way. The millionaire financier, Cyrus Field, one of whose companies played a large part in the laying of trans-Atlantic cables, requested the Royal School of Mines to recommend a bright, competent young man who could go to Newfoundland and locate coal and other minerals believed to exist there. Milne was the obvious choice and was told to report to the great man at his London office.

'I am glad to see you, sir,' said the millionaire when the young geologist was shown in, and in a matter-of-fact tone continued, 'we want to know if you can sail for Newfoundland on Tuesday next?'

For once Milne was at a loss for words. He was only twenty-two and had had little experience in business matters. Finally he managed to ask about salary.

'There will be no trouble on that point,' was the terse reply, 'you can leave a memorandum on Monday of what you want for your services — I daresay it will be satisfactory. The point now is — can you sail on Tuesday?'

It was then Friday afternoon and Milne ventured to observe that the shops closed early on a Saturday and on Sunday he would be able to get nothing so was uncertain whether he could be ready in time. At this, Mr Field leant forward on his desk and with a half-serious, half-quizzical look on his face remarked, 'My young friend, I suppose you have read that the world was made in six days. Now do you mean to tell me that if this whole world was made in six days you can't get together the few things you need in four?'

Milne was silent for a moment and then blurted out: 'I'll be ready, sir, on Tuesday.' And he was.

For obvious reasons the work of the expedition of which he was now a member could not continue during the winter months and had been planned to take place in the summers of 1873 and 1874. Despite the difficult terrain young Milne laboured hard and long to justify his selection for this task in what was then Britain's oldest colony. To examine and assess its rock formations and collect the quantities of specimens needed meant lengthy journeys into the then almost unknown interior of the island. He also circumnavigated it twice, exploring remote bays and coves: in some of these the seals he startled were probably observing a European for the first time.

Not all of the expedition's findings were made public but in his paper *Notes on the Physical Characters and Mineralogy of Newfoundland*, (*Journal of the Geological Society, 1874*), the basic geology of the island was described and comment made upon its unusual surface configuration. Later, for the same publication, this was supplemented by *On the Rocks of Newfoundland*, written in conjunction with Alexander Murray.

It was during these extensive field studies that Milne had become curious about the action of ice on rock and, as was now becoming a customary feature once his interest was aroused, began a prolonged in-depth study. During the next few years, even though preoccupied with other pursuits, he returned to the subject, formulating his eventual conclusions through a series of papers. *Ice and Ice-work in Newfoundland* for the *Geological Magazine* was quickly followed by *On the Action of Coast-Ice on an Oscillating Area* and *Considerations on the Flotation of Icebergs* for the *Journal of the Geological Society*. In these Milne brought a fresh approach not only to the factors which affect the floating and stability of icebergs and on the abrasive properties of ice on rock, but also highlighted the superiority of coastal ice over the iceberg as a rock transporting agent. Coastal ice had been a new feature to him as it had not been present during the visit to Iceland two years earlier and he was intrigued by it. He wrote:

> My first sight of large masses of ice was on my arrival at St John's, Newfoundland, in the spring of 1873. On the morning of the 16 May we found ourselves wrapped in a fog, through which a high, bold coast was dimly visible. At length it lifted, and we saw ourselves in a cliff-bound bay, at the head of which a narrow entrance showed us a harbour filled with ice and ships. Near us floated two great icebergs, whilst the sea around was covered with smaller lumps jostling against each other as they rose and sank upon the swell.

Although his papers were praised by some of his contemporaries they were faulted by others since he was dealing with a subject on which there had already been much research, and the controversy aroused continued for some time.

It is not known in which of the two summer expeditions to Newfoundland Milne visited the remote Funk Island for the purpose of collecting bones of the great auk (*Alca impennis*), the extinct bird of the *Alcidae* family. Most probably it was in 1874 after the bulk of the mineralogical survey had been completed. In an article *Relics of the Great Auk* printed in *The Field* in 1875, he stated only that he landed on 20 July.

The island is situated about thirty miles from both Cape Freels and

Cape Fogo, two of the most eastern headlands of Newfoundland. 'On account of its being thus placed far out in the Atlantic, unsheltered by any neighbouring land,' he wrote, 'it is only in exceptionally fine weather that its open, weather-beaten shore can be approached.' He went on to remark that the islet is a little more than half a mile in length and about a quarter of a mile in breadth, with no cliff higher than fifty feet, and the land for the most part shelving gradually towards the sea. 'At no point is there anything like a beach to divide the solid rock from the water.'

After emphasising the danger to shipping that this low-lying outcrop of Laurentian rock could be in the foggy conditions which occur so frequently off the coast of Newfoundland, he continued with a short account of the natural history of the little island. Among the birds he found there were terns (*Sterna hirundo* or *S.Wilsoni*), the fat, round, black and white puffins (*Fratercula arctica*), the razorbill (*Alca torda*) and great numbers of guillemots (*Uria troils* and *U. arra*).

> During the season that these birds are laying it is the custom of fishermen and dwellers on the island of Fogo and the adjoining mainland to make repeated visits to this island for the purpose of securing eggs. This they do very successfully and return with whole boatloads. Those which cannot be eaten when fresh are salted down for winter use. At one time eggs found a ready market in St. John's; but this trade has now very rightly been prohibited, for fear it should end in the extermination of the golden goose — a lesson learnt by the annihilation of a former inhabitant of the same spot, the great auk.

He listed the small number of plants and insects which were found there; tiny patches of soft thick grass; plants such as the Alexander (*Haloscias scotium*), Cochlearia (*C. fenestrata*) and a lone chickweek (*Stellaria media*). He also saw both plantain (*Plantago maritima*) and the common dock (*Rumen maritima*). There appeared to be a few mosquitoes from the mainland and, in addition to a small black beetle he picked up, (*Pterostichus (platysma) luczotii*), there was a lone white butterfly (*Pieris oleracea*), too exhausted to fly, giving him the opportunity to discuss at some length how the island could have been colonised by these plants and animals since none were indigenous.

On the nesting habits of the puffins he wrote that they made the ground like an immense rabbit warren. The greater number of these holes simply descended in a sloping direction for a foot beneath the surface, and then ascended in the same line, this making a small U-shaped passage undergound, at the bottom of which the puffin had its nest, in this way so constructed as to have two doors.

There was much in the same vein and for the naturalist of that day no doubt it made interesting reading, but it was not for a general survey of the wild life of the windswept island that he had come, but for personal evidence of former occupation by the great auk. (It is not true, as has sometimes been suggested, that Milne discovered the last breeding ground of this extinct bird.)

Having a strong wish to secure some relics of this bird, and my time for their discovery being limited to less than an hour, it was with considerable excitement that I rushed from point to point and overturned the turf. At nearly every trial bones were found; but there was nothing that could be identified as ever having belonged to the bird for which I searched. At the eleventh hour the tide turned, and in a small grassy hollow, between two high boulders, on the lifting of the first sod I recognised an alcine beak. That rare element called luck was in operation. In less than half an hour specimens indicating the pre-existence of at least fifty of these birds were exhumed. The bones were found from one to two feet below the surface, and in places even projected through the soil into the underground habitations of the puffins.

He was puzzled that the bones should have been heaped together and because he could find no evidence of cuts or blows thought that the birds had died peacefully, but added that it may be they were the remains of some great slaughter where the birds had been killed, parboiled and despoiled only of their feathers, and then thrown into the heap he had discovered.

In half an hour our work was ended; the wind was rising, and with it the swell of the ocean. Necessity drove us to our boats, and with reluctance we turned our backs upon Funk Island and its treasures. This singular repository may cause some future wanderer to halt, otherwise the island might be unnoticed; but should chance favour him, and time permit, there probably remains a much better harvest to be reaped than has yet been gathered.

The article concluded with the question as to whether the great auk was really extinct and contained a long account of the gradual disappearance of the birds, the last of which he thought had been slaughtered by man about thirty years earlier. Milne acknowledged that his information came in part from the writings of more than a dozen other ornithologists and it is obvious he had studied these thoroughly before compiling his own informative account.

Always interested in legend he took the opportunity of quoting Charles Kingsley, who, in *The Water Babies*, makes the last of the 'gairfowl', while standing on the 'All-alone-stone', relate the eventful history of its own expiring story:

'Thousands of years ago we came from Shiney Wall, where it was decently cold and the climate fit for gentlefolks. Once we were a great nation, and spread all over the Northern Isles; but men shot us, knocked us on the head and took our eggs, till at last there was none of us left except off the old Gairfowlskerry, just off the Iceland coast. Even there we had no peace — for one day the land rocked, and the sea boiled, and the sky grew dark, and the air was filled with smoke and dust, and down tumbled old Gairfowlskerry into the sea. Some of us were dashed to pieces, and some drowned, but those who were left got away to Eldey; but the dovekies tell me they are all dead now, and that another Gairfowlskerry has risen out of the sea close to the old one, but that it is such a poor flat place that it is not safe to live on and so here I am left all alone.' This was the gairfowl's story, and strange as it may seem, it is every word of it true.

By the inclusion of this tale Milne reveals he was among those who, in the days when even the idea of conservation was yet in its infancy, deplored the wanton destruction of wild life by man. In later years his concern for the welfare of animals is a discernable theme which runs through much of his writing.

At the end of the summer's work in 1873 Milne returned to England. For him the experience had been useful, exciting and worthwhile, but after being home for only a few weeks reaction set in. Life became something of an anti-climax. He felt at a loss and wondered how to spend the next few months before returning to Newfoundland in the Spring. Fortunately, a further opportunity for adventure quickly came his way.

The explorer and biblical scholar, Dr Charles Beke, was on the point of setting out on another of his expeditions to the Middle East, this time in search of what he considered to be the true location of Mount Sinai, where, according to the Old Testament, the Law had been delivered to Moses.

Beke felt certain that his mountain was near Aquba, then known as Akaba, about one hundred miles to the north-east of Jebel Musa, the traditionally accepted site in southern Arabia. As a result of the many differing translations of the Old Testament he had become convinced that Sinai was an extinct volcano and more than forty years earlier had written a book, *Origines Biblicae*, in which he developed this theory at length. The Ordnance Survey of Sinai in 1868 tended to confirm the position of the traditional site but did little to convince him that his own theory was wrong. Certain that he was right, Beke felt an imperative desire to clear up the mystery once and for all.

As he was now aged seventy-three and had recently recovered from a serious illness, he decided to take along a young geologist

who could shoulder some of the more laborious tasks and climb the
mountains which were now clearly beyond his capability. So it says
much for the reputation that Milne was rapidly making for himself
when, at a meeting of the Royal Geographical Society, his name was
suggested to Beke in the warmest possible terms by Professor
Tennant, a senior member and one of Milne's former lecturers.

Although not particularly interested in the religious theories held
by the explorer he quickly realised that here was an exciting
opportunity which was not only too good to miss but would also
greatly add to his geological knowledge. After it was agreed that his
travelling expenses would be the responsibility of the expedition's
leader, and that the trip should not take longer than three months, a
contract was signed. They arranged to start from Folkestone on 8
December 1873. Both men felt a certain amount of anxiety and
wondered if they would be compatible, but their fears were
groundless for Milne's lively humour soon captivated his aged
employer and they became firm friends. The first thing Beke found
out about his assistant was that he was a particularly poor sailor on
any sea that was not as smooth as glass.

In Paris, Beke suggested that his companion should visit the
Palace of the Tuilleries which was then in the ruined state to which it
had been reduced in the terrible days of the Commune. A sight, he
said, well worth seeing. Milne went, but as a devoted geologist with
no sentimental fancies. He came back laden with fossils he had found
in the stones of the palace which seemed to interest him more than
the building itself! The next day they left by train via Turin for
Venice. On arrival they spent the night ashore before sailing on the P
& O steamship *Simla*. Beke had been to the city previously but the
place was new to Milne so the Doctor showed him the sights and
later wrote:

> . . . the zest with which he views the novelties among which he
> passes is very refreshing and amusing. But the best of all is that
> his first thought is the mineralogical character of each object
> that presents itself to his sight. As in the case of the Tuilleries, it
> is not the form, or age, or historical character of the buildings,
> so much as the stone of which it is built. It is the same with him
> all along; it is not landscape in which he is interested but the
> character of the rocks. He will even make *me* a geologist in time.

They travelled across the Mediterranean to Alexandria and thence
to Cairo where there was a long delay while Beke endeavoured to
obtain both a boat and a firman, or safe conduct pass, from the
Khêdive of Egypt. He experienced much difficulty in persuading the
ruler to lend him the boat he needed to get to Akaba. Without it a
double crossing of the hot desert of Arabia would be necessary,
which would have been a sore trial for the old man. There was also

the question of the cost of such a journey. Although sponsored, the expedition's finances were never really sufficient and he was relying heavily upon the generosity of the Khêdive at this stage. Milne accepted the delay reluctantly but used this time to explore the area with his usual thoroughness, roaring with laughter at the way he was fleeced by the guides when he visited the great pyramids and mosques. Although these were interesting, it was the museums and rocks that claimed his attention. The delay continued and Beke wrote in his diary:

> I shall be glad to get away from here on Milne's account as well as my own. He wants to be actively employed. Having used up all the *geological* facts that this bare region presents to him, he is now hard at work, studying Arabic, Italian and French.

In fact, the young geologist was growing uneasy, now believing that he would not be back in England by the end of February as had been agreed in the contract. Yet he had become so valuable to the explorer that his services had to be retained at all cost and so a new agreement was drawn up to Milne's eventual satisfaction.

Beke discovered that his assistant was developing into something of an artist and reasoned that, if he could not obtain the services of an illustrator to accompany them, Milne could fulfil this task in addition to his geological work. It was the nature of the old man to be careful with money. He was always grumbling about the expense of the journey in his letters to his wife, exhorting her to find more sponsors while trying himself to find some in Egypt. He even took Milne to task for the way the latter was spending his own money!

At long last the Khêdive sent the written permission to proceed and provided transport. The expedition resumed its journey after an irritating delay of nearly a month in the Egyptian capital. The party crossed the delta of the Nile to Suez where Hashim, their guide, took them to a tiny boat, the *Erin*. Its captain was instructed to take the travellers wherever they wanted to go but there were many unavoidable delays over money for the crew, coal and essential repairs to the almost unseaworthy ship before they finally left harbour in mid-January.

They proceeded somewhat leisurely down the Gulf of Suez, calling in at several places on the way, including Tor, a small port near the foot of Jebel Musa, which Beke considered to be the pseudo Mount Sinai, although the traditionalists regarded it, and still regard it, as authentic. They crossed the mouth of the Gulf of Akaba to Ainunah on the eastern side where the explorer told Milne that he believed the Israelites had campled 3,000 years before. During this short crossing a strong wind whipped up the sea and, as usual, Milne became sick and was forced to go below to his cabin.

Turning into the gulf itself the *Erin* anchored at other places which seemed to the Doctor to lend weight to his theory, Milne doing most of the exploration ashore, making copious geological notes at every opportunity and collecting many fossils and shells, while Beke checked these observations against his belief that the Israelites' journey into the Wilderness took place where *he* thought it to have occurred.

The little ship again met with delays and it was not until nine days after sailing from Suez that anchor was finally dropped at Akaba at the head of the gulf. This was their disembarkation point from which the start of the most important part of the expedition was to be made. Camels were assembled, a local sheikh, his son and some more Arabs joined the party which, three days later on the morning of 30 January, finally got under way.

Milne rode a camel and amused himself by reading Macaulay's *Biographical Essays*, but Beke travelled in a *takhterawan*, a strange contrivance. In shape it was not unlike a London hansom cab of the period, but without wheels, fixed sides or top. It had a mattress and a cushion to sit upon and a sloping board on which to rest the feet. Two long poles protruded at either end to which camels were harnessed. As one would expect Milne found the whole contrivance hilarious but, in fact, if the camels were not driven too fast, and kept in step, it was not uncomfortable.

They slowly made their way across the desert and eventually came to the mountain called Jebel Baghir and camped there for the night. This was the area in which the Doctor thought his Mount Sinai should be. But this mountain did not look like a volcano and he was convinced that the true Mount Sinai was one. Still, it was in the position where the Mountain of the Law should be according to his theory, and it was decided that the next day Milne would set off to climb it and make a thorough investigation of the summit.

During the night a tremendous storm blew up and thunder rolled round the mountain, accompanied by lightning and torrential rain. The flashes behind the clouds which hid the top of the mountain seemed to Beke equivalent to the 'fire' in *Exodus* and he began to believe his theory that Sinai was a volcano was indeed correct. However, before finally making up his mind, he would await Milne's report.

The next morning the geologist and his party set off to climb the steep slopes while Beke remained in camp. From the summit it might be possible for them to see the pseudo Mount Sinai far to the south-west, and if there really were volcanoes in the vicinity these should also be visible. In his diary Beke wrote:

> He (Milne) took a telescope and other instruments with him, a hammer, a drawing block, a box of paints and my flask . . . he was pretty well loaded for such an ascent. But he is a famous

fellow when there is work in hand, and turns to it like a man. He is really a very clever young man, and invaluable to me on this journey, and I am anxious to give him full credit for all he does. He feels that he is working for himself not less than for me, and in a good cause.

Later, with a touch of sadness at his inability to go himself he added:

I hope and trust it may bring us both good; but I am more than fifty years older than he is, and my life is now almost spent. I gave Milne my pocket-flask filled with whisky, as he may want it, for he will find it dreadfully cold up there: in this respect I do not envy him his trip. How thankful I am to have someone so competent to do my work for me.

So for the old man began a long period of anxious waiting. Now convinced that he had found the true Mount Sinai he reasoned that, if it did not turn out to be a volcano this was not now important. It was a very long wait for it was not until late in the afternoon that the tired party returned to base. Milne had reached the summit and found horns and skulls of animals slaughtered there as Beke expected. It had been cloudy but a large plain to the north-east had been seen and this, reasoned the Doctor, could have been the Great Plain on which the Israelites had camped while Moses 'went up the mountain'.

Milne's own purely factual report is incorporated in Beke's book:

At 8 a.m., although it was cloudy and thundering, I mounted the Sheikh's horse, which he lent me, and with five others, two mounted (Hashim the guide and the Sheikh's son), and the three Arabs on foot, started for the summit of Mount Baghir . . . Our way was, for a mile, up a narrow wadi, which grew narrower and narrower until it became a gorge. On the way we passed a stone near which the Bedouins come to say their prayers . . . At the gorge we had to leave the horses with two of the Arabs, and going up a steep ascent to the left, we came to a low wall across the gorge, which was filled with boulders; and close above the wall on the right hand side is a well about three feet across.

Beke, referring to the well later, quoted an appropriate passage from *Exodus* as additional proof.
Milne continued:

Vegetation may here be said to cease for, with the exception of a few stunted plants and bushes, nothing seems to live.
    Our ascent was now a climb, the rock in places being nearly perpendicular. On reaching the summit of the mountain we found numerous skulls and horns, and a few bones of animals

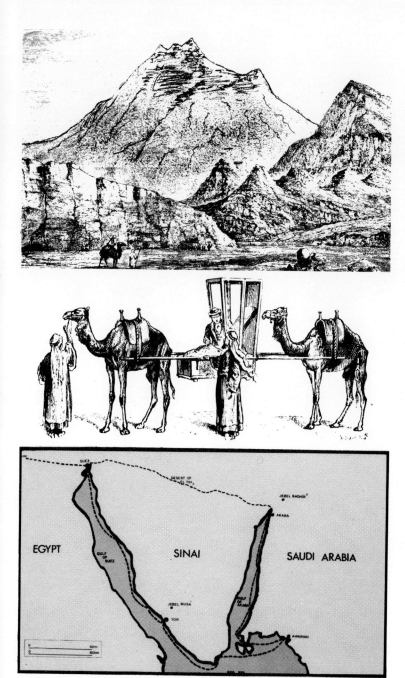

Top: *An example of Milne's sketches for Dr Charles Beke's book.* Middle: *Milne's drawing of a takterawan (Beke's book).* Bottom: *Simplified map of Beke's expedition to find the 'true' Mount Sinai.*

Map showing Milne's epic overland journey across Europe and Asia (1875-76).

— it being the custom of the Bedouins to come up here and pray, bringing with them a lamb, which they kill and eat on the spot . . . we came to a pile of large rounded boulders of granite, on several of which were inscriptions, which I copied as well as my cold fingers would allow me . . . Before reaching the summit we found snow in the crevices, and, for the sake of saying I did it, I snowballed Hashim, who joined warmly in the sport. Whilst we were at the top it hailed and snowed, and was bitterly cold, and it was as much as I could do to take a few angles with the azimuth compass. My companions made a fire, and it was only by continually warming my fingers that I could do anything. Akaba seemed just below my feet, but on so diminutive a scale that I failed to detect the castle among the palm trees . . . the landscape in other directions was almost blocked out by banks of cloud, rain and fog.

They came back down the far side of the mountain, which is some 1,700 metres in height, and reached a valley where some Bedouins were encountered. Thinking it was the Sheikh who was coming, these had killed and cooked a lamb which was offered to the weary party. Milne wrote:

I had to partake. It was a filthy, dirty mess, quite tough and scarcely fit to eat; but I was afraid I should offend them if I refused. It is the custom whenever a Sheikh comes to give him mutton and milk. As it was not the Sheikh, but only the Sheikh's horse, they daubed the animal's back with stripes of blood, to show the Sheikh what they had done for him. We went into one of the miserable tents to partake of their feast, and squatted down in front of a small fire, and nearly got smothered in smoke. The tent was so low that one could only crouch down in it . . . I never *saw* such a picture of dirt, misery and want. Their all would seem to consist of a few dirty rags, a bit of cloth for a tent, and a cracked wooden bowl in which they served the meat which, of course, we had to tear in pieces and eat with our fingers . . .

The report then goes into geological details and from these and other observations he made after climbing another mountain a day or so later he was able to deduce that the country was not of volcanic origin. Beke later wrote in his diary:

He does not at all like our returning without a volcano. I say that the volcano, though almost a vital object to me, is in truth but of secondary importance. My desire is to interpret the Scripture History truly. I *believed* I should find a volcano where I placed Mount Sinai. I find the 'Mountain of Light', but no volcano. I therefore confess that I am in error as regards the physical character of Mount Sinai, and that the appearances mentioned in Scripture were as little volcanic as they were tempestuous. Milne, who looks at the matter in a purely scientific point of view, says he would find a volcano first and then endeavour to see if Scripture History could be fitted into it. But this I cannot do.

This was not quite the end of the expedition. Milne spent one more day searching for a volcano without success and then the party returned to Akaba. On the way, Beke hoped to find the place where he thought the Israelites crossed the sea and Milne was required to make another long expedition to find the cave which is stated in *Exodus* to be close to the head of the Gulf.

Beke wrote:

It was not until six o'clock that Milne came back, heartily tired with a journey which has taken twice as long as he anticipated. His day, he said, had been thrown away: there was no maghara (cave), nothing, in fact, to see. But when I came to enquire particulars, I found that there *is* a maghara though *he* does not care to call it one; but he has made a sketch of it which will be one of the most effective in my book! But what is more important by far is, that he has seen a salt marsh at the head of the Gulf over which the sea sometimes runs, with *a passage of dry land between the two*. Here it is that the Israelites passed! I must go and see this tomorrow.

As though to give credence to the Scriptural story, during the night a terrific wind arose, almost blowing over the tents so that all had to rise and make them more secure. At daybreak the scene was one of confusion. The wind drove the sand with such violence that they were almost smothered with it. Beke described the scene:

The sea was perfectly wild, coming up far above the ordinary limits . . . *the wind was blowing from the south, or south-west, which naturally heaped the waters up in our direction, so that they ran up the beach, and filling the hollow ground behind, left a tongue of dry land between the two*. This, as the storm increased, and the waters also rose, was soon covered; but when I first saw it *the water was on both sides* of the land. How forcibly then and wonderfully did this portray and confirm the Bible narrative.

Milne later said that it was at this point that Beke was at last satisfied for he had 'found' his Mount Sinai in the position he had always believed it to be, and although it was not a volcano, Beke was quite prepared to admit he had been wrong in this assumption. Several other things had been found which tended to prove rather than disprove the site and the doctor was happy. The party withstood the rigours of the ten-day return journey to Egypt across the Sinai desert with a deal of fortitude despite the intolerable heat by day, intense cold at night and the discomfort of continuous dry winds. By now Milne was heartily fed up with camels and walked much of the way back. He would have been horrified to have known that he was to undertake a far longer journey on the back of a camel in the course of the next few months! The expedition arrived back in Suez on 15 February and Milne sailed for England leaving Beke in Egypt to make a report to the Khêdive.

The discovery of the 'true' position of Mount Sinai made by Beke aroused tremendous controversy in Britain, ranging from acceptance by some, to furious disbelief by the traditionalists, and many letters were penned to *The Times* and journals in consequence. Unfortunately, the old explorer was unable to defend himself adequately against the literary attacks and died soon after his return to England. Thus it was left to his widow to edit much of the book, *Beke's Discoveries of Sinai of Arabia*, published four years later. In it, she, too, paid warm tribute to the work of Milne during the expedition. The illustrations are from Milne's sketches and it also contains his geological report as one of the appendices.

Milne, himself, took no part in the dispute which raged for months; the work he had done was purely geological and he was content that it should be seen as such. The exploration proved to be another success for him since he had been able to prepare and have read important papers before the Royal Geographical Society which, in turn, increased his growing reputation as a competent geologist who was prepared to travel for the sake of science. Moreover, his collections of fossils and shells from the Sinai Peninsula were accepted by the British Museum and he had been able to see at first hand some of the places in the Middle East seldom visited by Europeans which made him something of an explorer in his own right. John Milne was becoming 'known'.

3

The Long Journey

John Milne went on to complete his geological survey for Cyrus
Field with a second summer in Newfoundland, and in the autumn of
1874 again returned to England hoping to obtain further employment. None was immediately forthcoming so he occupied the time
by writing up his notes, preparing papers and classifying the many
rocks and fossils he had collected during both expeditions.

Then came the offer of a three year appointment as Professor of
Geology and Mining at the Imperial College of Engineering in
Tokyo. He accepted with an enthusiasm tempered with some
apprehension at the thought of the long sea voyage. Possibly it was
this reason as much as any other which made him decide to travel
overland through Europe, Russia and Siberia to the distant port of
Vladivostok from whence a relatively short sea voyage could be
undertaken without too much distress.

Today, with the modernised Trans-Siberian railway in operation,
this journey is still long and tiring, but before its construction the
route was believed to be fraught with danger, too frightening even
to contemplate. Many of his friends and acquaintances poured scorn
on his proposal but Milne was by now an experienced traveller,
something of an explorer, physically fit and filled with a sense of
adventure. He realised that such an opportunity to increase his
already considerable geological knowledge was too good to miss. In
consequence he was undeterred by the general consensus of opinion
that he would be unable to complete the journey and was mad even
to try. Commenting some years later upon this derisive attitude he
wrote:

> Before leaving England I discovered that the popular opinions
> respecting a journey across Siberia were very vague. In China
> and Japan, where every member of a community must have
> travelled more or less, the idea of an overland trip across Siberia
> is by no means preposterous, — almost everyone, if he does not
> actually know somebody who has made the journey, is at least
> acquainted with someone who has discussed it. In England,
> however, where the name Siberia is to ordinary individuals but
> seldom associated with more than gangs of exiles, packs of
> wolves, and dreary plains of frost and snow, the idea of starting

on a journey across such a country is received with astonishment and a supplement of ridicule.

After appealing unsuccessfully in *The Field* and other publications for a travelling companion Milne left London for Hull on 3 August 1875. Here he was irritated to find that he had been misled by a newspaper advertisement as the passenger ship he expected to find waiting there turned out to be no more than a coaling steamer. 'Not wishing to beat a retreat at this early period of my journey,' he recorded in his *Travelling Notes*, 'I took my passage amidst clouds of coal dust and next morning was sailing down the muddy estuarine waters of the Humber *en route* for Gothenburg (Göteborg).'

He spent two days here exploring the little town and roaming the hills that overlook it. In the small geological museum he was intrigued by a fine collection of Scandinavian and other animals. In particular, he noticed that the Swedish elk had a taller, thinner, altogether more gaunt appearance than the American moose, 'with which, by some,' he reported, 'it is thought to be identical.'

On the evening of the 8th Milne boarded a train for Stockholm. Questioned later as to why he had chosen this roundabout route at the beginning of such a long journey he explained that, although a direct sea-passage from Hull to St Petersburg (now Leningrad) could have been made in six days, and in rather less than four by rail across France and Germany, he had selected the Swedish route chiefly on account of its newness and variety to him. Besides which, he thought there was a possibility of meeting friends in Stockholm.

Except for difficulty with the language, a factor which was to plague him throughout most of his trip and often reduce him to pantomimic gestures at which he became particularly adept, he found Sweden a pleasant enough place. In Stockholm he looked round all the museums he could find and after having his passport viséd, a lengthy procedure needing several visits to the Russian Consulate, he obtained a berth in a well-filled steamer bound for St Petersburg. Most of his fellow passengers were Americans and with the sea as smooth as glass the voyage was an interesting experience.

'It occupied two or three days,' he wrote, 'and was almost altogether through an archipelago of little pine-clad islands. Very often these islands were so thickly packed that there was land on all sides, and in no direction could the sea be seen.'

The ship called at several places, one of which was Helsingfors (Helsinki) then a small port, and during this tortuous passage among the islands off the south and south-western shores of Finland, many of which he was able to observe at close quarters as the little ship steamed slowly past, he developed a theory that the ice-worn character of the Baltic shores of both Sweden and Finland, so similar to those he had studied closely in Newfoundland and Labrador, was the result of the abrasive action of coastal ice and not caused by sheet ice and glaciation as was then generally believed. His somewhat lengthy but well-reasoned argument supporting this hypothesis, however, acknowledged the lack of definite proof since he went on to comment, 'The agent which moulded this country into its present form, and strewed it so thick with boulders, would, I think, be identified by most geologists as ice, and the only argument that would probably arise would be as to the way it acted. A universal covering of ice forming one huge glacier, like that which is supposed to cover the greater part of northern Greenland, might be the first suggestion. To explain this a colder climate than that which now exists in these latitudes would be necessary, and this in its turn would require some great astronomical change, as a variation in the obliquity of the ecliptic, the eccentricity of the earth's orbit, the temperature of space, or some great natural revolution in the distribution of land and water, all of which would involve difficulties in their explanation.'

This part of the world being new to him, Milne's writings reflect an intense interest in his surroundings:

'At about 4 p.m. on 13 August', he noted at this point, 'we ran between the formidable-looking forts of Cronstadt (Kronstadt) and shortly afterwards sighted the huge gilt dome which crowns St Isaac's cathedral, the glory of St Petersburg.' But he was not impressed with the site of Peter the Great's 'window looking out into Europe', commenting adversely on its low elevation in marshy surroundings which, he was told, gave rise at certain seasons to a mild malaria. Nor did he think highly of the Russian Government's School of Mines, criticising the curricula for the preponderance of theoretical studies to the detriment of those offering practical experience. Yet he acknowledged that the courses were severe. Of the 450 students starting the first year only some 18 to 20 would go on to complete the fifth successfully. The wealth of minerals there, however, made him very envious and he described the large block of malachite, weighing 1½ tons, which was said to be the largest ever extracted.

During a stay of six days in the city Milne spent much of his time sightseeing and visiting museums. At the Winter Palace he inspected the Crown Jewels. 'For size and number,' he wrote, 'the display of diamonds, emeralds and sapphires is perhaps unrivalled in any other court in Europe. A large spinel or ruby in the Imperial Crown is very conspicuous and the great Orloff diamond, weighing 194¾ carats, is also here.' But, in his opinion, the collection as a whole was very poorly displayed, the rooms ill-lighted and the cases affording no protection whatever to their contents.

He had a similar criticism about the Museum of the Academy of Sciences where he went to see the relics of the great Mammoth. 'The room in which the skeleton has been placed is one that, if the creature were alive it would find it impossible to walk out of.' The clubbed feet were an inexplicable puzzle to him and he also noted that the animal was covered with something like long red horse-hair. Eventually he was to see many specimens of this animal and declared that he never saw any wool on them in the way they are often illustrated in books. Along the Siberian rivers, especially the Ob and Lena, immense numbers of these remains have been found and he was told on good authority that they are often in such preservation that the natives eat the flesh.

Although the geologist in Milne made him critical of the site on which the city stood he was impressed by the fine buildings and statues which met his eye at every turn, and in his *Travel Notes* commented:

> Many of these, especially the churches and palaces, give some wonderful examples of modern masonry. The most conspicuous of these is St Isaac's Cathedral. Here there are four porches, each of which is supported by double rows of tall cylindrical columns capped by Corinthian capitals. These columns, which are composed of red granite, are each 60 feet high and 7 feet in diameter. The steps leading up to these porches, each a single mass of granite, are equally striking from their megalithic proportions. Inside the building there are many tall columns of malachite and several of lapis lazuli. These, however, are only columns with an external coating of these minerals; nevertheless, when they are seen they serve to give an idea of the quality and quantity of these substances which have been obtained from Russian mines, and also serve to remind one of the insignificance of the displays of similar materials in our own and other countries.

Milne stayed in St Petersburg, then the Russian capital, for almost a week while he made final preparations for his journey. At the very least he knew that it would be difficult. Before him lay thousands of miles of arduous travel, much of it in little-known territory and with the likelihood of physical danger the further he went from European civilisation. Could he but have known the perils ahead of him it is not unlikely that even his staunch spirit would have quailed at the very outset! But the formalities required for his passport were completed and he sought for and obtained several letters of introduction which were to prove valuable. By paying much of his money into one of the banks he obtained a circular note for its withdrawal at towns along his proposed route through Russia thus reducing the amount to be carried on his person. Yet Milne's efforts to find someone to travel with him through Siberia again met with no success and on the evening of 19 August, somewhat dispirited, he left by train from Moscow. His Trans-Siberian adventure had begun . . .

By no means could it have been considered an auspicious start. Bored as always by train journeys which, he often said, gave no chance for worthwhile observation, he stared gloomily through the dirty windows at the flat, marshy landscape. So long as daylight lasted he could see that much of it was covered with corn-fields where the reaped crops were still standing in sheaves. Here and there were clumps of birch, thickets of spruce and alder, and small woods of fir and juniper. In the morning the country became slightly undulating and, as the line was as straight as it could be made, the train took on every gradient as it came. Explaining the reason for this Milne wrote:

> The design of the engineer had been that the track should pass in the vicinity of several large towns but the Emperor Nicholas, to whom the plans were submitted, laid his rule upon the paper between the two extremes and drew a straight line, intimating that it was between St Petersburg and Moscow that *he* wished to travel. And thus originated the straightest railway line in Europe.

Milne spent several days in Moscow trying to persuade someone to accompany him, but even here his idea was not considered feasible. One English resident to whom he had letters of introduction would, on every occasion Milne visited him, tip back his chair and roar with laughter at the absurdity of the scheme. But others were more sympathetic and tried to help. Mr Leslie, the English Consul, advertised in several daily papers and this resulted in five or six applicants, three of whom were young ladies.

'As it happens in England and other countries so in Russia, young ladies have often to make long journeys alone,' Milne recorded, 'but in Russia where the distances have to be overcome by driving day and night in carriages over rough and lonely roads, it is more necessary in this country that the lady should have a companion. From this, coupled with the fact that it is almost as cheap for two to travel together as one alone, the custom of ladies travelling with *unintroduced* gentlemen has originated.'

Finding none of the applicants, or rather the conditions they suggested, to be suitable, on the night of 26 August he left Moscow by train for Nijni Novgorod (Gorkiy), where a great fair was being held and there was the distinct possibility of falling in with merchants returning to Siberia.

Twenty-four hours in this little town was enough for Milne. The fair disappointed him, being carried on in a series of one-storied houses and sheds built on flat ground near the river Volga. These buildings were filled with bales and boxes of various materials and

there was hardly anything approaching a shop or stall. Everything
for sale was very dear and there seemed to be nothing of value being
offered. Moreover, his search for someone to join him was fruitless
and by now it was clear that he would have to continue alone with
the hope that, from time to time, an encounter with a casual traveller
in the same direction might occur.

His route now took him by steamer along the rivers Volga and
Kama to the town of Perm.

> About 10 a.m. the next morning the whistle sounded three
> times, the captain gave his orders, and we pushed out into
> mid-stream. After doffing of hats, and crossing themselves (I
> suppose for a favourable voyage) we started off in a driving rain
> against a head wind down the Volga.

For Milne there were now eight days of delays and irritations. The
river had as many shoals beneath the surface as there were sandbanks
above it and two men were kept constantly in the bows to sound.
This they did with a straight rod marked with alternate bands of
black and white. When less than 3½ feet was called the signal to stop
was given and if it was not too late the vessel went into reverse and a
new course was tried. Early next morning they collided with a small
steamer and stove in its bows. After this, many frustrating hours
were spent finding their way between sandbanks when the ship was
not aground as so often happened. The steamer itself frequently
broke down and repairs had to be effected while it was secured
against the river bank.

Life and arrangements on board a Russian steamer were very
different from those he had anticipated and in consequence he was
somewhat uncomfortable. Although most of the passengers were
on board for at least three or four days, no beds were provided. A
number of cushioned seats had been arranged in parallel rows across
the saloon on which the passengers rested as best they could, for
most of them took a plentiful supply of pillows and rugs whenever
they travelled along the atrocious roads or in the primitive river
steamers. On the upper deck there was a small cabin where meals
were served from a buffet. People always brought their own tea and
sugar with them and often some of their food. Such foresight was
the custom everywhere, and away from large towns food was even
taken into the hotels.

During this tedious passage Milne was pestered by a young Jew
who kept a kind of small shop on board, selling trinkets, pocket
books, and a variety of articles for the benefit of passengers. This
man tried to buy Milne's clothes, particularly his coat, for which
daily bids were made. Sometimes money was offered, or goods,
even the Jew's own clothes, for the coat so obviously coveted.
'Altogether he succeeded in making himself the most persistent

nuisance which I think I met on my journey,' Milne recalled. As life on board the steamer had been so tedious it was with pleasure he greeted the sight of Perm when, on 3 September, it at last came into view.

Even so, Milne did not find the town impressive, and although he paid tribute to the ideas of the original planners, the eccentricities of individual enterprise had taken over to a large extent and either lack of money or energy had resulted in a number of one-storied wooden houses scattered here and there. The streets were deep with mud and bordered with planks, the remnants of sidewalks. His criticism was a little harsh for such conditions as he described could be found almost anywhere where poverty exists. One or two buildings towered above the rest indicating either a theatre or a club or, more likely, a church.

Even the poorest village he had so far seen had its churches with their green roofs and multitudinous cupola-topped spires. Milne's reference to the famous church in Moscow is amusing, 'Called, I believe, the Cathedral of St Basil, which has domes like turnips and spires like carrots, it is so peculiar in design, and magnificent in its colours, that, by an agricultural mind, it might be aptly compared to the closely packed contents of some vegetable garden' — scarcely the kind of remark that would have endeared him to most Muscovites!

At the time of Milne's visit Perm was known to the Russians as Woolwich once was to the British for it was then the centre of their armaments industry. The main factory employed some 4,000 workmen and was the largest establishment of its kind in the country. Here he was shown several huge steel guns and also the largest steam hammer in the world. He learned that at one time the coal used in the massive furnaces came from Newcastle which amazed him. 'Especially,' he wrote, 'when we consider that the neighbouring Urals are full of coal, one seam discovered in the nearby district of Solikamsk being no less than forty feet in thickness!' Even now, he noted, coke was being purchased from England at a cost, in 1875, of £5 per ton!

It was here also that he had his first introduction to real Russian travel, in the vehicle called a *tarantass*, a seatless, four-wheeled carriage with a body suspended on three of four longitudinal poles instead of springs. A tarantass usually had room for two people but some carried four. He was advised that if making a long journey it was better to buy one for between one hundred to two hundred roubles since otherwise it would be necessary to change vehicles at every post-station, and when travelling both day and night this would become extremely objectionable. Milne took this advice and purchased one. He also took bad advice by buying a mattress to place on top of the luggage to ward off some of the jolts.

I left Perm at midnight on the night of September 5th, and before daybreak the novelty had ceased to be a source of pleasure, and I realised the miseries of the roads. In the first place, being always well provided with horses, we were whirled along at a rate regardless of both ruts and stones. My mattress instead of acting as a relieving pad, acted as a spring, and bounced me so unmercifully, that as soon as I had the opportunity I exchanged it for a quantity of straw. At each post-station it was necessary to turn out and present an order for horses which had been received at the starting place at the rate of so much per verst (three versts are approximately two miles, or just over three kilometres), in order to obtain new horses. As this was often in the middle of the night, and you had to wake up the station master, who perhaps told you in return for the annoyance you had given him that all the horses were taken by the previous traveller, getting up to be thus treated was really very unpleasant. By threats or persuasion you may induce him to procure horses from the village, or, if there is no village, from some neighbouring peasant. Having by some means or other obtained your horses, you pay for them at a fixed rate, or so much per verst, up to the next station. To insure yourself against being cheated you can, when not too sleepy, refer to a table of charges hung in a glazed frame against the wall, where these distances are distinctly written down.

There is a special room for travellers at these wayside stations furnished with a wooden bench, two or three chairs, a table, an *icon*, a huge brick stove which when lighted gives out an intolerable heat, and thousands of cockroaches. Usually the stations are located in villages but many of them are solitary buildings amongst the woods. Distances apart vary considerably but it is generally possible to reach one of them every two or three hours. It is usual to stop about every third station to get something to eat and there is seldom anything better than black bread, milk and eggs, and not always even that. It is not only customary to carry tea and sugar with you, but also your food. However, at all stations where is one thing you will find, and that is a samovar. This is a huge tea-urn, with a central pipe filled with red charcoal. It is full of hot water, which, from the way it steams and spurts, appears to be boiling under pressure. You also get a tea-pot and some glasses. Being provided with these materials you are left to your own devices. To make tea, there is no difficulty, but should it be winter and you are provided with food, which will certainly be frozen as hard as any stone, you may at first be somewhat perplexed. Soup may be thawed by placing a lump of it in a glass, and standing this in the slop basin, which you fill with hot water. To thaw your bread or a piece of chicken you can place it on the top of the samovar, taking care that it does not fall inside. Proceeding in this way, and exercising a little ingenuity, which never fails the hungry when in search of food, you will no doubt eventually manage to procure a meal.

Travelling continuously day and night for three, four, five or even ten days, the whole time being jolted in a manner which it would be difficult to describe, every two or three hours having to look after the changing of horses and the signing of papers, was somewhat trying, even for a twenty-five year old. If two men were travelling together the duties could be shared, each taking alternate nights in endeavouring to sleep. But, as Milne discovered on the way from Perm to Ekaterinburg (Sverdlovsk), his next stage, acting as an 'unintroduced' gentleman had serious drawbacks.

'Should a gentleman travel with a lady,' he recorded tartly, 'the duty of turning out to wake up sleepy post-masters, or of generally fighting the battles of the road, must, according to the usages of European society, fall on the gentleman. For twenty-four hours to thus wait upon a lady, is an act of gallantry which is pleasing; but after that, when both passengers have aching bones, and wish to sleep but can find no rest; when only moans and growls are to be heard at every rut you cross; when at a post-station you get out to find fresh horses and are unmercifully grumbled at for creating a disturbance in the internal arrangements of the carriage, bodily and mental aggravations will have arrived at such a pitch that I think most natures would succumb, and a gentleman when travelling with a lady would see that there are more troubles than had been anticipated.'

When later he again had the opportunity to act as an 'unintroduced' gentleman, the offer was hastily declined!

For Milne the chief point of interest during the uncomfortable stage between Perm and Ekaterinburg was the crossing of the Urals, the traditional dividing range between Europe and Asia. Seeing these mountains for the first time proved something of a disappointment as they were much less impressive than his imagination had visualised: 'As we ascended, small streams grew smaller and told us that the water parting which divides the two great continents was near. Large, fat magpies, lively water-wagtails and an occasional woodpecker were the chief birds we saw. A few flowers remained in bloom.'

Butterflies such as the Camberwell Beauty, brown Fritillaries and a single white *Pieris* all reminded him of home but, notwithstanding the cheering aspect of these bright relics of a fading summer, a yellow tinge on the leaves of the drooping birches told him autumn was near. During the nights now it was cold and in the mornings everything had a coating of hoar frost.

The town of Ekaterinburg (Sverdlovsk) was reached late in the afternoon on 9 September and in 1875 Milne described it as one of the finest in Siberia with a population of 30,000. Having been told of the Russian custom when travelling to abstain from ablution for fear of causing a cracking and peeling of the skin his immediate need, before making a preliminary tour of the town, was to have a thorough wash, his first for several days. Although impressed with the fine open streets and large buildings built mostly of wood he soon became highly critical of the primitive hotel facilities both there and in other Siberian towns through which he passed:

> First there is a room which may or may not be papered, generally not; a little whitewash upon the rounded logs which form the walls being considered sufficient in the way of decoration. The floor is carpetless. Two chairs, a table and a bedstead complete the furniture which often seems to have withstood in a greater or less degree the wear of many ages. Projecting from the wall or reared in the corner of the compartment there is a huge brick stove which is supplied by fuel through a door in the outside passage. Five minutes after this has been lighted you realise its capabilities and I can easily imagine that in the depth of winter it would be possible to dispense with bedclothes. This may be perhaps in part an explanation of the fact that at all these hotels you find your bedstead destitute of such accessories. I may also mention that towels, soap, wash-hand basins and other small necessaries which are found in most hotels are without representatives in Siberia.

Milne stayed in Ekaterinburg for two or three days to rest and investigate anything of interest in the immediate neighbourhood. He had been under the impression that the town was the centre of the Urals mining district but this was no longer true. Some ten miles distant in the village of Berezovski there were some large gold mines and to these he made several visits. But to see other mineral workings it was necessary for him to travel to Nijni Tagil (Nizhny Tagil) some 150 miles to the north. He wrote:

> On account of the snow and sleet, the cold, the disgraceful conditions of the roads, and being obliged to travel on a system which compels you to change carriages at every post-station, this was one of the most disagreeable journeys I experienced whilst in Russian territory. However, the mines of copper, iron, gold and platinum together with the insight I had into the geology of the Urals and the entertainment which I received from Russian and other officials who are employed at Tagil well repaid me for my trouble.

The great feature of Tagil at this time was its ironworks. Milne observed that many of the shops and foundries were lighted by a gas made from wood, some 200 cubic feet of which produced 800 cubic feet of gas. The roots of pine and rind of birch furnished the largest quantity of gas, and although the light obtained was less bright than that of coal gas, approximating to an illuminant equivalent of ten candles to fourteen from coal, it was very cheap, one jet costing, in 1875, half a kopec per hour.

His description of the Russian methods of mineral extraction, although lengthy, is informative as is his dissertation on the appearance, age and structure of the Urals themselves. Not only did he deal with their geographic and geological formations but he also discussed in some detail the flora and fauna of the area. He listed some of the animals and plants peculiar to the western but not the eastern flanks of the mountains and *vice versa*, concluding:

> Thus we see that the Urals, although not forming a formidable barrier in the physical configuration of the globe, still play the part of one in preventing an unlimited mixture of the species — a fact which when regarded geologically is of considerable significance, more especially when we reflect upon their great antiquity.

For the next section of this journey as far as Tomsk, Milne had the choice of travelling directly overland across the Barabinsk steppes or by road to Tumen and there joining a steamer which would convey him to the town along the rivers Toufa, Irtish (Irtysh), Obi (Ob) and Tom. The former trail represented a distance of about 1,200 miles and the latter more than 2,200 but by now he had had his fill of Russian roads and chose the longer route, preferring the discomfort of eight to ten days in a steamer to five unpleasant days and nights being jolted unmercifully in a carriage. The decision having been made he left Ekaterinburg on Wednesday, 22 September.

A Jew called Kaib, a penniless tailor's apprentice, offered to become a travelling companion for a while and after 36 hours of continuous misery along the road they arrived at Tumen (Tyumen). A small steamer carried them down the shallower reaches of the river Toufa to a point where they could embark on a larger one. Their progress was both slow and difficult as behind them the boat towed a barge overcrowded with nearly a thousand convicts. It was unwieldy and slowed their progress considerably by running on to sandbanks. Every day the steamer stopped once or twice to take on firewood but rarely was there a settlement along the river banks large enough to be called a village. During stops Milne had an opportunity of inspecting the convicts. The sides of the barge were fitted with iron bars making it look like a huge bird-cage. Although their feet were shackled the prisoners did not seem unhappy; some had their wives, or husbands if the women were the malefactors. They had their samovars and were quite free to talk to one another or to anyone who would pause for a chat.

On board the steamer the passengers amused themselves with card playing, a pastime in which the ladies seemed to be particularly successful, having each night a lap-full of paper roubles to count over as the proceeds of the day. When not so occupied the time was taken up with smoking or cracking small nuts, 'which', noted Milne, 'from the monotonous gaps they often fill in Siberian parties is called by the Russian word which means "Siberian conversation".'

But as a geologist it was for him personally a boring journey. His observations recorded daily became depressingly similar as they traversed a great plain composed of either sand or loam. The terrain was often marshy and there were few trees to break the skyline.

At Tobolsk, where the muddy Tobol joined the clear black waters of the Irtish (Irtysh) Milne was able to go ashore for a few hours. He noted that everything, including the pavements, was made of wood as no stone of any kind could be found in the vicinity. He was shown a momument to the memory of Yermack, a robber chief, who is regarded as the first conqueror of Siberia. There was also another monument of a different kind commemorating the folly of Ivan the Terrible. This was in the form of a bell, which having been ringing at the time of one of his butcheries, or else not having been ringing on that occasion, was shipped as an exile to Siberia and, after having a small piece broken from it, was ordered that never so long as it was a bell was it to ring again.

After joining the river Obi (Ob), which in places was about three-quarters of a mile broad and with the steamer still towing the convict barge, Milne saw for the first time a number of Ostiacks who form a portion of the original inhabitants of Siberia.

'These were short in stature, had large heads, heavy bodies and thin legs. Their eyes, which point inwards and downwards,' he noted, 'are not deeply sunk in their heads but are so placed that the eyelids run smoothly up to the eyebrows, which latter are well up above the eyes themselves. Notwithstanding a general chubbiness in their faces, the cheek-bones are very prominent. Their hair is long and black and their complexion chocolate.'

These natives by the river were extremely dirty, lived in small huts made from rough pine sticks with a covering of birch bark, and appeared to exist on fish some of which they would barter.

On 5 October the mouth of the river Tom was reached. As this was very shallow it was necessary for the passengers to join a smaller steamer. Along the banks were many bushy trees on which a few autumnal leaves yet fluttered. On the evening of that day it was warm enough without an overcoat but next morning with Tomsk in sight it was bitterly cold and the decks were thickly covered with frost. Milne felt a certain unease when he was told that the Tom generally became frozen about 22 October and would remain closed to shipping until 20 April, but consoled himself with the knowledge that he would soon be travelling in a more south-easterly direction. Eventually, on 6 October, Tomsk was reached. Here he wasted no time in sightseeing for on the ship he had become acquainted with a General Smirnoff and a Baron Stackelburg and as both they and he were anxious to proceed without delay he purchased a tarantass and joined their party en route for Irkutsk. Travelling arrangements were much the same as he had experienced earlier; fast, uncomfortable and continuous, with stops every two or three hours to change horses. On either side of the road there was generally a strip of cultivated ground but beyond that only black woods of scrubby woods and fir. The roads were extremely slippery and both day and night they had to dismount from their carriages frequently to help the horses struggling up the steep hills. Going down a particularly tricky slope they over-ran one of the animals and had to leave it to die at the side of the road. After a wearisome journey of some 1,500 versts (1,000 miles) they finally arrived at Irkutsk, the St Petersburg of Siberia.

The first real major set-back in Milne's plans now occurred for there was a delay of about a month before it was possible to continue on his way as the winter roads had not yet formed and the ice on the rivers was not thick enough for sleighs, although sufficient had accumulated to prevent the passage of boats. On the advice of his Russian friends he took private lodgings in the town as the hotels were far too expensive. There was nothing he could do but wait with as much patience as he could command. In fact the enforced hold-up gave him the opportunity to study the way of life of these Siberian Russians who lived so far from their European counterparts. They seemed to him to be very self-contained, knowing little about the outside world and apparently caring less. They were quite content with their theatre which opened every other night; the two clubs where once a week there was generally dancing; a flourishing geographical society; the local newspaper and other means of education and enjoyment much as could be found in Western Russia. Without doubt it was a civilised society in isolation. Although in the half dozen or so hotels dinner could be chosen from a list of 50 dishes the high cost ensured a limited clientele and strangers were an object of interest. It was a little embarrassing:

'A foreign visitor is, if I may judge from the lengthy description he elicits in the local paper, and the battery of glasses which are brought to play on him in the theatre, a *rara avis*,' he commented.

The long delay in Irkutsk provided the newly appointed Professor of Geology and Mining with opportunities to discuss the earth-

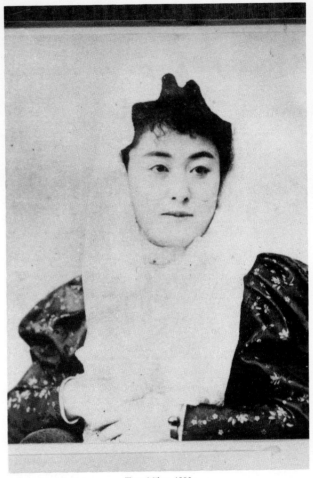

Tone Milne, 1883.

The Milne-MacDonald Vibration Recorder

John Milne (extreme right) featured with a group of Ainu taken on Shumushu Island in the Kurils, 14 August 1878.

quakes which frequently disturb this central Asian area. He learned that the whole locality was one of ancient volcanic activity and in places there were still hot springs and mineral waters. Not long before his arrival several sharp shocks had been experienced, but fourteen years earlier the disturbances had been particularly severe. Much structural damage to buildings had been caused and the waters of Lake Baikal had risen to flood many miles of farmland. Thousands of cattle had been drowned and 40,000 hayricks swept away. In some wells water had risen like a fountain two metres high and it was noted at the time that barometer readings were very much lower than usual. The earthquakes were preceded by sounds like those of a powerful wind. Animals had been affected; frightened cattle had bellowed, horses neighed and dogs howled incessantly.

But Milne's interest in earthquakes at this time was governed by the fact that his knowledge was theoretical only and thus was no more than that of a competent geologist seeking and recording information before turning his attention to matters which at this stage intrigued him more, such as the various gold-mining techniques in the alluvial deposits around the town, and in investigating the geological reasons for the differing quality of gold extracted from mines in the vicinity. He was not to know at this juncture, of course, that very soon the strange underground earth movements would virtually come to dominate his life. It is doubtful if he would have much cared anyway as he was daily growing more and more anxious about the possibility of completing his journey at all since the friends and acquaintances he had made in the Eastern Siberian town startled him with their serious recommendation that his present venture be abandoned. If it was his intention to reach Japan quickly he should return to England and go on via America. Milne recorded:

> When I was at home and travelling in imagination across a Mercator's chart, on which I staked out the distances with a pair of compasses, I always thought that if ever I was fortunate enough to reach Irkutsk I could consider myself as being almost in Japan. I had reached the expected goal and then to be told that I was further off my destination than I was three and a half months ago was most disheartening. For numerous reasons, being settled that it would never do to retreat, I made enquiries and found that from Irkutsk I had two courses open to me.

These were to go either to the river Amor (Amur) which, by the time it was reached would be frozen over, necessitating a long journey by sleigh, or to Kiachta (Kyakhta) and thence by camel train across Mongolia to Pekin. Although these friends advised that little trust could be placed in the Mongols, Milne chose this latter route for, despite the probably dangers when crossing Mongolia, had he undertaken the sleigh trip to Vladivostok it was likely that he would have to remain there until the end of April before the ice melted and a ship could sail for Japan.

> It was with a feeling of sorrow that I took leave of Irkutsk. This was partly on account of leaving the friends who had shown me so much kindness and partly because I knew something of the Miseries before me.

So, on 23 November, in a sleigh and for the first time for thousands of miles quite alone except for his Russian driver, Milne left for Kiachta. The roads were very rough and travelling by sleigh did not have the easy gliding motion that he had expected; it was, in fact, quite the reverse. There was just as much bumping as in a tarantass.

His route now led him directly to Lake Baikal whose dark blue waters contrasted strikingly with the small white peaks of the distant hills. This huge stretch of water had not yet frozen over and so could not be crossed by sledge, and as there was too much floating ice for steamers to effect a safe passage John Milne was forced to take the road which skirted round the southern shoreline. The scenery here was picturesque with high pines flanking the steeper portions of the road and clumps of birch which swung their drooping branches, thick with hoar frost, in the breeze.

At night, however, what with charging down deep gullies in the dark, the roaring of the waters of the lake on the shore, the intense cold, the loneliness and the generally cramped position he was obliged to adopt, he became miserable and depressed. On one occasion he was even a little frightened:

> As I never met any travellers on the road the sudden appearance of two men one night somewhat alarmed me. The driver had stopped to do something to his horses when in front of me I heard a whistle which was immediately replied to. This roused me from my drowsy state and I sat upright in the sleigh and ordered the man to drive his fastest. This he did. Dashing down into the bottom of a ravine we rose quickly upon the opposite side where I saw the men standing beneath the trees! We passed between them: nobody spoke and nobody did anything.
>
> Before starting I had been told that this portion of the country was very dangerous, being filled with escaped convicts. This, together with the general desolate character of the district through which I was passing, may have aroused fears which likely as not were groundless.

Soon the snow became less preventing further use of the sleigh. It had to be left at a lonely post-station along the road where the official in charge willingly gave him a receipt. Later, in Japan, Milne would sometimes wave this at his students saying if any of them were ever passing that way they could collect the vehicle. He would then go on to explain how annoyed he had been, not only because at Irkutsk he had been told repeatedly that the only possible method of travel to Kiachta at that time of the year was by sleigh, but that it was cheaper to purchase one than to travel *pereclodnoi*, that is, by staging between post-stations along the road. Then, with a flash of wry humour he would add that at least he owned property in Siberia!

The Professor's route now took him south-eastwards away from Lake Baikal and through the old volcanic district of Kalenishnaya where he passed one or two caravans carrying tea. He wrote: 'The flat faces and oblique eyes of the men who drove these told me my European associations must soon end and I should shortly be among the Mongols.'

That night he reached Troitskosarsk, the old Russian fortress town which lies near the head of a sloping valley bounded on either side by hills. About two miles further down was his goal, Kiachta, the Russian frontier town which, although small, was in those days one of the only three official entry points into the country, Leningrad and Riga being the others. The palisaded Chinese town of Miamachin, now known as Altan Bulag in the People's Republic of Mongolia, lay just across the border. It was 28 November and he had now travelled over 4,000 miles from St Petersburg. During this last stage of this journey the cold had often been intense and on occasions his moustache and beard had frozen so tightly together that, without thawing off the ice, he had been unable to open his mouth. All food, including wine, was frozen solid and in spite of many skin covers and sheep-skin clothes he had often felt bitterly cold.

At Kiachta Milne suffered a further delay of several days before he could complete arrangements for crossing Mongolia. His intention had been to travel with a Russian officer whose acquaintance he had made in Irkutsk and whom he encountered here again. This man was travelling on Government duty and so could go by a special route, much longer than that taken by the camel-trains, but accomplished more quickly as riders were sent on ahead of him to collect horses. In winter this was seldom possible along the caravan routes as the summer herdsmen had by this time left the area. Although both influence and persuasion were applied to the Frontier Commissioner on the Russian side, Milne's idea of travelling with the courier was vetoed. It was explained by this courteous official that there was an agreement between Russia and China that only one Russian courier at a time could be allowed to take this special route. Clearly, if the form were filled up for presentation to the Chinese governor of Maimachin for two couriers instead of one, and one of these an Englishman, this would have been a breach of regulations. They were told firmly it was impossible, and the only alternative was for

Milne to say goodbye to his friend temporarily and to make preparations for the extra twenty days crossing the tract of snow ahead. With difficulty he hired camels and joined a camel-train which was soon to cross the Mongolian frontier.

At noon on 9 December, some eleven days after arrival in Kiachta, he left to continue his journey with a Cossack as an attendant, and five camels, one of which was harnessed to a small two-wheeled Chinese cart called a *telega*, or *turga*. The contract made with the Mongols for crossing this difficult terrain was that they should take him to Kalgan on the Chinese border in 30 days for 100 silver roubles. 'For every day under that time I was to pay three roubles extra and for every day beyond that time they were to pay me. There was also a clause that a tent, fire and water should be supplied.' In the train there were nearly 100 camels which were looked after by five Mongols and their families.

In the first eight hours they travelled only 30 versts. The temperature was −26 °C. After a mug of tea around a fire the journey continued until 2.30 a.m. when they slept in a yourt — the name for a Mongolian felt tent. Inside, in addition to the men, women and children, were three goats and a pig.

During the day they travelled continuously until early evening when they stopped for a hot drink, after which they continued until midnight or later when a halt was called for sleep, and by 7 a.m. they were on the move again. During the night he usually rode in the wagon but was compelled to walk up the hills. To withstand the cold his clothing was covered by a suit of sheep-skin and felt boots. In the wagon, in addition to a large wolf-skin robe, two rugs of sheep-skin were also necessary.

On the night of 11 December they were on a slippery snow-covered road through the Makatah Pass when they met a caravan of about 200 camels travelling in the opposite direction. Milne wrote:

> To pass this train and get to the top of the pass was a troublesome struggle. The camels, and the two oxen which it had been necessary to hire before entering the pass, slipped and fell continuously. I found walking at night very trying, from the cold being intense enough to continually bridge icicles across my mouth and freeze my beard tightly to my coat. At about 2 p.m. we reached a place called Barsh, after 27 hours travelling and with only half an hour's rest. During this time the camels were without food, and it was 18 hours since I myself had eaten. Eating only once a day is at first trying, but it is almost impossible to do otherwise when travelling in the winter months. Our travelling was so arranged to take advantage of the moonlight.

They reached Urga (Ulan Bator), the religious centre of Mongolia
on 14 December. Milne noted that the houses there were small and
made of mud, very much like those of an Arab village, and were
surrounded by palisading some ten feet high, with clay between the
joints as an added protection from cold winds. There were many
churches in the town

> . . . most of which in shape are like very large circuses. They
> are the life of the place and the thundering boom of a Mongolian
> service may be heard issuing from them at all hours.

Round an open square in the town were several small stores kept
by Russians where many things were for sale, from walking dolls to
camels and ponies. Small huts of felt, about the size of large packing
cases, were placed around the square and used as shops which at
night could be carried home. Blacksmiths with portable forges plied
their trade, hawkers sold hats, and pious Mongols turned the great
vertical drums which were set up in many places as 'praying
machines'.

Leaving the town the next day they entered terrain which was
very rugged; there were no trees, the magpies which had so far
accompanied them disappeared and for companions they were left
with large black ravens. These were so bold that they rode on the
camels' backs and tore open the provision bags. Yourts could not be
expected in this particularly inhospitable area and now Milne had to
live with the five Mongols in a small canvas tent. During the day the
temperature was usually well below freezing and at night sank as
low as −31 degrees C. Between noon and 3 o'clock daily during this
part of their trek the caravan was halted and the Mongolians scraped
a piece of ground clear of snow to pitch their tents and cook their
daily meal in the pungent smoke of a fire made from camels' dung.

As this was going on the camels were turned loose for an hour or
so to ramble about in search of food, after which they were brought
back to the tent and made to sit down between their packs to rest
while the men slept. Every evening between 8 or 9 o'clock they
moved again, travelling all night and through the next day until the
noon rest period came round. The country now was very wild and
sparsely populated. Sometimes they rested on the site of a previous
encampment and in such places often they were able to pick up a
little cow and horse dung, which made a much more cheerful fire
than that from camels — a scientific observation which later Milne
sometimes used to start a conversation at a particularly sticky party!

Eventually they reached Teck-sha-Buinta, a small place of about
150 buildings, including four churches.

> Immediately on my arrival my Cossack and I were surrounded
> by an inquisitive crowd. Although we endeavoured to take all

in good part, this inquisitiveness soon led to impudence and those at the back tried to push those in front on top of us. Fearing lest this should lead to hostilities which, under the trying position of being buffeted and jeered at were difficult, I hit upon the happy expedient of diverting their attention. I had in my pocket a number of small Russian coins and brass buttons. Showing one of these to the crowd, I threw it in the air and let them scramble. With this they were so attracted, that before I had tossed away 40 kopecs and a few brass buttons, our caravan was on the move out of the village. This was the largest sum of money disbursed upon the road and I always thought that it was well spent.

That evening they reached Kooistelroi which, although it had only five or six yourts, was the headquarters of a Mongolian Mandarin. The camels, through sore feet and other causes, were unfit to go any further and they had to stay three days until fresh animals could be obtained. Milne lived in a yourt during this time. It was used as a kitchen so he shared it with two cooks, several girls and a number of passing visitors, all of whom examined his property and watched his actions which apparently were interesting and amusing to them.

Of the Mongols themselves, he wrote:

I had but little opportunity to gain much idea of their character. Two features were, however, too prominent to be overlooked, even by the most unobservant. The first of these was their light-heartedness, which contrasted very strongly with the stolidity of their neighbours, the Chinese. They were ever ready to make and enjoy a joke, and the more especially so if it were in any way practical. The other feature was their hospitality. When visitors came to our tent they were apparently always welcome, and seldom went away without having taken part in a meal.

When I was in Russia, the Mongols had always been represented to be as characters of the blackest dye, amongst whom it was hardly safe to travel. This was the chief reason why I was urged to take the Amoor route rather than the one via Pekin.

At noon on Christmas Day 1875, the camel-train left Kooistelroi and the trail again became very rough with so many boulders that during the night it was necessary to have a lantern. The hard ground began to tell on the feet of the camels and several hours were spent every night in doctoring them and stitching small pieces of leather over the sore parts to act as shoes.

On 2 January, a high wind from the north-west began to blow, increasing the cold, the thermometer again falling to –31°C. Driving snow prevented them from seeing many yards ahead but it did not stop their steady progress.

On 5 January Milne and his Cossack left the caravan and forged ahead, and on the morning of the 9th descended at last from the high plains and through the steep, rocky pass towards Kalgan.

> This descent was down one of the roughest roads on which up to this time I had had to travel. In the upper portions we passed between many beds of red earth, but lower down there was nothing but high boulders and perpendicular cliffs. At times the distances between these cliffs was not more than 60 yards, and as this space was in many places covered from side to side by a sheet of smooth ice we had difficulties with our camels.

Now and then they saw a tower of the Great Wall of China standing upon a peak and looking like the dilapidated base of a truncated obelisk. Little gardens appeared wherever a pocket of soil had collected, often in seemingly inaccessible places. On 9 January, just before entering Kalgan, which is divided from Mongolian territory by the Great Wall, is a little village called Yamborshaw. Here they halted, thirty-one harrowing and dangerous days after leaving Kiachta.

Difficult though the crossing had been Milne had still found time to make geological notes of some importance. The part of Mongolia from Kiachta to Kalgan through which he had struggled appeared to him to be a saucer-shaped plateau of mainly volcanic and granitic rock the outer edges of which were about 5,000 feet above sea level and the inner area sloping down to between 2,000 and 2,400 feet. He noted that burrowing animals were scarce and in consequence buzzards were absent also. Trees and vegetation generally were few and far between. Even so, he decided that the country was interesting and one which would repay the geologist who could visit it at a more favourable season of the year. Milne wrote:

> After spending a day and a half in washing, sleeping, visiting temples, admiring the Great Wall and having a general introduction to Chinese life, I started for Pekin in a palanquin carried by two mules.

He arrived in this ancient city four days later. Compared with the hardships endured across the bitterly cold plateau of Mongolia, the final stage of the journey was relatively easy. After spending a week in the city, resting and seeing the sights, Milne left Pekin and travelled overland again by mule for Tientsin, arriving there two days later. Here he spent a further week in making preparations for the overland journey to Shanghai and waiting for the Russian officer with whom he had hoped to travel across Mongolia and who had travelled the official courier's route.

Had it been summer the trip could have been made by river steamer, but the ice had not yet broken up and was not expected to do so for another three weeks. They finally left for Shanghai at noon on 5 February, in two-wheeled Chinese wagons, each harnessed to a pair of mules, travelling for fifteen days until the Grand Canal was reached. Here a boat was boarded and two days later they were in Chinkiang, nearly 500 miles from Pekin. The country through which they travelled was alternately mountainous, undulating and flat, and intensively cultivated wherever possible.

The villages were all similar in appearance. Entrance was generally through a gateway in a mud wall; the streets were narrow, uneven and dirty. Milne described some New Year festivities in one of these. A large paper dragon from 20 to 30 yards in length was the chief object of attraction. Its body was made of long cylinders of paper, each of which was carried on a pole. These were united by bags of linen which gave it flexible joints. Its interior was lit with candles and a band accompanied it through the streets.

Many travellers were encountered on the roads along the plains, most of whom, if not on foot, were riding in wheelbarrows. Sometimes one barrow carried two persons! Everywhere there were people, who, like themselves, were on the move from sunrise to sunset. The country roads were as much thronged as the streets of many small towns at home on a busy day. These were so numerous that often the pair had to wait at the entrance to narrow defiles for the passing of a long line of barrows coming towards them before it was possible to enter. There were many beggars, old and young. Many were half-clothed and the children naked, all very dirty and covered with sores. Several times they saw freshly decapitated heads hanging up by the side of the road in wickerwork cages.

They had unpleasant experiences at some of the villages through which they passed. Great crowds of people followed them and at all the inns they were refused entry, as 'foreign devils' could not be admitted. Often it was not until they reached the outskirts of a village that they found someone to accommodate them for the night, and then they either had to put up with the worst chambers or were given an empty outhouse in a yard. At almost every town they had to put up with impertinent curiosity and insulting remarks from these crowds which always followed them.

The weather was gradually becoming warmer now and on the rivers the ice was slowly melting. Once on the Grand Canal their journey proceeded rapidly, the stream being with them. Junks were to be seen everywhere and sometimes became so numerous as to give the appearance of the activity of London Docks. Fishermen and beggars were plentiful. The latter collected alms in an extremely novel manner. They had several long bamboo poles lashed together forming a rod of great length at the end of which a small, deep bag was attached. In order to lift this immense rod and present the bag to passengers on the various levels of the passing junks, the whole was supported on the top of a post driven in the shore and turned about upon it like a swivel. The master of this begging machine stood on the shore and, whilst beating a small drum to attract attention, worked the rod, raising, lowering and swinging his bag into any position where he thought a return might be expected.

On 23 February 1876 a tired but triumphant John Milne reached Shanghai after a crossing of China which had taken 19 days during which time he had covered 1,600 kilometres (1,000 miles). It was a satisfying end to an undertaking which many of his friends had considered impossible. Most of these had already begun to fear for his safety and some had even given him up for dead. Some less well disposed among his contemporaries criticised him for taking 203 days to travel the 13,000 kilometres (8,000 miles), but these he ignored for initially at least he had been in no great hurry.

In his two accounts of what was undoubtedly a feat of considerable endurance Milne tends to minimise the many difficulties encountered on this long overland winter expedition across half the world. In his notes he prefers instead to comment on geological features, describe the flora and fauna encountered and compile tables listing snow and rainfall, temperatures, barometric pressures and the times of freezing over and breaking up of the ice on the various Siberian, Mongolian and Chinese rivers, the whole of which was an invaluable contribution to the western world's scant knowledge of these then remote areas. His summary included an account of how Siberia was then being colonised. Perhaps the most fascinating of all the appendices was the one entitled *Observations for persons intending to make the overland journey*.

'A strong constitution is needed,' he wrote. 'For the journey I should allow 70 to 80 days. The rate at which you travel will depend greatly on the season of the year. The best times are either summer or winter and the worst times between these seasons when there are roads for neither sleighs or carriages and when rivers are obstructed with floating ice.' He went on to advise that large quantities of provisions should be carried, preferably in a frozen state. In winter he strongly warns against crossing Mongolia at all unless 'they wish to taste hardships which I strongly suspect are very little inferior to those of an Arctic expedition.' He said it was cheaper for two to travel together and suggested that two portmanteaus of moderate size should be sufficient to contain the clothes needed if it were intended to mingle with the inhabitants of the town, but warned that in the matters of dress the Russians were very punctilious, even to wearing a dress-coat for a morning call. Persons crossing Siberia should not imagine they are diving into unknown regions, where they will meet with untold dangers and accomplish heroic deeds. On the contrary they will find themselves travelling on good roads, between good towns inhabited by a refined community. Inhospitable frozen plains, packs of wolves and gangs of exiles are to the observer upon the ordinary post-roads of Siberia almost mythical in existence. At times the traveller may be uncomfortable and cold, but if he mingles with his fellow travellers he will probably meet with kindness and hospitality which will obliterate all unpleasant feelings and leave behind an impression which will always make him think with pleasure of the days he spent in Russia and Siberia.

Despite Milne's apparent conscious attempt to minimise his achievement it is not difficult to imagine the hardships brought about by language problems, frequent long periods of loneliness, hunger, extreme discomfort and at times even personal danger. These factors, either singly or combined were his constant companions throughout his journey and more particularly during the latter stages when transversing Mongolia and China.

There is little doubt that the somewhat brash young man who had set out so defiantly from Britain some seven months earlier had by now matured considerably. There is evidence that he was much more sure of himself. His writings from this time onward have the stamp of authority. Quite clearly his earlier comprehensive training, together with the experiences of Iceland, Newfoundland, Sinai and this extended Trans-Asian expedition had by now ensured that he was destined to become an eminent British geologist — a young man whose recent election to a Fellowship of the Royal Geographical Society had already been more than justified.

4

The Professor

While its role undoubtedly was important, the Imperial College of
Engineering in Tokyo to which Milne had been appointed was but
one of the essential training units established by the Meiji
government in its determination to achieve rapidly at least parity
with western industrialisation. A major factor in the authorities'
ambitious programme was the employment — albeit with some
dissension — of large numbers of foreign specialists to train Japanese
nationals for virtually every area of social, economic and political
activity of the emerging nation.

It is not practical to discuss at length here the many controversial
theories centring around the precise function of these foreign
employees who were invited to Japan from 1865 to 1900 in numbers
which have been conjectured variously as between 2,000 and 5,000.
Although officially known as 'oyatoi-gaikokujin', a literal translation
of which is 'honourable foreign menial or hireling', this apparently
derogatory title reflects less a desire to humiliate the newcomers by
ensuring they were made aware of their standing in the hierarchy
than a fear that foreign technology, backed by overseas finance,
might eventually subjugate the strongly nationalistic Japanese to the
status of colonials as had happened elsewhere.

Thus, in the main, selection of these western 'helpers and
servants', the 'living machines' whose end-product would be carbon
copies of themselves, was a prudent affair. Each nominee was
subjected to extensive investigation before employment was offered
and thereafter was sensibly bound by a contract hedged with many
restrictive clauses. In the case of mining engineers, to cite but one
example, the Ministry of Public Works, under whose aegis the
Imperial College was founded in 1873, imposed strict qualifying
standards which Milne was able to satisfy. This was followed by the
presentation of a contract the signing of which ensured that, when he
was engaged in activities concerning the mining industry, he was
authorised to deal only in technical matters. Like other foreigners he
would not be allowed to own or invest money in any of the
country's mines either operational, discontinued or projected, nor to
lend money to Japanese nationals as a way of circumventing this
prohibition. By such means the Meiji government was able to

protect valuable mineral rights from falling into the hands of foreigners.

Not a shred of political power was given to the alien. He soon became aware that, while his advice could be sought at all times it would also be asked of others and the matter then considered carefully. Decision-making was never to be his province. Thus those westerners who tried to become the masters through their technological superiority would be courteously but quietly 'dropped' as soon as it was convenient. Only those who were prepared 'to work fully, honestly and in a spirit of brotherly love' were successful. From the start the Japanese showed themselves more inclined to adaptation rather than adoption and only those foreigners who grasped the philosophy behind this Asiatic attitude and respected it could hope to succeed. Some of these latter came to regard their tasks almost as a vocation and as a result of this understanding between the different cultures there developed a mutual respect and trust. For the foreigner who had this type of mentality Japan became a land of great opportunity.

One of the important qualities required of these 'advisors' was wholehearted enthusiasm. Milne's colleagues at the new Imperial College of Engineering were, like himself, young. Most were in their middle or late twenties and each was extremely competent within his own specialisation. This academically exciting group quickly developed into a team as effective as those in some of the older educational establishments in Europe, yet was unfettered by the latter's enduring conservatism and often time-consuming traditions. In Japan they retained and developed the idealism generated by the young when they sense a successful future opening to them. Among Milne's contemporaries were those men who, like himself, were later to become famous in the world of technology but who, for the most part, left Japan within a few years to continue their various careers elsewhere. Milne did not leave. He remained for almost two decades during which time he fostered the new science of seismology and became its acknowledged leader throughout the world.

When he joined the staff in 1876 the College was a relatively small establishment. He was welcomed by Henry Dyer, who, at the age of twenty-five, had been appointed Principal prior to its opening three years earlier. A Whitworth Scholar and graduate of Glasgow University, this Scottish engineer undoubtedly was responsible for much of the high standing that the College was to achieve. He remained in his appointment for ten years before returning to Britain and a long, active life in engineering, education and social welfare.

Milne was also glad to renew his acquaintance with John Perry whom he had known in England and who had preceded him to Japan to become Professor of Engineering. Although often giving the impression of being something of a dreamer by nature, Perry not only had a flair for invention but also a deep interest in electricity. An impulsive, warm-hearted Irishman, he had a decidedly amusing outlook on life which attracted Milne greatly as it was complementary to his own Lancastrian humour. Thus it was almost inevitable that the two men should become close companions and develop a lifelong friendship.

Another colleague with whom Milne became friendly was William Ayrton who was both an electrical engineer and inventor. Ayrton had taken up the appointment of Professor of Natural Philosophy and Telegraphy in 1873. When John Perry arrived later these two formed a partnership which continued long after both had returned to England and resulted in the production of a number of successful scientific instruments. Ayrton was regarded as the practical member of the team being a man of much restless energy. Both he and Perry interested themselves in the problems of earthquake motion. Among the more important papers they wrote together were one dealing with a scheme for seismic measurement and another considering proposals for building construction in an earthquake country. But after leaving Japan in 1878 and 1879 respectively their more active participation ceased although both retained a deep interest in the subject.

Established as it had been to produce the skilled manpower which Japan so urgently needed if it were to succeed in matching the industrial capability of the western world, life at the College was hard for students and staff alike as a copy of an early timetable shows:

6.00– 7.30	Private study
7.30– 8.00	Breakfast
8.00–noon	Class
noon– 1.00	Lunch and recreation
1.00– 4.00	Class
4.00– 5.00	Gymnasium
5.00– 6.00	Dinner
6.00–10.00	Private study and recreation

Although class-contact hours finished for the lecturers at 4 p.m., thereafter they were expected to be available to answer the many queries raised during private study as well as to undertake their duties of marking student work, prepare lectures and assist in the development of new courses. There was considerable administrative work in addition and they were also required to assist with games. The College year began at the beginning of October and lasted until the end of June with only a small break around the New Year and the occasional one-day national holidays.

When Milne began teaching there were about one hundred students in their preliminary year; a two-year course was running in basic science and a number of more advanced four-year courses had just started in mechanical, civil and telegraph engineering. Mining, architecture, chemistry and metallurgy subjects were also being taught. Milne lectured to all these groups except the telegraph and mechanical engineering students.

The staff consisted of twelve professors who were supported by six assistant lecturers, three librarians, a museum keeper and a gymnastics instructor. There were also interpreters and secretaries as well as wardens for the hostels.

As the academic staff was mainly British, English was the teaching language and a high standard was demanded as the following shortened extracts from an early entrance examination paper reveals:

> *Dictation.* '. . . that man, I think, has had a liberal education who has been so trained in youth that his body is a ready servant of his will, and does with ease and pleasure all the work that, as a mechanism, it is capable of.'
>
> *Use of English.* Show the difference in meaning between members of each of the following pairs of words:
>
> (a) speak and tell   (b) teach and learn
> (c) raise and rise   (d) hear and listen
> (e) say and tell   (f) science and art
> (g) push and press   (h) beautiful and admirable

By any standard the curriculum was not an easy one for the Japanese youngsters. Such was the pressure of work that only those who could cope with this foreign language had any chance of completing the course. These future engineers were obliged to study for seven years to obtain an M.E. (Master of Engineering). They were then required to accept government employment for a further seven. Failure to honour this commitment was heavily penalised as their college fees then had to be refunded in full by the student's sponsor.

So intensive was their instruction in English that eventually all classes were ordered to receive lessons in the Japanese culture and language in addition as it was found that, so keen was their determination to complete the course and help their country, many students were neglecting their own tongue and way of life. Like those of today, some neglected their health and physical well-being. To off-set this, gymnastics became an optional part of the curriculum and a number of sporting activities were also introduced. An early college calendar shows these to have been; 100 yards, 200 yards, 500 yards and one mile running, (note the British measurements); walking one mile; putting the stone; hop, step and leap; hurdle race, steeple chase; long jump, pole jump and high jump; base-ball; throwing the hammer; drop kick with football; swimming; football; shinty; rounders; quoits — if this was the same game as that played today one wonders which 'athletic' British lecturer introduced it — leap frog; prison race, and two others called 'smugglers' and 'bonnety'. Later, cricket was introduced as well as lawn tennis, bowls, fives and golf.

The Imperial College grew rapidly until, before it became part of Tokyo University in 1886, it was for a time the largest technical college in the world. Milne took his duties there seriously: his material was always carefully prepared; his lectures delivered in precise language his students could understand and the notes he gave them ever a model of clarity. But as he considered some of the textbooks he needed were inadequate he was forced to prepare much of his own material. Thus it was not surprising that, towards the end of 1877, he sent to a number of his former teachers and friends in Britain lithographed copies of his written notes on crystallography hoping 'that they would try to have them published in the *Geological Magazine* or elsewhere' as his covering letter explained. Among these friends were Professors Maskelyn and Tennant of King's College, London and Drs Woodward and Davies at the Department of Mineralogy at the British Museum, the latter being a well-known petrologist and mineralogist. Eventually it was decided between them that Davies would edit the manuscript with the assistance of Woodward and then, because of Milne's absence in Japan, shepherd it through the many stages of publication. In a letter dated 20 March 1879 to Mrs Arnott — John Milne's mother had remarried after the death of his father — Woodward wrote that 500 copies of the book had been printed and suggested that, initially at least, 250 of these should be bound. He advised that it would be a good idea if Davies were to be paid a sum of £5 for reading and correcting the proofs, and tactfully submitted that this should be sent by Mrs Arnott, together with a personal word of thanks. No doubt the money was well earned as Milne's writing never was, or is, easy to decypher!

There was an unexpected hold-up in the publication of this textbook, *Notes on Crystallography and Crystallo-physics*, (Trubner & Co) due mainly to the lengthy postal delays to and from Japan. Although the manuscript was completed in 1877 the introduction to it was not written by Milne until a year later and the book itself was not ready until 26 February 1879. As a result of this a Mr Gurney stole some of the author's thunder with his own pamphlet on crystallography which reached the booksellers before that of Milne.

The young professor's slim volume of only some seventy pages was generally well received although one unnamed critic, writing in the *Geological Magazine* took him to task for some minor errors but added:

> Whilst taking exception to the way Mr Milne has tried to avoid some of the difficulties of the subject, we cannot but admire his

courage in publishing what has evidently been a labour of love, though beset with difficulties . . .

The woodcut figures are clear and exceedingly well chosen. As to the rest we consider that Mr Milne has displayed considerable ingenuity in putting before his students in the way he has done a confessedly difficult subject, but into which those not versed in higher mathematics may yet hope to gain a fair insight.

Whether or not the mistakes referred to in this review can be attributed to Milne or to the assistant to whom, through pressure of work, he was obliged to delegate the task of preparing the final draft of the manuscript may never be known, but Professor John Perry is on record as saying that he never heard Milne criticise anyone unkindly and it is in keeping with the author's integrity that he himself accepted the blame for such errors that were made. As a matter of interest, throughout his life Milne was scrupulously fair in acknowledging his sources of information and in this particular work he expressed himself indebted to Professor Miller's *Treatise on Crystallography* and Professor Maskelyn's *Lecture-notes on the Morphology of Crystals*. His modesty about his own contributions in all scientific matters was always to be one of his more endearing qualities.

For its time the book had some excellent illustrations; twenty-five extremely clear diagrams with white lines on a black background. Compared with his later works the style was unusual in that it was largely mathematical in content. It was centred around the accepted three co-ordinates for planes, a system instigated by Professor Miller.

As there was to be only one printing, copies of the book are today something of a rarity. Milne did not, however, lose his interest in the subject — in 1880, for instance, he wrote a lengthy paper entitled *Experiments on the Elasticity of Crystals* for the *Mineralogical Magazine*, but he was soon to be too preoccupied with other interests to continue work in this direction. He had discovered that his active mind needed stimuli greater than teaching could give him and on occasion the rigid confines of the classroom tried his patience sorely. At this period of his life Milne missed the excitement of active adventure and he welcomed the arrival of holidays which allowed him to range far and wide through a country then so little known to the West. There were so many things to do in a land of fascinating people, frequent earthquakes and many active volcanoes, especially for someone physically fit and not yet thirty years old!

Two open-air pursuits began to attract his attention — volcanology and archaeology.

Volcanoes had a fascination Milne could never resist: before seismology finally claimed most of his attention he was attracted to them as a moth is to a candle. His interest had begun in boyhood, the direct result of a book he had won as a prize at school. Eventually it took him to Iceland to study their activity at first hand. Later, in Arabia, Dr Beke's idea that Mount Sinai was a volcano sent Milne eagerly climbing several mountains there in the hope of confirming the theory. Now, once again, he was in a part of the world where opportunities to renew the acquaintanceship were plentiful. It is little wonder, then, that whenever his lecturing and other duties permitted, he could be found at the summit of one or other of the many Japanese volcanoes or carrying out some of the experiments which made his contribution to volcanology of some importance. Each one he explored added something new to his knowledge of the way they were formed — as often as not gained as a result of an almost complete disregard for personal safety as he clambered down into their smouldering craters.

His reports of these surveys make fascinating reading since they invariably contain comments upon the people, animals and plants which inhabited the surrounding districts as well as notes on interesting geographical and geological features. Extracts from two have been selected. In the first he describes a visit made early in 1877 to the volcano of Oshima, a small island to the south of Tokyo:

Ships coming into Yokohama brought news that the island was on fire. One captain reported that flames 200 feet in height were seen. Although Oshima was an island which three years previously had been giving out clouds of smoke, and seven years before that had been actually in eruption it was thought by many that the conflagration was due to the burning of grass or wood, and it was not until some days had passed that the true state of affairs became fully recognized.

After some trouble, a party was organised and a steamer engaged to visit the scene of the eruption. We left Yokohama on the afternoon of 19 January, and in the evening reached Kanasaki, a village situated at the extremity of the peninsula upon the south side of Yeddo Bay. After staying here a few hours, we continued our course and reached the island shortly after daybreak on the following morning. During the night there was an uninterrupted view of the volcano from the summit of which high clouds of steam, lighted up with the glow from the crater beneath, could be distinctly seen. It was a veritable 'pillar of fire'. . . . All the sides of the harbour in which we lay were thickly covered with underwood and small trees, whilst in many places near the shore, some fair-sized pines rose to a considerable height.

Excepting birds, the fauna of the island is represented by rats, mice, weasels and snakes. At one time there was a large wild goat-like animal, but this has been exterminated by the Japanese natives. Foxes, and many other animals which are so abundant on the mainland, do not exist. Frogs are also conspicuous by their absence, but this is probably owing to there being a scarcity of water on the island. In whatever way, however, this island may have been colonized since the time of its formation, both the fauna and flora are sufficiently large to guarantee the assumption that it is of considerable age, which, as I have before stated, is probably that of the volcanic cones which so thickly cover the mainland.

From the people on shore we learnt that the eruption had commenced on the 4th of the month and therefore it had been sixteen days in action. The only notice they had of its outburst was a loud explosion, which was described as having produced a slight vibration. This appears to have been all that was felt of the nature of an earthquake, and so far as the inhabitants of the island were concerned, all was going on quietly . . .

Information, however, was difficult to obtain and uncertain in its character. None of the inhabitants, although not more than four miles distant, had visited the crater, and, as we shortly afterwards found out, did not appear even to know the way to it.

Securing the assistance of six men, we set out by a zigzag road towards the top of the old crater in which the village is situated and where our vessel was lying at anchor . . . After struggling along for nearly two hours, we found that the men we had engaged as guides did not know the road and were leading us round the island rather than up towards the crater . . .

We now directed our course towards the highest peak before us at the back of which we hoped to see something of the eruption. After a tough scramble through black, scoriaceous ashes, we reached the top where we soon saw we had much further to travel. We had in fact reached the rim of an old crater whose sides at this point descended perpendicularly, I should think, at least 400 feet. Walking along this rim, which was covered with large weather-worn whitish boulders which looked not unlike material torn from the perpendicular faces below us, we found a slope of ashes down which we descended into the bed of the old crater. . . The explosions we had heard when at a greater distance were now more audible and occurred rapidly in succession. As we neared the top, which was about 800 feet above the plain from which we started, the noise, which was like that of immense jets of steam, was sometimes accompanied with a tremulous motion of the ground. It was not long before we reached the rim of this second crater which

we did to behold a sight defying my powers of description.
Instead of looking up at a crater we were looking down at one
. . . before us there was a short descent of loose, black ashes,
somewhat steeper than that up which we had climbed,
terminating suddenly in perpendicular cliffs, which formed an
amphitheatre of rocks about half a mile in breadth, the walls of
which, upon the opposite side, were about 300 feet in height. At
the bottom of this pit, on the side nearer to us, a small cone with
an orifice of about 50 feet in diameter, was belching masses of
molten lava to a height of more than double that at which we
were standing.

The explosions, which varied in intensity, occurred about
every 2 seconds but sometimes there was a pause of 15 to 20
seconds. At the time a strong wind was blowing at our back
which kept any of the lighter lapilli from driving in our
direction. Coming, as we did, so suddenly upon the precipice-
like edge of a huge black cauldron, roaring, shaking the ground
and ejecting a dense column of red-hot stones and ashes, the
wild and dismal aspect of which was heightened by dark clouds,
driving rain, and a heavy mist, produced at first a feeling of
timidity which was so strongly shown by our six so-called
guides that it was with difficulty they were prevented from
taking to precipitate flight . . .

The greatest interest in this eruption lay in the fact that·we
were able, on account of our position, to look down into the
crater. In the intervals between the ejections the interior could
be well seen, and it was observable that the sides had a slope of
nearly the same inclination as the exterior. Now and then large
masses of these interior sides, which were black, would slide
down towards the throat of the crater and reveal a red-hot
interior, showing that the cone itself was probably internally
red hot throughout. One side of the cone had been blown away,
leaving a breach, almost level with the plane from which it rose.
This opening greatly facilitated our observations. Looking
down into the crater on this side, molten lava, approximately
level with the base of the cone, could be seen. At each explosion
it rose in waves and swayed about heavily like a huge basin of
mercury, a little of it being apparently pushed forward through
the breach to add to a small black-looking stream on the outside.
The explosions which I have referred to as resembling outbursts
of steam, might be compared to the escape of steam from a
slowly-working non-condensing steam engine greatly magni-
fied.

On listening attentively, a rattling could sometimes be heard,
reminding one of stones and pebbles on a beach driven forwards
and drawn backwards by the advancing and retreating surge.

Each explosion, as I have said, produced a fountain-like column of red-hot ashes and volcanic bombs. The height to which they sometimes rose must have been nearly 1,000 feet. Many of them appeared to be of feathery lightness. As they rose their velocity became gradually less and less, until they seemed to pause and float in mid-air before turning to descend which they did with an augmenting speed . . .

Looking at some of these bombs which had fallen on the level where I was standing, they appeared to have done so while in a pasty condition, because some of them showed a decided flattening, as if produced by impact. Both the bombs and the lapilli were of a black colour, and pumiceous texture. Although I believe each of these explosions to have been the result of a sudden bursting of steam through the molten lava I did not see any aqueous vapour which I could recognise as having been evolved whilst I was standing near the crater. This may have been perhaps due to the intense heat keeping the vapour in an invisible state until it became hidden in the fog and murky atmosphere which enveloped us.

Notwithstanding a strong ice-cold breeze blowing in the direction of the eruption, which was about 150 yards distant from us, the effect of radiation was distinctly felt, especially when the ejected column of ashes was large.

Independently of variations produced by unusually large ejections, two thermometers in boxes were each raised 3°C so long as we remained in this position. The warmth was all that made our position bearable, as otherwise it was bitterly cold, with a sleety rain pouring down, and we were all wet through. Once or twice a little fine ash fell upon us and a slightly sulphureous smell could be detected. The journey down the mountain was accomplished in about two hours, which was half the time it had taken us to ascend . . .

From the inhabitants we learnt that the mountain is regarded as being holy, and that at certain seasons they make solitary pilgrimages to its summit. We, however, had been the first to see the eruption.

Earthquakes, although so common on the mainland are said not to occur here and the only shocks that have been felt are those which were produced at the time of the breaking out of the volcano . . .

Next morning we set sail for home, a distance which in coming had been traversed in only six hours but in returning, through the roughness of both wind and water, occupied two days.

As would be expected, this report contains considerable geological detail concerning lava flow and deposition yet clearly emerging is the beginning of Milne's decision to discover not only the way volcanoes are formed but also to question the then current belief that in their active periods they were the principal cause of major earthquakes in Japan.

Among other volcanoes he was able to climb that year was Asama Yama, the 8,300 feet active cone some 75 miles north-west of Tokyo. On that occasion he did not remain at the summit long, for, as he explained:

> The crater looked like a bottomless pit, with perpendicular sides. It was audibly roaring and belching forth volumes of sulphurous vapour, threatening suffocation to any living thing it might envelop.

Nine years later, with two companions, he tried again. The object of the expedition was to satisfy a curiosity which had arisen regarding the depth of the crater. Other visitors to the summit had reported that, at favourable moments when the wind had blown the steam to one side, they had been able to see downwards to an enormous depth, some estimates putting this at between 1,500 and 2,000 feet. Milne's party provided themselves with sufficient wire and rope to solve this problem, but the weather was so bad, and the great mass of snow then lying on the mountain so deep, that the expedition was a failure. One of his companions had to give up the attempt at 6,000 feet and, although Milne and his other climbing acquaintance continued, they reached the summit only with great difficulty. He recalled:

> Our stay was very short. The wind, which at times was so strong that we were compelled to lie down, rendered it impossible to approach the crater. After a few minutes rest we beat a retreat, worn out with fatigue, across the snow-fields towards our starting point.

Other people who went later disagreed among themselves about both the depth of the crater and its diameter. These widely differing reports as to the dimensions of the volcano, together with his own increasing curiosity, finally led Milne, accompanied this time by three friends, Messrs Dun, Glover and Stevens, to face the fatigue of ascending Asama for the third time. Of this expedition he said:

> We left our resting-place, Katoukake, at the foot of the mountain, at 4.30 a.m. on the morning of October 2, and in company with five coolies we reached the summit at 11 a.m. After a short rest, we commenced our measuring operation, the general arrangements of which were entirely the suggestion of Mr Dun. When these are explained, they are no more remarkable than the manner which Columbus caused an egg to

stand; but before Mr Dun made his suggestion, the various schemes which were proposed would, to my mind, have been unpractical and unsatisfactory. One suggestion was to roll a cannon-ball, with a string attached, down the crater; another was to shoot an arrow carrying a string into the hole; a third suggestion was to fly a kite across the crater, etc., etc.

In the event, they established a rope across part of the crater's rim and paid out a copper-wire sounding line which ran through a brass ring secured to the centre of the rope.

The getting of the rope into position was a matter of no little difficulty. First was the fact that clouds of vapours not only prevented us from seeing from station to station, but also from seeing far out into the crater. Secondly, on account of the hissing and bubbling noises in the crater itself, we could only communicate with each other by sound for short distances. And thirdly, there was the difficulty of clearing the cross-rope from the ragged edge of the crater, which involved considerable risks in climbing.

The first attempt at sounding failed, the wire breaking through tension, but the probes it carried, which were made from metals of low melting point like antimony and zinc, together with those of wood, india rubber, sealing wax, and so on, were recovered. From these objects it was hoped to gain some idea of the temperature in the depths. Saved, too, was the small net, christened the 'automatic laboratory' which contained pieces of blue and red litmus paper, Brazil-wood and lead papers. 'I had planned a number of chemical tests,' he said, 'but from previous experience I had learnt the impossibility of carrying out anything but the simplest of experiments when working on the summit of a live volcano.'

The second sounding reached the bottom (side?) at about 440 feet and the metals came up unchanged although the sealing wax showed signs of softening. The automatic laboratory had a strong smell from the action of acid vapours, the blue litmus was turned red and the lead papers well darkened.

The third attempt was an unfortunate failure for this time the line gave way at 200 feet carrying with it a mercury thermometer and other apparatus which Milne had reserved for what he hoped would be the best sounding.

In the final effort the copper wire was replaced by a strong twine and, allowing for errors, it was concluded that the depth at this particular spot was at least 700 feet.

Before we left the summit, we were fortunate in obtaining views of one side of the bottom of the crater. This we did by cautiously crawling out upon an overhanging rock, and then, while lying on our stomachs, putting our hands over the edge. The perpendicular side opposite to us appeared to consist of thick horizontal-stratified bands of rock of a white colour. The bottom of the pit itself was white, and covered with boulders and debris. Small jets of steam were hissing from many places in the sides of the pit, while on our left, where we had been sounding, large volumes of choking vapours were surging up in angry clouds.

After this we descended the mountain, reaching our hotel at 8 p.m. after fifteen hours absence.

Milne referred to this episode as a 'holiday excursion', partly undertaken with the object of making a few scientific observations. The results which were obtained were undoubtedly few in view of the risks incurred. 'All that we did,' he added, 'was to solve a problem chiefly of local interest, to learn a little about the nature of the gases which are given off by one of the most active volcanoes in this country, and to enjoy the spectacle of a phenomenon which is the lot of very few to witness. When a stranger gazes for the first time down upon the burnt and rugged sides of an apparently bottomless pit, which, while belching out enormous clouds of steam, roars and moans, he receives an impression never to be forgotten.'

The terms of reference under which Milne was employed meant that he was required also to travel extensively to familiarise himself with the geological structure of many of the islands which constitute Japan so as to be able to advise on mineral extraction using modern mining techniques. During the long journeys he undertook in the next two decades, however, he seized every opportunity to examine volcanic activity at close quarters. In the early years of his appointment he climbed more than fifty different volcanoes and observed the sites of many others as he trekked about the countryside in the College's long summer recesses.

He made one such extended trip in 1878 in order to visit the Kurils, a line of some thirty small islands then recently placed under Japanese control. These extend from the Kamchatka Peninsula south-eastward towards Japan's northern island of Hokkaido. Entangled in a vast net of seaweed they are the home of innumerable birds, and in Milne's day, were the haunt of seals and sea otters later driven away by unregulated hunting. The climate is severe with cold, snowy winters and, as he found to his cost, cool, foggy summers, a point which he brought out in the first of the papers he later published on the Kuril volcanoes:

Owing to a continuance of foggy weather, which I do not think would find an equal even in Newfoundland, the want of harbours, and the strong currents, although I was almost a month steaming amongst these islands it was seldom that we could affect a landing.

It is safe to assume that during this period the weather must have remained calm as, for once, he makes no comment upon the state of the sea or any reference to the chronic seasickness to which he was always prone.

Even though he was unable to land on as many of the islands as he would have wished he could not have been too disappointed for he commented:

> . . . the bulk of the material embodied in the following notes was written from what I saw from the deck of our vessel. However, as I had good opportunities for seeing nearly every island in the group, and many of these from several points of view, the following notes may not be altogether without value. One advantage which was gained by viewing these islands from a distance was that I was thereby better able to judge the number and the general form of the mountains they contained, and to roughly make comparisons of their relative heights, than I could have done had I been actually on the islands themselves.

When explaining his methods of working he sometimes unconsciously reveals his resourcefulness:

> In a few cases I endeavoured to estimate the heights by means of sextant observations. I also made measurements of the slopes of the mountains which I saw; but as these were made with a small hand clinometer from the deck of a rolling ship, the measurements may only be regarded as rough approximations.

By holding a sextant horizontally he was able to carry the reflected image of one mountain and place it in juxtaposition with the image of its neighbour seen directly. It soon became apparent to him that the true form of the slopes of these newer volcanic mountains of the Kurils were approximately exponential, and confirmed a theory he had already formulated as a result of earlier observations on the Japanese mainland.

The outward journey ended at the southern extremity of Kamchatka which is terminated with high black snow-capped peaks, looking, Milne thought, as cold, cheerless and uninviting as the most dreary part of Iceland.

His paper goes on to describe in detail many of the islands themselves; their physical features, geology, flora and fauna are all commented upon and he wrote too of the few inhabitants of this desolate archipelago:

> Here (at Myrup) there are three wooden houses which had been built by the Russians, and quite a number, perhaps a score, of

half-underground dwellings. On landing we found that all these were deserted and in many cases difficult to find owing to the growth of wormwood and grasses.

The inhabitants of the island, who call themselves Kurilsky, are twenty-three in number. They live chiefly at a place called Seneno about four miles distant. In addition to their own language they speak Russian fluently, and also know something of the Aino language. For the last three or four years they have lived on fish, a few blay-berries and the various animals they could shoot. I mention these people as they appear to be the only inhabitants of the Kuriles north of Iterup.

Throughout this biography Milne's modesty has been mentioned frequently. Unlike many of the Victorian explorers who hastened to perpetrate their fame by naming some newly discovered prominence after themselves, he resisted temptation whenever the opportunity arose. On one of the islands of the group, Paramushir, for instance, he discovered a new volcano.

An irregular mountain, forming the northern end of this group, is giving off steam. It is covered with reddish scarps and patches of snow. As this mountain, which is remarkable as being one of the flickering embers of those fiery furnaces which raised the Kuriles appears to be without name, either on the charts or amongst the inhabitants, I have ventured to name it Mount Ebeko.

Thus, on the maps and charts of the world there appears no Mount Milne, or Milne Island on any feature he named for himself: the river with his name in Australia was not discovered by him.

In his lengthy account of this voyage, *A cruise among the volcanoes of the Kurile Islands*, he concludes that the volcanic mountains there are of more recent origin than those of Kamchatka or Japan since they are less denuded and possess a more well-defined form.

On his return to Tokyo he began many experiments to determine the form which a heap of loose material automatically will assume. He allowed a stream of sand or gravel to fall through a funnel upon a level floor, varying both the material and the height of the fall and then sprinkled the resulting heaps with water to stimulate rainfall in his efforts to imitate the effects of denudation. Rectangular cases were sometimes filled with gravel, their sides removed and the materials within left to determine their own movement. From this he discovered that denudation does not play an important part in giving a volcano its form. Much time was spent in investigating other factors which might affect its regularity such as the position of the crater, the direction of the wind during eruptions, and the nature of the eruptions themselves. The results of these intensive studies are recorded in many publications. He formed the habit of describing each volcano he studied in great detail and sketched its profile from a number of angles.

In time he came to feel that there was really very little that was unknown to him about the volcanoes of Japan. The vast knowledge he gained enabled him to become the first to demonstrate conclusively that contrary to the current belief, most of the country's earthquakes were not caused by volcanic activity and that the reason should be sought elsewhere.

'In Japan', he wrote eventually, 'the majority of earthquakes which we experience do *not* come from volcanoes nor do they seem to have any direct connection with them. In the centre of Japan there are mountainous districts where active volcanoes are numerous, yet the area is singularly free from earthquakes.'

As near as it is possible for a man to become captivated by mountains and to understand their moods, so Milne grew to regard volcanoes with something akin to affection, particularly so with Fujiyama, the great 3,886 metre cone which rises above the heavily wooded mountains near Tokyo with an almost perfect symmetry. More than most westerners in Japan at that time he understood and respected the reverence which many Japanese held for this now quiescent, beautiful peak which other volcanoes, for all their awesome activity, cannot match. He climbed it on several occasions and once spent five days and nights on its summit. Doubtless he would have been delighted with the majestic views on clear days and would have noted the glint of sunlight on the beautiful lakes that skirted its lower slopes, observed the emerald green rice fields on the plains below stretching endlessly towards the distant Pacific ocean, and enjoyed the solitude so difficult to find in the busy cities.

At intervals during the years 1876 to 1879 when young Milne was still seeking hobby interests which could satisfy his insatiable need to extend his knowledge of Japan, he focussed his attention on the study of the country's pre-history. Thus he could be found unearthing 'kitchen middens', burrowing into tumuli and exploring natural and artificial caves. Despite not being a trained archaeologist his remarkable ability to absorb quickly the ethics of disciplines not entirely dissimilar to his own enabled him to grasp far more than mere basic essentials. Soon he was something of an expert in his own right.

He had the undoubted advantage of being able to benefit from his work with men of experience one of whom was the renowned Professor Morse. The two appear to have joined forces on more than one occasion, particularly in Hakodate and Otaru on the large northern island of Hokkaido. Although Morse was regarded as the leading authority on Japanese archaeology at that time, rightly or wrongly Milne found himself unable to accept a number of assumptions made by this American and outlines these areas of disagreement in a comprehensive paper, *The Stone Age of Japan*, read to the Anthropological Institute in May 1880.

Although now dated, this is still interesting to read if only to emphasise the general lack of knowledge of the subject which then existed. In it Milne maintained that many facts relating to the early history of Japan could be drawn from the shell heaps or 'kitchen middens' scattered about the countryside. Tumuli offered other clues as did natural and artifical caves; so, too, could a study of the language, the names of places, the types of people encountered and their customs, religions and traditions. Even the geological positions of the islands which form Japan yielded valuable information about the earliest inhabitants of which, at that time, little was known in the western world. He itemised in detail the various 'middens' he had excavated and listed the genera of sea-shells found therein as well as classifying pottery, bones, arrow-heads and ornaments recovered.

Recalling that the Stone Age of Japan was of a more recent origin than that of Western Europe, existing as it did until 660 B.C. he gave his reasons for suggesting that the original inhabitants were the Ebisu, ancestors of the modern Ainos. Traces had also been found of the existence of Alutes and Kamchadales. The aborigines had migrated northwards before the invasion of the Japanese coming from the south, and he drew a parallel with the northward retreat of the Gaelic-Celts before the advancing Danes and Saxons in England. The origin of the Japanese people was then a subject of controversy among westerners, and Milne suggested they could have come from Polynesia in the south and east:

I venture this remark on account of the many similarities which are so very observable between the inhabitants of many Pacific islands and Japan. It is needless to say that the origin of the Japanese is a subject which yet remains to be investigated, and what I have said is as yet only a suggestion.

Milne's supposition is not now accepted and it is generally believed that Japan was populated mainly from Asia.

The origin of the Ainos was even more obscure at that time and being unable to advance a constructive theory, he chose instead to relate one of the dozens of myths then current:

In Japanese history we are told the story about an Asiatic princess who, fleeing from her father, took refuge in a canoe, and in company with a dog was drifted to Japan. The result of the union were the hairy Ainos. Originally, the Ainos were called Ebisu, or barbarians, and the word Aino is said by some to be derived from the circumstances of the above story, — 'Inu', which became corrupted into Aino, meaning a dog.

He loved to lighten his work with some such intriguing piece of information and this biologically impossible fable with its highly scandalous overtones concerning the immoral behaviour of the young princess is a typical example.

Concluding the story, he remarked:

> From the vast amount of material, geological, archaeological and literary which remains to be exhumed, I see it would be easy to spend years in continuing to examine new mounds, and in extracting from manuscripts and histories . . . Several explorers are now in the field who have already collected together a vast amount of material. When this is published it may modify many of my conclusions, but I trust my materials have been sufficient to maintain the general outline of the geological and ethnological changes which have taken place during the more recent periods in this interesting country of the 'Rising Sun'.

He did not continue with these investigations after the publication of this paper as an increasing involvement with earthquakes, stimulated by personal experience, left him too little time.

From his earliest student days Milne was aware of the esteem held for the Royal Society, for like others, he respected the learning and eminence of its Fellows, particularly those he had met in his post-graduate days in England. Although he and Thomas Gray, working together in Japan, had tentatively forwarded to the Society a paper on their experiments which had been read and favourably received, he little thought then that he might be one of the lucky fifteen who, in those days, were elected annually to a Fellowship. However, such was the case for, in 1887, on a proposal by William Thomson (later Lord Kelvin), H. Woodward, J. W. Judd, G. H. Darwin, R. Etheridge and John Perry, most of whom played significant roles in the development of the new science of seismology, he was elected to 'The Royal Society of London for the Improvement of Natural Knowledge', to give its full title. Since it was one of the oldest and most exclusive societies in the world, with a long history going back to the heydays of natural philosophy; to Newton, Boyle, Hooke, Halley and many others, even to its Royal Patron, Charles II, for him to become an F.R.S. before his thirty-seventh birthday, must have given immense personal satisfaction.

Yet there was no doubt about his right to selection for this honour as the record shows:

Professor John Milne, Tokyo Japan. *FGS, Associate and Hon Fellow of King's College, Lond., Royal Exhibitioner at Royal School of Mines, Lond., Professor of Mining and Geology in the Imperial*

*College of Engineering, Dept. of Public Works, Japan. Studied in
Freiberg; travelled in Iceland; engaged in 1873-74 in mining in
Newfoundland; accompanied Dr Beke as geologist to North-West
Arabia; travelled across Russia, Siberia, Mongolia and China to
Japan; visited the Kurile Islands, the Korean frontier, California, etc,
author of many papers . . . on volcanoes and earthquakes . . . .
Entrusted with three grants from the British Association for
investigating Earthquake Phenomena. Author of numerous other
papers on Geology, Mineralogy, Mining, etc. Has especially devoted
himself to the study of Earth Movements.*

Although the work he was doing in Japan was useful he had often
wished to be back in the main stream of academic life: to have the
opportunity to discuss problems at first hand with other experts,
for, confined as he was to a relatively small group of intellectuals in
Tokyo, he occasionally felt isolated from the outside world. He
began to wonder if he was forgotten. His election to this exclusive
'club' convinced him this was not so and he now knew that the many
contributions to knowledge he was making in this far-off country
were respected by his contemporaries in Britain and elsewhere.

Milne's study of the effects of earthquakes on buildings, which are
discussed more fully in the next chapter, also led to the design and
production of instruments which could monitor vibratory motion
elsewhere. By 1889 he had developed a series of vibration recorders,
one of which is of particular significance.

Some time earlier a Mr MacDonald of the Locomotive Department of Tokyo Railways commenced a series of experiments in an
endeavour to find a method of reducing vibrations of the steam
engines then in use on the rapidly expanding Japanese rail system.
He had begun by observing the movement produced by water in a
bottle placed in the cab of an engine in motion but it immediately
became obvious that, unless this could be recorded in some way for
analysis, the experiments were of little practical value. The need was
for an instrument able to register the three components of the
oscillations which occur in a moving train in such a way that each
could be identified from a permanent record sheet.

Naturally, this problem was of immediate interest to Milne and he
and MacDonald lost little time in setting to work. They decided that
the vibrations of a locomotive originating from an imbalance of the
moving parts could lead to a serious loss in efficiency and
consequently to greater consumption of fuel.

Ordinary earthquake instruments Milne and others had invented
were found to be too sensitive, their working being interfered with
partly by the suddenness of the jolts to which they were subjected
and partly because they were affected by changes in inclination. It
soon became clear that, especially for the horizontal movements,

apparatus with considerable stability was required and that it must be both compact and portable. The final form adopted, the Milne-MacDonald Vibration Recorder, although involving the same principles as many seismographs, was not suitable for recording earthquakes also. It was novel as applied to the vibrations of rolling stock and at the same time somewhat different in its construction from any earthquake measuring device.

The typical simplicity of a Milne invention is apparent. A clockwork motor slowly drives round a recording drum. On to this drum is wrapped a sheet of paper which is marked by three black-lead pencils attached to the tips of pointers which produce traces representing the vertical and horizontal vibrations made by the locomotive and the movements backwards and forwards. Two separate principles are used in this recorder; one for sensing the vertical vibrations and the other for the horizontal movements. Any vertical jolt displaces the weight and is recorded on the paper by one of the pencils. The horizontal record is produced by the movement of two metal cylinders.

After a long series of trials on various locomotives on different tracks in Japan had been made, Milne and MacDonald demonstrated that their recorder could indicate not only imbalance but also variations in the speed of trains. It was able to show those parts of journeys where time was gained or lost; stoppages which had occurred and their duration, and, in addition, could indicate the average speed when the distance between stations was known. More importantly, after the basic track characteristics had been established, variations on their mean would pin-point faults on the permanent-way such as the irregular yielding of the railway lines on bridges, the softening of a track bed, and other signs of misalignment. By interpreting the traces made by a locomotive in motion, imbalance could be rectified — a major step forward, this, as incorrect balancing of an engine reduces its safe working speed and might lead to derailment through excessive swaying.

After several improvements to the original model had been made the apparatus proved to be satisfactory, and as a result of this invention Milne was able to offer concrete suggestions for reducing vibration of their rolling stock to the Japanese railway authorities.

While on a visit to Britain in 1889 Milne met his friend Sir William Thomson and on a railway journey from Largs to Glasgow, demonstrated his 'new instrument for registering the three components of oscillation on a railway train'. Much interested by the explanation of its principles and on learning from Milne how it had been developed with the cooperation of John MacDonald, Sir William suggested that a paper should be presented by them to the Institute of Civil Engineers in London, and to this Milne readily agreed.

Subsequently, Paper 2468 by John Milne FRS, and John MacDonald of the Locomotive Department of Tokyo, *On the Vibratory Movement of Locomotives and on Timing Trains and Testing Railway Tracks*, was read at the meeting of the Institute in November 1890.

This very factual paper was only about twenty pages long; the discussion and correspondence it engendered accounted for three times as much space in the 'minutes'. Both paper and discussion are still worthwhile reading material for any engineer with an hour or so to spare. The contents of the paper aroused so much interest among the eminent engineers of the Institution that its committee honoured the authors with a coveted prize — The Telford Premium — a money award that took its name from the Institute's first president, the famous engineer who was responsible for, among many other engineering feats, the Caledonian Canal. The sum of money donated was far outweighed by the academic prestige it gave to the recipients and Milne, in particular, was quietly pleased to add it to his growing list of achievements acknowledged by the scientific and technological worlds.

Although not the first attempt to produce an instrument to measure the vibrations of railway trains, the Milne-MacDonald Recorder was by far the most successful and sophisticated. A later model of this device was manufactured by the London firm of R. C. Munro & Co. and was employed on railway systems in Britain and other countries. It was also used on a number of paddle steamers of the day, including the famous *Royal Sovereign*, which plied for years on the river Thames as far as Margate.

The techniques used for the detection of vibrations for transport generally have improved tremendously since the introduction of the Milne-MacDonald Recorder of course, but the pair must be given credit for their ingenious invention. In the case of Milne it was an object lesson of how the application of skills and knowledge gained in one specialist field could be used to good purpose in another.

While, as we shall see, the work he did in laying the foundation of modern seismology must always take pride of place whenever John Milne is discussed, his contribution to the world's knowledge of volcanoes, his exploration of the mineral wealth of Japan, his influence on that country's mining industry and the many other benefits arising from his resourcefulness must also be taken into account when assessing his value to mankind.

Not unnaturally, his work had its critics. Some raised valid points and these he respected. But there were those, sometimes eminent scientists themselves, who seemed to spend much valuable time in finding fault with the work of others, possibly to elevate their own importance. Milne could afford to ignore these even when he knew he was right and usually did so.

When convinced he was right he might be tempted to offer a mild rebuke, especially if his opponent was a person of considerable specialist knowledge. After the publication of Milne's paper *On the form of volcanoes*, O. Fisher, a well-known geologist of the time, wrote a letter to *Nature* complaining that, when referring to the differential cooling of the earth's crust beneath the atmosphere on the one hand, and that below the seas on the other, Milne had written: '. . . without entering into calculations on the subject . . .' 'Why *not* enter into calculation, when, as in the present case, that was so easy?' he asked.

It was John Perry, newly returned to England, who took up cudgels on Milne's behalf 'as he is too far away to reply for himself.' Perry explained that he had raised this very point when the paper was being written and Milne had told him firmly:

> I wish to keep myself from committing a common error of many geologists who know a little mathematics, the error of imagining that I can create a mathematical theory for a phenomenon when I am only acquainted with part of the cause of the phenomenon.

Fisher was not satisfied and, replying to Perry to whom he referred as 'Milne's apologist', went into even greater detail and making sure that attention was called to the number of papers *he* had written on the subject. Perry did not deign to answer and Milne, obviously feeling that his friend had made the point for him, also refused to be drawn.

Differences of opinion between academics were as common in those days as now. Accepted as a way of life, they are of value in opening up fresh lines of thought and new areas of investigation. An attack on one's personal integrity, however, is a different thing altogether. A charming and kind man, John Milne was also sensitive and could be hurt as much as anyone on such occasions. But, if the accusations were false, he was capable of a swift counter-attack. An example of this occurred at the end of the summer vacation of 1877 when he returned to College two days late from a geological expedition to Hokkaido. He apologised to the Principal, Henry Dyer, and settled down to his lecturing without delay. To his astonishment he received the following letter:

Kobu-dai Gakko
Oct 8th, 1877

Prof. Milne.
Dear Sir,
    I have received a letter from the Kobusho of which I enclose a copy and request your consideration and reply.
        Yours truly,
            Henry Dyer, Principal.

The enclosure from the Kobusho (Ministry of Public Works) was a communication typical of any government department:

Kobusho, Oct 8th, 1877

Henry Dyer, Esq.,
Principal,
Dear Sir,
I beg to inform you that the Minister of this Department requests you will communicate with Messrs Milne and Perry to produce a document respectively stating satisfactory reason for the delay of their returning on duty from the recent travelling and especially so with Mr Perry because his case is somewhat different from Mr Milne in some respects.
I am, dear sir,
Yours very truly,
K. S. Otiri.

Perry's reaction is unknown but Milne was livid. The draft 'document' he prepared in reply clearly indicates his anger. Almost unreadable, there are missing words which had to be inserted later and other furiously slashed out of existence. Icily polite, it must have caused something of a stir when forwarded to the Kobusho.

Kobu-dai-Gakko
Tokyo Oct 11th/77

To Henry Dyer, Esq.,
Dear Sir,
I have the honour to state that the cause of the detention referred to in your note and that of the Kobusho was, as I have already mentioned to you verbally, that the steamer by which I had intended returning from Otaru to Tokyo was diverted on duty different to that which had been anticipated.
It may not be out of place to mention here that I was detained 2 weeks at the commencement of the vacation on college work whereas on the present occasion I was but 2 days late, this, too, whilst partially on arranged college work.
Under the circumstances the criticisms which Mr Otiri's note are open to, are, I think, too trivial to need any comment.
Believe me,
I am, sir,
Yours truly,

There could be no answer to that and the matter does not appear to have been referred to again. Milne was satisfied as he had shown he was not prepared to be criticised unjustly.

As far as is known there is only one recorded incident where he really lost his temper over an academic issue. This was the affair of the 'aseismic tables' — an invention used primarily to provide Japanese lighthouses with a stable platform for their lamps which were often extinguished when any earth movements took place. Whilst on a journey to Australia in 1885 Milne was at first incredulous and then extremely angry when he read in the magazine *Nature* details of a particularly unpleasant personal attack then being mounted upon him back in Britain. The editor of this august scientific journal had been requested to print a series of letters:

> *Royal Observatory, Edinburgh*
> *June 5, 1855*
>
> My Dear Mr David Stevenson,
>   At p.248 of the new British Association volume for 1884 there is a section on 'Experiments on a building to resist earthquake motion', which reads amazingly like your paper of twenty years ago; but yet it is not that, for your name does not enter and they have in a way got round the letter of your invention by employing, in place of your bronze balls in shallow bronze basins, cast-iron balls and cast-iron plates, 'with saucer-like edges', for the lower basins; and for the upper basins, 'cast-iron plates slightly concave but otherwise similar to those below.'
>   Against such men would any patent be safe? though you may not have taken out a patent for your philanthropic invention for saving life in earthquake-persecuted countries; but the whole section is the most indubitable approval of your methods and principles that could well have been proposed by anyone. Certainly it transcends anything that could have entered the mind of
> *Yours very sincerely,*
> *C. Piazzi Smyth.*

Replying for his father who was indisposed, D. A. Stevenson thanked Professor Piazzi Smyth for his letter and asked permission to publish it 'to give the honour of the invention to whom the honour was due'. Professor Smyth agreed, adding,

> for in so far as I wrote it at all, I am ready to stand by it before many or few,

and went on to castigate 'the B A Man' for inferring it was *he* and not David Stevenson, who was the inventor of the system.

Milne was a prolific contributor to *Nature* and the editor, knowing his man, sat back, tongue in cheek and prepared to weather the inevitable storm. He had not long to wait.

> Dear Sir,
>   While on a visit to Melbourne Observatory I saw Nature of July 2 containing two letters from Prof. Piazzi Smyth, intended to expose a piratical attempt on the part of a 'B A Man' to adopt an idea of Mr David Stevenson with regard to the construction of houses to withstand earthquake action . . . The piracy referred to by Prof. Smyth is a brief note in a paper written by myself . . . Prof. Smyth complains that I have not taken notice of a paper written some twenty years ago by Mr

D. Stevenson. I regret to say that I am not acquainted with that paper, and how Prof. Smith expects that I should be when living 10,000 miles away from collections of European books, I fail to see. I am, however, acquainted with very much relating to aseismic tables, and if I made reference to the work of Mr Stevenson, I must necessarily have referred to the work of others. As every report I have hitherto written to the B.A. has been in the form of notes which have subsequently been expanded in special papers, an historical account of aseismic tables would have been out of place. Prof. Smyth is apparently only acquainted with the work of Mr Stevenson . . .

After listing several methods of construction, Milne continued,

All these involve the same principles, and only differ in their dimensions.

He went on to itemise plate and ball instruments, of which he had constructed several types and stated that all had been failures. They had, he wrote, been independently invented and described as original by many and followed this statement with a list of people, of whom Mr Stevenson was one, who had claimed to be the inventors. With regard to lamp tables, as he had been an officer in the Department of Public Works of Japan for the last ten years and where he had every facility of knowing what the performance of the lamp tables at the lighthouses had been at the time of severe earthquakes, he trusted that some credence might be given to what he had to say on the subject.

When I last made enquiries about these tables, I found they were all regarded as failures and one and all had been clamped.

After discussing models where he ridiculed Prof. Smyth's experiments, Milne turned his attention to buildings.

The only building placed on free foundations with which I am acquainted is the one I have erected in Tokyo. At first it rested on balls, and like Mr Stevenson's lamp tables, it was for certain reasons a failure. Now it rests on spherical grains of cast-iron sand. It is now astatic, and I regard it as a success . . . From what I have now said it will be clear that I have no desire to claim the authorship of the aseismatic joint. Detailed reference to the obscure and manifold authorship of what has hitherto proved a failure would certainly have been out of place in the report to which Prof. Smyth has referred. Had Messrs Stevenson and Smyth been acquainted with the nature of earthquake motion, a few of the more important facts in the history of the ball and plate joint, and the details of the failure of the tables in the Japanese lighthouses, I feel sure that much of the objectionable innuendo to which I have been subjected would never have been penned.   John Milne, s.s. Waihora, Hobart, Tasmania.

> *PS — The above has been written whilst at sea and I have had opportunity to refer neither to books or papers. On my return to Japan I shall be glad to continue the history of the ball and plate joints, should it be required.*

It was a strong enough reply and there the matter could well have ended. In the event it was but a ranging shot in the bitter battle which followed. Milne grew more and more angry with his accusers as evidenced by the many underlined passages in his other letters to *Nature:*

> *The only occasion on which I have posed as the author of the aseismic joint in question was when Messrs Stevenson and Smyth promoted me to that quasi-enviable position.*
>
> *Had these gentlemen recognised the fact that they were only reading a brief note about plate and joint, intercalated in a collection of notes on other subjects, and had they been well acquainted with recent literature relating to aseismic tables, they would certainly have refrained from the objectionable accusations made on July 2.*
>
> *On more than one occasion I have referred to Mr Stevenson's work in Japan. As an example of such a reference, Messrs Stevenson and Smyth may turn to the 'Times' of May 26 — a date which it will be observed is prior to the date of their unwarrantable attack. In that paper there is a long letter on 'Building and Earthquakes' signed with my name. When speaking of my house on shot, there I say, 'This experiment was very similar to one carried out by Mr David Stevenson with regard to the lamp-tables in several of the lighthouses on the coast of Japan' . . . I will further other references if required. I think it would be only just for Prof. Piazzi-Smyth and Mr D. A. Stevenson to withdraw their accusations.*

There was more — much more. The controversy went on for months. To his chagrin, Milne did not get his apology before the editor terminated the correspondence. The matter rankled with him for years and his references to it were always bitter. In view of the fact that he had made it a personal rule always to quote original sources when not himself the inventor, to be accused of not doing the very thing upon which he prided himself was most hurtful and his anger understandable.

Nearly a century has passed since this storm in a tea-cup took place. It was not very significant then and is unimportant now, referred to only to indicate that Milne was not always the mild, utterly charming gentleman some would have us believe. He might well have been for most of the time but when the occasion arose he could be as human as most.

Milne's work at the College, now part of the University, continued throughout. He never neglected the original terms of his contract even though his seismology was such an absorbing hobby that it began to dominate his life. Often he would emphasise this very point to his friends when they remonstrated with him for working so long into the night, saying, 'After all, I am trained in geology and mining and, you know, these things still fascinate me.'

Thus it was with little surprise that his colleagues learnt of the publication of *The Miner's Handbook*. This was an enlarged version of his lecture notes which were first printed in Japan about 1879. It was subtitled *A Handy Book of Reference on the subjects of mineral deposits, mining operations, ore dressing, etc, for the use of students and others interested in mining matters*. It contained updated tables, formulae, definitions and many useful facts together with a six-page bibliography listing the works on mining, etc, to which he had made reference when compiling the book. Its first full edition, printed in Japan in 1893, was quickly exhausted and by 1902 his London publishers, Crosby and Lockwood, were issuing a third. Modest as ever about his own contribution Milne wrote in the preface:

> Although here and there a few notes, collected when visiting mining districts in various parts of the world have been added, the book as a whole is little more than a collection of well-known facts put together in an order following the writer's lectures.

Be that as it may, the reviewer for the magazine *Nature* commented:

> During his long stay in Japan Professor Milne seems to have acquired the deftness of a native in packing, for it is difficult to conceive how more could have been crammed into a book no bigger than a cigar-case and weighing only 6½ oz. It is a veritable miniature compendium of mining which is likely to find its place not only on the shelves but also in the luggage of most mining engineers.

Many men would have been content to have pursued a teaching career in mining and geology, especially when supplemented with extensive opportunities for field studies in both disciplines. To have added a major in-depth study of volcanology and maintained a deep interest in archaeology with considerable time-consuming explorations in each to their work-load would have taxed the majority severely. To have become involved in the founding of a new science into the bargain was something surely only a man such as Milne would have been capable of undertaking so successfully.

5

The Seismologist

When John Milne arrived in Japan in March 1876 he could not have been aware that the slight earthquake he experienced on his first night was eventually to determine the course of his life, or that at that moment the future 'father of modern seismology' had been 'born'.

It was almost as if he were being welcomed by the phenomenon and invited to give it serious attention. But there was no time for intensive detailed study as he had to settle down quickly to the task of teaching his first group of eager Japanese students the intricacies of mining and geology. He also felt impelled to complete his series of reports on the geology of countries he had visited — Newfoundland, Egypt and Siberia — and to finalise the manuscript of his first text book, *Crystallography*. Nor, at this stage, was the young professor at all certain in his mind that he wanted to become too immersed in a study of earthquakes, fascinating although he knew it would be, for the subject was already being enthusiastically tackled by Ayrton and Perry. In fact, quite a number of the foreigners in the country as well as some Japanese were beginning to take the topic seriously and when Ewing and Gray joined the College soon after, they were similarly attracted.

Milne may have considered that, if he wanted to make a name for himself, he should turn his attention and talents elsewhere. As we now know, he began a comprehensive investigation into the formation and geological distribution of Japanese volcanoes, and also developed a brief interest in archaeology with some useful field research into ancient stone implements and other Japanese prehistorical remains. Yet he soon found himself becoming more and more intrigued by earth movements. The problems they presented were something he could not resist: before long he was as much involved as his colleagues in trying to solve them.

In that year earthquakes seemed to be almost daily occurrences, and Milne later was to write:

> In April, the month following my arrival, there were no less than ten shocks recorded, whilst in the following twelve months there were fifty-three in all.

So it is not surprising that, when it was possible, he would turn his attention to what was for him and the rest of the British staff a new experience. The phenomenon presented them with a challenge which could not be ignored. Conversation at mealtimes and in the common rooms often centred round the latest series of alarming tremors and when he commented, 'We had earthquakes for breakfast, dinner, tea and supper', he implied more than just the physical experience. In order to discuss the subject sensibly, background knowledge was essential. Here Milne was at an advantage for his geological experience stood him in good stead and his interest in museums, together with a penchant for wide reading, had enabled him to accumulate a vast store of relevant facts. In the broad Lancastrian accent which he never lost throughout his life, his skill in presenting a good tale, told with inimitable humour, gave him the ability to hold his listeners spellbound when he recounted stories of mythical monsters and gods whose subterranean movements caused these disasters.

In Japanese mythology these movements were made by a large earth spider and later in that country's history by a catfish buried in the ground. At Kashima, some sixty miles north-east of Tokyo, there was a rock which was said to rest on the head of this creature to keep it quiet. As a result, earthquakes in the vicinity were infrequent but the rest of the islands were shaken by the wriggling of its tail and body. In Mongolia the earthshaker was a subterranean hog; in India a mole; the Mussulmen pictured it as an elephant while in other parts of the world equally unlikely animals bore the responsibility for the movements.

Sometimes he would tell the legend of the people of Kamchatka and their god Tuil, who, like themselves, lived amongst the ice and snow. Their dogs were infested by fleas and when they stopped to scratch, these actions produced the earthquakes! In Scandinavia, too, a land of much mythology, there was an evil genie called Loki who, having killed his brother Baldwin, was bound to a rock face upwards, so that the poison of a serpent should drop on it. Loki's wife, however, intercepted the deadly liquid with a vessel and it was only when she had to go away to empty the dish that a few drops reached the prostrate deity and caused him to writhe in agony and shake the earth.

Among his stories were those which dealt with the numerous shocks which were felt throughout Britain in 1750 and the great disaster of Lisbon five years later, as a result of which many sermons were preached from pulpits to emphasise that God was warning about man's increasing wickedness: the Book of *Revelation* was well thumbed in many a vicarage and rectory. After the earthquake in Palermo in 1706 a similar series of incidents had occurred and Milne told his listeners, 'The people seemed to be extremely humble and penitent, scourging themselves and doing penance.'

He would also recite a poem written in 1750:

What pow'rful hand with force unknown,
Can these repeated tremblings make?
Or do th'imprison'd vapours groan?
Or do the shores with fabled Tridents shake?
Ah no! the tread of impious feet,
The conscious earth impatient bears;
And Shudd'ring with the guilty weight,
One common grave for her bad race prepares.

'Earthquakes were sometimes used to show how one religion was better than others,' he would continue, 'for even during my own times in Japan, evidence of a selective providence was found in the fact that a few of the houses tenanted by Christian converts happened to remain standing amongst the ruins of their Buddhist and Shinto neighbours!'

In academic papers and in popular articles for magazines, and later still in his book, *Seismology*, he was to write of early philosophers such as Aristotle, Pliny and others who, because they had observed steam and gas exhalations escaping from volcanic vents, held that earthquakes were due to the working of the wind or imprisoned vapour beneath the earth's crust — a view which finds its parallel in the early history of the Chinese. Theories of this order were met with until late in the Middle Ages. He proved his point by quoting from Shakespeare's *Henry IV*:

Diseased nature oftentimes breaks forth
In strange eruptions: oft the teeming earth
Is with a kind of colic pinch'd and vex'd
By the imprisoning of unruly wind
Within her womb; which, for an enlargement striving,
Shakes the old bedlam earth, and topples down
Steeples and moss-grown towers.

Theories concerning the origin of earthquakes other than those attributed to pure mythology were frequently put forward by philosophers and early scientists. The electrical discharge theory, for instance, had its distinguished advocates in the eighteenth and nineteenth centuries, particularly in Italy. The hypothesis centred around the idea that electricity, by causing the explosion of subterranean gases indirectly produced earthquakes. Others expressed the view that earth motions were due to chemical explosions; bitumen and sulphur were quoted as possible explosive materials, while the vapours produced by the action of water on quick lime or on iron pyrites were similarly favoured. Still others contended that earthquakes might in some way or other be connected with volcanic action. Steam under pressure below the surface, they reasoned, could cause an explosion while the passage of lava along the strata planes could inflict earth movements above ground. These were but a few of the many theories and beliefs which had been advanced. The truth was, said Milne, that no-one really knew.

The little group of interested people in this earthquake-troubled land, so far from their own, soon acknowledged Milne as their leader. All were determined to see if something could be done to understand the phenomenon better and they discussed endlessly the facts and theories currently known or believed. 'Better instrumentation,' Milne told them, 'is the key to the problem and the path we should pursue.' So began a concentration on ways and means of recording and analysing the tremors which came to them almost daily.

This was an obvious course to follow for, although many so-called earthquake measuring devices had been constructed in the past, few, if any, could claim to have been particularly successful. To understand the kind of instruments needed by Milne and his colleagues, some knowledge of the motion of the ground during an earthquake is necessary. It is not, as many then believed, a single disturbance, but rather a number of them, preceded and followed by vibrations which increase in intensity as the moment of fracture occurs, decreasing thereafter in much the same way as echoes die in time and distance. If all that was needed was a record that an earthquake had taken place then such devices were already in existence. These seismoscopes, as they are called, were available in a variety of forms, but in order to study the phenomena correctly, the frequency, amplitude, extent and direction of the 'waves' as well as the exact time of the occurrence need to be known. The group at the College immediately found themselves in difficulty because seismographs, the instruments capable of recording these factors, had not yet been invented. Indeed, as Milne explained, all they had were really only elaborate seismoscopes.

'The earliest seismoscope of which we find any historical record is one which owes its origin to a Chinese called Chôko (Chang Heng),' wrote Milne. 'It was invented in the year A.D. 136.' Milne then notes that a description is given in the Chinese history called *Gokanjo* and a translation runs as follows:

In the year of Yoka, A.D. 136, a Chinese called Choko (Chang Heng) invented the seismometer. This instrument consists of a spherically formed copper vessel, the diameter of which is nearly three metres. It is covered at its top, and in form resembles a wine-bottle. Its outer part is ornamented by the figures of different kind of birds and animals, and old, peculiar-looking letters. In the inner part of the instrument a column is so suspended that it can move in eight directions. Also, in the inside of the bottle, there is an arrangement by which some record of an earthquake is made according to the movement of the pillar. On the outside of the bottle there are eight dragon heads, each of which holds a ball in its mouth. Underneath these are eight frogs so placed that they appear to watch the dragon's face, so that they are ready to receive the ball if it should be dropped. All the arrangements which cause the pillar to knock the ball out of the dragon's mouth are well hidden in the bottle.

When an earthquake occurs, and the bottle is shaken, the dragon instantly drops the ball, and the frog which receives it vibrates vigorously; anyone watching this instrument can easily observe earthquakes.

With this arrangement, although one dragon may drop a ball, it is not necessary for the other seven to drop theirs unless the movement has been in all directions; thus we can easily tell the direction of an earthquake.

The story continues:

Once upon a time a dragon dropped a ball without an earthquake being observed, and the people therefore thought the instrument of no use, but after two or three days a notice came saying that an earthquake had taken place at Rosei. Hearing of this, those who doubted the use of the instrument began to believe in it again. After this ingenious instrument had been invented by Chôko (Chang Heng), the Chinese Government wisely appointed a secretary to make observations on earthquakes.

To Europeans in Japan at that time, the study of earthquakes was a pleasant hobby. For Milne it became an obsession. It is impossible to give here a full account of his great contribution to seismology, for his writings on this subject alone exceed two million words — a massive output. The examples of his work which follow have been chosen to illustrate the range of his interest, the character of the man and the reason many consider to him to be the true father of the science. Those interested in a more detailed appraisal of his academic work will find of value the comprehensive lists of books and papers in the bibliography.

To appreciate more fully the tremendous stimulus resulting from his work in this field a number of points must be borne in mind. The state of experimental seismology throughout the world in the 1870s was negligible. Those few who were so engaged were 'back-room boys' in the true sense of the word. Even in the basic sciences teaching laboratories were rare; none existed solely for the study of earthquakes. In no country was there a scientific society devoted solely to this discipline and to provide a forum for discussion and the

development of ideas, while departments of seismology in universi-
ties were unknown. In Japan, therefore, it is not surprising that
before the arrival of the western technologists little was being
attempted.

Yet it was to be in this earthquake-ridden country that the place,
the time and the man finally coincided. Milne's contribution to the
rapid development of the new science at this stage was crucial, for,
although he seldom went into deep mathematical analysis, he alone
seemed to have the insight needed to identify those problems
demanding investigation: he could see clearly the path to be
followed if progress were to be made. He was a true pioneer, totally
absorbed with what he was attempting to the extent that some
considered him to be a fanatic. Yet 'Earthquake Milne', as he soon
came to be known, had the personality to stimulate others not only
to take an interest and provide practical help with his complicated
experiments, but to carry out their own. Of all his many
contributions to seismology perhaps that could be considered the
greatest.

He used his training as a geologist and a practising mining
engineer to establish disciplines in the new science, and, if some of
his contemporaries felt that his fundamental understanding in
certain fields was suspect, they were carried along by his tremendous
enthusiasm and drive since he was able to convince most of them
which would be the most valuable areas of research. Needless to say
he, and they, made mistakes. It is easy for modern sophisticates,
armed with the wisdom of hindsight, to be critical of some of his
work but, viewed alongside his contemporaries, the great leap
forward in seismological knowledge which began at this time was
almost entirely due to his utter dedication to the immense task before
him.

The major turning point in Milne's life, the final conversion to
seismologist, was the direct outcome of an earthquake which shook
the Tokyo-Yokohama area at about ten minutes to one o'clock on
the morning of Sunday, 22 February 1880. Of this he wrote:

I was asleep. It, however, quickly woke me and by means of my
watch and a lamp which was burning close to my head to enable
me to observe the time of the earthquake shocks, I obtained
very fairly the time of commencement and the duration of the
shock. At the time the house was swaying violently from side to
side, and even when I thought the motion had finished the
distance through which the building was oscillating was so
great that I was unable to walk steadily across the floor.
Immediately after this I visited two long pendulums which,
with various other apparatus, I had been using for making
experiments on earthquakes' motion. At the time when I saw

them, which was within a minute of the cessation of the shock, they were swinging violently through a distance of two feet. They would have swung further had they not been prevented by catches. From these and the swinging lamps I obtained an approximate direction of the shock.

Next morning, having much to do in collecting records from various instruments, I sent a messenger to Yokohama carrying watches to compare the difference in time of observation of the shock, and to make general inquiries about the damage.

It being evident that much damage had been done, I drew up a series of questions, which were printed on sheets of paper and, through the kindness of the editor of the *Japan Gazette* who was interested in earthquake phenomena, were issued to the subscribers of that newspaper.

Milne devised twelve questions in all, seeking information on the time of the shock; the direction of the first swing of any movable object and that in which chimneys fell; the damage done to the house of the reader; the width and direction of cracks in walls; whether the shock had been felt and if it produced feeling of sickness, headaches, etc., and if a rumbling sound had been heard before or after the earthquake.

He analysed these replies, as well as those he received as a result of writing to several other local newspapers, and the answers to many letters he despatched to friends and acquaintances in the immediate vicinity. In all, this mammoth task involved five hundred printed forms and over one hundred letters and was the earliest recorded use of a mass-questionnaire technique in seismology. The response was good, and together with the information he obtained from a number of instruments and contrivances with which he had been experimenting, and from a series of visits he made in and around Tokyo and Yokohama, he was able to produce a most comprehensive report. He wrote:

What I have endeavoured to do has been to give the history of an earthquake from the sudden jar which gave it birth, to the time it passed our dwellings to fill us with alarm, until finally, spreading outwards in ever-widening circles, its energies and motion became dissipated, and it died. Although its life was ephemeral, perhaps not existing as an earthquake for more than ten minutes, its energy was sufficient to shake the largest mountain.

Milne's conclusions ranged beyond the disaster itself. Because of the many inconsistencies in the information sent to him, he now knew for certain he was right in his contention that better seismological instrumentation was essential, and that immediate intense research was vital if meaningful progress was to be made.

Even of greater importance was his realisation that, if this full-scale, detailed and accurate study of earthquake phenomena was to take place, then the services of many other people were needed; there was so much to be done that it was far beyond the capabilities of the few enthusiasts then working on the problem. It was time to enlarge the scope of investigations and this could best be done by the formation of a society with many dedicated members all working in their specialist field and pooling their knowledge.

He called a few of his friends together to discuss the feasibility of the idea, and a small committee was set up. Milne was asked to become the first president of the proposed society which shows the esteem in which he was already being held, but he demurred and insisted it would be better to have this place filled by a prominent Japanese official. His Excellency, Yamao Yozo, the then Minister of Public Works, was invited, but owing to pressure of work had to decline the honour and so the position was eventually offered to Mr I. Hattori, a Japanese gentleman.

The first working meeting of The Seismological Society of Japan was held on Monday, 26 April 1880, in the lecture hall of the Kaisei Gakko and was well attended. John Milne had the honour of delivering the opening paper to this, the initial meeting of the first seismological society in the world. In a long and carefully prepared address he developed what he thought should be the aims of such a society, reviewed the current knowledge in the field of seismology, and made useful suggestions as to how their investigations should proceed.

The following extracts demonstrate his understanding of the situation and the future development he envisaged:

> Gentlemen: Today I have the honour of addressing a society whose main object is to collect and systematize facts which are in any way connected with earthquakes and volcanoes. It is intended that the society's chief work shall be to gather and correlate phenomena which emanate from the interior of the earth; and whereas nearly all the learned societies, of which there are so many in European countries, chiefly study that which is on the exterior of our planet, the objects of this society are decidedly peculiar.
>
> The task is great, and one of the first problems which come before us is to determine how it is to be accomplished. No doubt the same end may be attained by different methods, but it behoves us always to strive after that which is the best. At the outset it would seem well to obtain first a clear idea of the goal we are endeavouring to reach. Next we might consider the roads it would be necessary to follow to attain it successfully, and finally, we might examine how far previous workers in seismology have advanced along the paths we desire to follow.

He then expressed briefly his own ideas as to the nature and cause of earthquakes and volcanoes confirmed by observations made in the previous four years:

> Earthquakes are to us the evidence of sudden jars or blows which, having been struck upon the earth, cause a vibration to travel through a portion of its mass. During elevations or depressions rocky masses may reach their limit of elasticity, and having been fractured, give such blows.
>
> Volcanoes are direct evidence of internal heat, and to those who study physiography they are most important factors in all considerations connected with the internal condition of the earth.

Milne went on to survey the findings of earlier investigators. He spoke of men like Perry and Robert Mallet each of whom had devoted much time to the study of earth movements; or Humbolt, Arago, Biot, Hopkinson, Schmidt, von Seebach, von Hoff, Falb, Fuchs, von Lasaulx, Credner, Vogt, Volger, Palmiori, Rossi and others each of whom had added something to the current knowledge then available. He stressed that geologists, physicists, mathematicians and men of science generally had always been attracted to a study of earthquakes; they had thought about them, and written about them. He emphasised that before beginning any investigation it was important to become familiar with all the earlier studies.

Putting forward reasons for the study of earthquakes, he said that students of seismology had always strived to discover some means of predicting when earthquakes would occur.

His outlook was always practical and he told his audience about a scheme to be carried out in the district around Tokyo and Yokohama:

> Through the interest taken in seismological science by Mr Yamao Yozo, the Minister of Public Works, fifteen seismometers of the pendulum type as designed by Mr Gray are now being constructed for distribution over the plain of Musashi. Through the kindness of the Director of the Telegraph Department, these instruments are to be placed in the telegraph offices, where by means of clocks which are every day regulated by Tokyo time, not only will the earthquake movement be recorded, but the time at which the shocks are felt will also be noted.

He concluded by saying that investigations like these were of the greatest interest to science, and the practical results of value to the geologist, the builder and the engineer.

The earthquake on the morning of Sunday, 22 February 1880, was not of large magnitude. In the great seismic catalogues it is confined to a mere line of figures; one of the thousands that find their way into such reference books. Its importance pales to insignificance besides the many, and yet this particular one should never be forgotten since the locally strong movements along the bluffs of Yokohama towards Tokyo are those which resulted in the establishment of the Seismological Society of Japan and Milne's emergence as the pioneer of a new science.

From this time onwards the Society's members, stimulated by his constant encouragement, began systematic observations of earthquakes on a scale never before envisaged. By the end of Milne's service in Japan there were nearly a thousand centres at which earth movements could be registered. All were invited to take part for he wanted to interest the layman as well as the specialist. Some of his papers, like the one he presented to the Society entitled *A Mantel-Piece Seismometer* explaining the construction of a simple indicator, illustrates this well. So determined was he to do all in his power to reduce the devasting effects of these natural disasters, and so great his powers of persuasion that many of his colleagues found themselves cooperating in schemes they would not have thought of initiating.

Once he had taken the decision to devote as much time as possible to the study of earthquakes his insatiable need to 'know everything there was to know' sent him searching the libraries for information, collecting material from all over the world, and arranging translations. As a result he was able to build up an impressive reference library. The lights of his study burned long into the silent Japanese nights as he read, thought, experimented and recorded. His papers began to tell of experiments with weights suspended on wires; weights supported on springs like a watchmaker's noddy; spiral springs and various types of pendulums; vessels filled with water and other liquids to measure tilting; overturned columns, and similar devices. It soon became apparent to him, as it had to others, that the principle of the simple pendulum could be employed as the more accurate measuring instrument they were seeking. In 1881 he noted:

For the last two years I have had a number of pendulums varying in length from 1 to 36 feet suspended in my house for the purpose of experimenting on earthquake motion there, together with others which are suspended in a building of the Engineering College. At that time I suspended three small pendulums in my dining room. One great problem which presented itself was to suspend a mass of material so that at the time of an earthquake it should remain practically at rest. The solution was first sought for in the bob of an ordinary pendulum. It being supposed that greater stability would be attained if the lengths of the pendulums were increased, three enthusiasts, in order to obtain a support from the roof timbers of their houses, cut holes through two ceilings, and the bobs of long pendulums were even to be seen in drawing rooms!

Insomuch as it was found that whenever a heavy earthquake occurred these pendulums were caused to swing in some instances so violently that apparatus in their vicinity was wrecked, attempts were made to make them dead beat and next astatic, and a series of experiments were started which it would require pages to describe.

Besides his work with pendulums he was concerned at this stage with a thorough investigation of all crude methods then available for earthquake detection and measurement, for he was personally convinced, and was to remain so for the rest of his life, that simplicity in the principle of instrument design was a key factor if success was to be achieved. By a systematic analysis of the worth of these earlier instruments he could determine upon their retention or rejection.

'At this time,' wrote Milne, 'Tokyo was in reality a city of many inventions, all of which were for the purpose of obtaining trustworthy information about earthquakes; their name was legion, and it is no exaggeration to say that of seismographs, seismoscopes and seismometers, more than one worked with fifty different devices.'

In all his experiments the conclusions to which he came were always recorded in meticulous detail. During the period he was investigating the movement of liquids in a vessel during an earth tremor, for instance, he felt it necessary to note even the following simple failure:

If a glass which has been smeared over with a tincture of gall be dried and partially filled with a weak solution of iron perchloride, this latter does not give a mark by washing up the glass. Also, the precipitate which is formed will not stick to the side of the glass.

For these experiments he was criticised by some of his contemporaries who thought them unnecessary. Undeterred, Milne commented somewhat tartly:

The records I have now given are the results of many experiments made during the last four years. Many of them are the records of failures and these have been referred to so that others wishing to record earthquakes may avoid similar errors. The unsatisfactoriness of the results obtained from many of the old simple seismometers has been pointed out. The reason why they have so long been repeatedly recommended would seem amongst other things to have been the want of sufficient opportunities to experiment with such instruments and also, perhaps, from the non-recognition of the true nature of an earthquake vibration. Many may think that since seismology has of late years made such great and rapid strides, investigations such as mine have been behind the times. Those who hold ideas like these need, I think, only to be reminded of the vast amount of valuable information which *might* have been gathered in if we had scattered around us persons provided with *simple* instruments in order that they should change their opinions.

He went on to point out that such instruments were needed if they were to be operated by laymen, and re-emphasised the need for establishing a vast network of recording stations throughout Japan, being fully aware that complicated and expensive instruments for the many would not be feasible at the time.

He pointed out, too, that not all of his experiments were simple. Some were technically well advanced for the period. For example, in the same report, he had stated:

For several months experiments were made with microphones whilst endeavouring to make a record of earth tremors, but I cannot say as yet these experiments have been attended with any great success. The microphones which I have chiefly used have been small, double pointed pencils of carbon about 3 cm long, saturated with mercury and supported vertically in pivot holes bored in other pieces of carbon which were the terminals of the circuit.

It is less than one hundred years ago that he was using these 'microphones' — a long way from the geophones used with modern seismic surveys in this, the latter half of the twentieth century, but it is thanks to Milne and others engaged in these early experiments that such rapid strides in mineral prospecting and subterranean knowledge have now been made.

He realised, as had Mallet and others before him, that one of the most important tasks which confronted the seismic investigator at that time was to find a way to determine the magnitude of earthquake 'waves' so that mathematical relationships could be formulated. Frequent though they were, earthquake movements could not be relied upon to occur at the bidding of humans at the right place and of suitable intensity. It was therefore necessary to simulate them. For many years, with the willing help of Japanese government officials and departments, notably the Minister of the Interior, the Meteorological Office, the Public Works Department, the Imperial Telegraph Company and the Naval and War Departments, Milne carried out a long series of experiments with this end in view.

Heavy metal or concrete balls of up to 1,800 lbs in weight were dropped from varying heights to 35 feet, and explosive charges which often amounted to several pounds were detonated so that parameters of the vibrations — including velocity; vertical, normal and transverse acceleration; and the attenuation of amplitude with distance when the structure of the sub-soil was known — could be measured.

During the course of such experiments many amusing things happened and Milne later recalled one particular incident where a heavy charge was used. 'I used dynamite often,' he said, 'which could be exploded at the touch of a button, and I also had a number of seismographs situated at determined distances from the charge which were interconnected electrically so as to show the rate of wave transmission. On this occasion I placed myself within twenty feet of the mine in a position barricaded by earthworks which had an old door on top to keep off the falling stones. When I was ready I signalled to my assistant, who stood some distance away, to press the detonating button. The dynamite exploded with a sound like the broadside of heavy cannon, and I had scarcely fixed my eyes upon the moving smoked-glass disc when about a ton of earth came smashing down upon the door, flattening me and the instrument alike, and bringing that experiment to an untimely end.'

He was fortunate not to have been killed or seriously injured and thus able to go on and conclude this series of vital experiments, as well as his other equally important work at that time which included the testing and development of seismological instruments without which this branch of geophysics would have been useless.

His report on these simulated earthquakes runs to some eighty pages with the detailed summary alone accounting for six of them. He decided that they were analogous to those of natural disturbances and was eventually satisfied that he had solved many of the problems connected with the physical properties of surface earth-motion.

Intent upon producing more realiable instruments to record the erratic movements, the young staff at the Imperial College between them constructed many different devices. Some were discarded after trials while for others only a limited use could be found. Milne systematically tested most of them and while making suggestions for improvement where needed, offered endless encouragement to the inventors. It was almost inevitable that success would eventually follow. Within two or three years primitive but quite effective seismographs were ready for use.

It would be wrong to convey the impression that Milne alone was responsible for all the upsurge of interest in Japanese earthquakes at this time although undoubtedly his infectious enthusiasm was a major factor. The work of two other engineers in particular must be mentioned. James Alfred Ewing had joined the College in 1878 as

Professor of Mechanical Engineering and Physics and a year later Thomas Gray took up the post of Professor of Telegraphic Engineering. Both men soon became prominent in the design and construction of seismographs, pooling their respective talents and each working with Milne. But although they retained much interest after leaving Japan in 1881 and 1883 respectively, Ewing's active participation, significant though it was, became progressively less as he began to turn his attention to other interests in the scientific world. Gray, too, was to produce little of note after leaving the country. Even so, their contribution to seismology cannot be too highly valued.

Soon after his arrival at the College Gray became interested in finding a method to measure the vertical movement of an earthquake shock. At this stage Milne and he formed a working partnership and between them constructed a seismograph incorporating several important new principles. Not only could it record all three components of subterranean vibration but could operate for long periods without attention. More significantly, it could record the time of disturbances with reasonable accuracy.

Known as the Gray-Milne seismograph, the operation of this successful invention is described by Milne in his textbook *Earthquakes and Other Earth Movements* (Kegan Paul Trench, Trubner and Co., 1883), as follows:

In this apparatus two mutually rectangular components of the horizontal motion of the earth are recorded on a sheet of smoked paper wound round a drum kept continuously in motion by clockwork by means of two conical pendulum seismographs. The vertical motion is recorded on the same sheet of paper by means of a compensated-spring seismograph.

The time of occurrence of an earthquake is determined by causing the circuit of two electromagnets to be closed by the shaking. One of these magnets releases a mechanism, forming part of a time-keeper, which causes the dial of the timepiece to come suddenly forwards on the hands and then move to its original position. The hands are provided with ink-pads which mark their positions on the dial, thus indicating the hour, minute and second when the circuit was closed. The second electro-magnet causes a pointer to make a mark on the paper receiving the record of the motion. This mark indicates the part of the earthquake at which the circuit was closed.

The duration of the earthquake is estimated from the length of the record on the smoked paper and the rate of motion of the drum. The nature and period of the different movements are obtained from the curves drawn on the paper.

Mr Gray has since greatly modified this apparatus, notably

by the introduction of a band of paper sufficiently long to take a record for twenty-four hours without repetition. The record is written in ink by means of fine siphons. In this way the instrument, which is extremely sensitive to changes of level, can be made to show not only earthquakes, but the pulsations of long periods which have recently occupied much attention.

In 1881 Milne took the instrument to Britain where an improved version was produced by Messrs White of Glasgow, the cost being met in part by the British Association. On his return to Japan the device was shown to the Emperor and at his bidding was placed in the Meteorological Observatory in Tokyo. There it gave many years of valuable service and the readings obtained from it were published annually in the British Association's reports and elsewhere.

It is not known how many of these seismographs were manufactured — probably only a few — but by now most have been destroyed. One is carefully preserved at the Geophysics section of the Science Museum in London.

Like several of the world's major seismologists Milne spent much time in the preparation of earthquake catalogues and whilst in Japan the various lists he made covered the disturbances in that country effectively. For instance, in one of them he tabulated 429 shocks which had occurred on the Yedo plain between 1872 and 1881, and then attempted to correlate their effect on buildings. Where the information was available he gave the time, date, force, direction and duration. In both his regular reports to the Sub-Committee of the British Association, of which he was the secretary, and in the journal of the Seismological Society of Japan he included catalogues and comments on recent earthquakes which had occurred there.

His last paper in the Society's journal was a catalogue of nearly 400 pages giving details of a staggering total of 8,331 earthquakes recorded between the years 1885 and 1893 — a labour of love, this, as the task was undertaken long before the days of modern data processing. Each entry contained all the relevant details available. Of this massive piece of work Milne commented: 'As it stands, it is only a tentative effort to provide investigators with a new kind of data which may lead to investigations not hitherto possible.'

In the spring of 1887 Milne read a paper entitled *Earthquake Effects, Emotional and Moral* to the now well-established Society. This fascinating report, based upon his own observations and those of others who had also studied the subject, emphasises the wide range of his intensive research into seismic phenomena. This particular paper commenced with a description of his own reactions and those of his friends to their first earthquake experience.

Among the first desires which seize a visitor in an earthquake country is to experience a shaking. Should he leave the country without the fulfilment of his wish he expresses regret. On the other hand, if he becomes a resident in such a country, after the first trembling he will often express pleasure at the sensation he has experienced, and it is seldom that alarm is created. These expressions, however, are not permanent, for as the shakings are repeated, rather than sinking into a state of indifference to the disturbances, as so many writers state to be the case, a feeling of timidity often arises, until finally he comes to the conclusion of those who have more experience than himself, that the oftener you feel earthquakes the less likely they are to be disregarded.

He described some of the world's classic 'quakes, remarking that between 1783 and 1857 the Kingdom of Naples lost 111,000 inhabitants, a yearly average of 1,500 out of a total population of only six million, and that in the Antioch disaster of A.D. 526 an estimated total of a quarter of a million people perished. He also dealt at length with the effect major shocks had on the religious outlook in many communities. Concluding, he expressed an opinion that, 'With the facts which have been given lying before us, further arguments to show that seismic forces have exerted a vast influence upon the human race are *not* required.'

The discussion which followed the reading of this paper was lively and a revealing remark was made by one of his colleagues, the Japanese Professor Sekiya, who said, 'Professor Milne had at one time written monographs on special earthquakes; next he wrote upon experiments he has made upon artificial disturbances; then he described instruments for measuring earthquakes and now he takes up the literary portion of the subject: in short, he threatens to exhaust all that there is for workers in seismology to investigate.'

This no doubt raised the laugh it deserved, but such a statement, made by a man who was already beginning to be known for his own work, and who was himself to become a leading seismologist, confirms that Milne was recognised by others as the one with the widest range of interest in earthquake phenomena. This point was emphasised two months later when Milne again stood before them with a paper entitled *Notes on the Effects produced by Earthquakes upon the Lower Animals,* in which he stated that observation had shown that some animals produced signs of agitation immediately before an earthquake. He dismissed out of hand as being purely accidental, however, that there were cases where animals exhibited strange behaviour patterns several days before an earth movement occurred. 'A few seconds before an earthquake,' he said, 'I have often had the opportunity of confirming the tact that pheasants scream. Frogs, which by their croaking disturb the stillness of the summer nights, suddenly cease their vociferation before an earthquake. The Japanese assert that moles show their agitation by burrowing. Geese, swine and dogs are said to show clearer signs than other animals of an approaching earthquake. Many birds are stated to show uneasiness, hiding their heads beneath their wings and behaving in an unusual manner. The alarm of intelligent animals like dogs and horses may be the result of their own experience which has taught them that small tremors are premonitory of movements more alarming.'

With this opinion his friend, Professor Sekiya, did not entirely agree saying that *he* kept pheasants to study their behaviour at the time of an earthquake and considered that observation of them had not yielded any definite results. In this context it is also of interest to note that another Japanese seismologist, Professor F. Omori, supported Milne, he too having observed twenty-two occasions when pheasants had so screamed: on about half of these he himself had not felt the tremor which had disturbed the birds, but the movements were confirmed later from the records of instruments.

It was from papers like these, most of which came from the pen of Milne, and the far-reaching discussions which followed, that the Seismological Society of Japan helped to lay the foundations of current sub-terrestrial knowledge.

One of the series of investigations Professor Milne made in later years in Japan was into the magnetic and electrical effects which might be caused by earth movements. Considering the matter to be of some importance, he prepared and read a paper to the Society in 1890, remarking that it was only the second of its kind ever written on this subject. In it he developed the first in much greater detail, saying:

> The object of this paper is to draw attention to a variety of observations which require extension and to express the hope that the systematic study of such observations may lead to the explanation of several phenomena which at present are not understood.

He confirmed that electrical currents flowed through the ground during an earthquake and offered several theories, two of which reveal the way his thoughts were then being directed:

> One cause possibly producing earth currents would be the inrush of steam into fissures and cavities produced in rocks at the time, or previous to, the resulting crash which might be the cause of an earthquake. In addition to this, deep down in the earth we may conceive of the existence of intense chemical action caused by heated steam or molten matter acting on each other and the materials they come into contact with, giving rise

to currents of considerable magnitude. The earth currents of an active volcano are a subject still requiring investigation.

He had been able to verify that similar currents had been set up in artificially produced earthquakes, but felt that the second explanation he had offered, the theory of chemical action, was less likely than the first and that the earth currents observed at the time of an earthquake may be due to mechanical disturbances in the earth.

He added that, to propound a theory of the electrical phenomena which may have been observed in the air was more difficult, for, 'In some cases they may only have been atmospheric effects which have accidentally synchronised in the time of their occurrence with earthquakes. Possibly perhaps sudden dislocations of strata may occasionally have produced static electricity manifesting itself as luminous discharges in the air.'

We may smile now at his use of the words 'possibly' and 'perhaps', but when we consider how far the science of electricity has developed since the period in which he was working, his theories deserve to be considered sympathetically and the originality of his thinking appreciated.   'If we admit that the earthquakes of certain regions are the outcome of volcanic energy, and at the same time bear in mind the intensely magnetic character of many lavas,' he commented, 'the possibility of a connection between local variation of terrestrial magnetism and seismic phenomena is apparent.'

When the Society's chairman closed the meeting he remarked:

. . . the Society and science generally are benefited distinctly by Professor Milne's peculiar faculty of ever opening up new lines of research.

The tremendous support Milne received from the Japanese was supplemented by grants from the British Association. The Geological Society of London also donated money from its Wollaston Fund, and later added more when it awarded Milne the Lyell medal. In his absence abroad this medal was accepted on his behalf by Professor J.W. Judd, a personal friend of long standing. In accepting the award Judd said of Milne:

The cheerful courage with which he faced unpromising surroundings, the resourceful tact with which he had met every difficulty, and the unconquerable energy with which he has surmounted the greatest obstacles are known to all of us. You, Mr President, have referred to the admirable work done by the Seismological Society of Japan, and it is not too much to say that during the long period Professor Milne might have justly asserted 'I am the Seismological Society.' The foundation of that Society and the *Seismological Magazine* was due to the wise foresight and the unflagging energy of Professor Milne himself, and to the efforts of the pupils whom he instructed, and whose enthusiasm he has fired.

Very early in the industrialisation of Japan it was realised that a great reduction in the appalling casualty figures and the widespread damage to property resulting from earthquakes could be achieved if the transmission of shock waves to buildings was better understood. From this point it was but a small step for some to begin to question the existing building regulations as well as the methods of construction currently in use. The need to do so was evident. For instance, in later years Baron Kikuchi was to write:

> More than 25,000 persons were killed or injured, 120,000 to 130,000 houses were demolished or burned, 45 kilometres of railway destroyed, and more than 520 kilometres of roads, bridges and irrigating ditches destroyed. In one day the fruit of more than ten years' continued effort in the building of drainage canals, reservoirs, etc., was swept away.
>
> The destruction caused by earthquakes is beyond doubt far greater and more appalling than the consequences of war. And what is still more serious is the fact that wars can be avoided; but earthquakes are beyond human control. Nevertheless, we can at least seek to devise means and use all possible efforts to preserve life and to avoid in some degree exposure to danger.

Milne's investigation into earthquake phenomena was exhaustive. He studied them not only as a geologist anxious to probe the mystery of their origin, but as a humanitarian determined to find ways and means of helping people unfortunate enough to live in seismic areas, where death or injury and damage to property is an ever-present fear. He considered that any progress in this field, however small, would help to reduce the pain, misery and terror that a large earthquake inevitably brought in its wake.

He was quick to notice the difference in both the construction and the subsequent damage caused by a strong earthquake upon Japanese and European styled buildings. The former often received little visible damage, being mainly light wooden structures resting loosely on boulders for foundations, while the European type of building the westerners had introduced relied upon bricks and mortar, and often heavy coping stones, all resting on solid foundations and needing many tie rods and iron hoops in an attempt to reduce the effect of the shocks. Such buildings were expensive and more likely than not to be death traps when disaster struck. Yet, on the other hand, large temples and other heavy buildings were common enough throughout the country. This was because beneath their heavy roofs and superstructures there was usually a multiplicity of timber joints which, at the time of earthquakes, yielded to the shocks and so did not communicate the whole of the movement to the stones.

When Milne turned his attention to a fuller investigation of this matter he discovered immediately that no specific apparatus existed to help him. Ever resourceful, he devised his own, starting with the simplest of experiments as was his custom. He wrote:

A wire was stretched along the springing line of several arches in the Kubu-dai-Gakko (Engineering College), and one end of this was fixed, whilst to the other end, which hung freely over a staple, there was attached a short length of thin brass wire at the end of which a weight was hung, keeping the whole line stretched. This weight was of a size that, if it were slightly increased, it was sufficient to break the fine wire which joined it to the thick one. It was anticipated that, if at any moment this wire should be *suddenly* stretched by the brickwork not moving as a whole, the weak wire would be snapped.

Dozens of similar experiments followed, all simple and direct, such as the one where he tried to determine whether walls of a building which had once been cracked still continued to give way during further shock. The extremities of the cracks were marked with pencil and subsequent movements could also be detected by using a stylus mark on smoked glass. He commented later:

I hope that my observations will at least be sufficient to attract attention to a subject which is of so much importance to all who dwell in brick or stone buildings put up in earthquake countries.

It is of significance that one of the last papers he published in Japan is a record of further experiments carried out in this field. Working with Professor F. Omori, he investigated the overturning and fracturing of brick and other columns by horizontally applied motion. But by now the test equipment had become more specialised. In his report he thanks the Professor of Architecture, Mr K. Tatsuno, for help in constructing a metal framed trolley on which columns, up to twenty courses of brick high, were built and vibrated by a system of cranks. The mathematical analysis in his work was more prominent, perhaps through the influence of Professor Omori.

But there is still the Milne attention to detail; the recording and publication of the results of experiments; the description of fifty-odd different types of column built on the trolley; how mortar had been allowed to mature before each test; the careful noting of fracture points; the maximum velocities and accelerations compared with the values obtained during shaking from natural earthquakes, and so on. Eventually his experiments reached the stage where it was possible to design and build a series of shock-proof structures for testing under actual earthquake conditions.

His first anti-earthquake building used a similar principle to that which had been tried earlier in lighthouses. It was small, about six metres by four metres, and constructed of timber with a shingle roof, plaster walls and a ceiling of lathes and paper. An unusual feature was that it stood on four cast-iron balls held between saucer-like metal plates separating the building from the pier supports placed at the corners. Instruments showed that slow-moving earth movements were transmitted to the building while sudden shocks were not. Later, he constructed a room which was attached to his own house. This also rested on pillar foundations but had a layer of cast-iron shot placed between the iron plates. It stood for many years and remained undamaged.

In 1885 the East Indian section of the Dutch Royal Institute of Engineers offered cash prizes for scientific essays. One of the questions was 'Describe the theoretical methods and calculations used when making deduction from observations on earthquakes, together with positive data as to the point of egress of a given shock.'

As Milne had completed the first major analysis of an earthquake 'from birth to death', for him the question was tailor-made and it was no surprise when he learnt he had been awarded the first prize of 150 guilders and a diploma. But for another essay in the same competition he received only an honourable mention. Even so, the prize committee asked his permission to use part of it in a study then being made concerning Javanese methods of architecture. This request gave Milne considerable pleasure as it was recognition that the earthquake shock-proof house he had designed and constructed in Tokyo was attracting attention in other countries where the need for such buildings was of paramount importance.

In 1888, His Excellency Arinori Mori, then Minister of Education in Japan, set up a committee of interested engineers, architects and others to advise on construction which could withstand earth-quakes. Milne played a considerable part in the work of this committee and many of his simple yet practical and common-sense suggestions were incorporated in the recommendations made. These were all extremely detailed and many of them are still included in the building regulations of earthquake-troubled coun-tries.

His views were treated with respect for as so often happened with investigations he undertook, he was able not only to distinguish the trees from the wood as it were; not only able to grasp the problem as a whole, but to isolate it into individual components and estimate the importance of each. Moreover he could explain facts in such a way that they were easily understood by all. As a first priority he emphasised that, for a small outlay on a seismic survey, or even by a closer look at local architectural history, lives could be saved and damage to property lessened by the choice of a suitable building site and that this must be the first priority. Basically this meant that, on firm ground, heavy buildings should be constructed to a certain pattern while on soils less solid, lightly constructed erections only were advisable. Also further experiments with loose, rigid, and deep foundations were essential.

In a country that was adopting western ideas it was important to preserve in its architecture local experience which had been gained over the centuries. In the first early years of over-enthusiasm for western culture such things as chimneys and other parts of factory buildings often suffered unnecessary damage as they were built without due regard to the traditional type of Japanese construction which had evolved with experience. Milne explained to the committee that although it still might seem desirable to keep all buildings as light as possible with an extensive use of timber, the risk of fire was increased disproportionately. Fire, he pointed out, was a great destroyer of life after a severe 'quake. Thus bricks and mortar, too, despite their weight, had an important part to play in providing strength and, if sufficient attention were given to the method of construction of such things as archwork, balconies and staircases, additional resistance could be incorporated in the building.

Partly for his work on this committee and also for his contribution to seismology in general, in 1888 Milne was decorated by the Emperor with the Order of Merit with the Cordon of the Sacred Treasure, and shortly afterwards he was elevated to the status of a Chokunin.

In 1891 there occurred one of the largest and most devastating earthquakes ever recorded in Japan. In his annual report to the British Association in 1892, here much abridged, Milne wrote:

> If we may judge from the contortions produced along lines of railway, the fissuring of the ground, the destruction of hundreds of miles of high embankments which guard the plains from river-floods, the utter ruin of structures of all descriptions, the sliding down of mountain sides and the toppling over of their peaks, the compression of valleys and other bewildering phenomena, we may confidently say that last year, on the morning of October 28, Central Japan received as terrible a shaking as has ever been recorded in the history of seismology. It is the subject that might be written about at interminable length and therefore in this short report (it ran to some 50 000 words) no attempt is made to give detailed descriptions of all that happened.
>
> The first notice that I received of the earthquake was at 6h 39m 11s on the morning of October 28, whilst I was in bed. From the manner in which the house was creaking and the pictures swinging and flapping on the wall I knew the motion

was large. My first thoughts were to see the seismographs at work; so I went to the earthquake room, where to steady myself I leaned against the side of the stone table, and for about two minutes watched the movements of the instruments. It was clear that the heavy masses suspended as horizontal pendulums were not behaving as steady points, but that they were being tilted, first to the right and then to the left.

Horizontal displacements of the ground were not being recorded, but angles of tilting were being measured. That whenever vertical motion is recorded there must be tilting, and therefore no form of horizontal pendulum is likely to record horizontal motion, is a view I have often expressed. What I then saw convinced me that such views were correct. Next I ran to a water-tank which is 80 feet long, 28 feet wide and 25 feet deep. Its sides are practically vertical. At the time it was holding about 17 feet of water which was running across its breadth, rising first on one side and then on the other to a height of about two feet. It splashed to a height of four feet. It seemed clear that the tank was being tilted first on one side and then on the other.

Whilst this was going on trees were swinging about, telegraph wires were clattering together, the brickwork of the tank was cracked and the College workshop, a few yards away, was so far shattered that it had to be partially rebuilt. The effect of the motion upon myself was to make me feel giddy and slightly sea-sick. The chimney of a paper-mill in Tokyo fell and also a chimney at the electric light works in Yokohama . . . Little by little the news of the destruction arrived from many towns and as it came it grew more terrible.

The scene of the greatest disaster was the Nagoya–Gifa plain which lies about 140 miles WSW of Tokyo and 80 miles NE of Koko. In this district destruction had been total. Cities and villages had been shaken down, the ruins were burning, bridges had fallen, river embankments had been destroyed, the ground fissured in all directions, and mountain sides had slipped down to dam the valleys. More accurate estimates of certain damages are now before us. The killed numbered 9,960, the wounded 19,994, and the houses which were totally destroyed were 128,750. In addition to these there were many temples, factories and other buildings. In an area of 4,176 square miles, which embraces one of the most fertile plains of Japan and where there is a population of perhaps 1,000 to the square mile, all the buildings which had not been reduced to a heap of rubbish had been badly shattered . . .

The immediate cause of this great disturbance was apparently a fault which, according to Dr B. Koto, can be traced on the surface of the earth for a distance of between forty and fifty miles. In the Neo valley, where it runs nearly N and S, it looks like one side of a railway embankment about 20 or 30 feet in height. The fields at the bottom of this ridge were formerly level with the fields now at the top of it. In Mino, where it strikes towards the east, it is represented by subsidences and mound-like ridges suggesting the idea that they might have been produced by the burrowing of a gigantic mole. Although there is only 20 feet of displacement on the surface, from what we know of surface disturbances resulting from the caving in of subterranean excavations, the maximum throw of this fault is in all probability very much greater than that which is accessible for measurement. Not only have the rice-fields been lowered, but, according to the peasants, the mountain peaks on the western side of the valley have decreased in height.

Not only is there evidence of subsidence along this line, but there are many evidences of horizontal displacements. Lines of roads have been broken, and one part of them thrown to the right or left of their original direction; whilst fields which were rectangular have been cut in two, and one half relative to the other half been shifted as much as 18 feet up or down the valley. One result of this is that landowners find there has been a partial alteration in the position of their neighbours. A more serious change has been the permanent compression of ground, plots which were 48 feet in length now measuring only 30 feet in length. It appears as if the whole Neo Valley has become narrower. A similar effect is noticeable in the river-beds, where the piers of bridges are left closer together than they were at the time of their construction . . . Along the railway-line many curious appearances were presented. It was almost everywhere disturbed, the exceptions being where it passed through small cuttings. Along these cuttings, although they might not be more than 20 or 50 feet in depth, the rails and sleepers were unmoved; from which it might be inferred that the movement on the free surface of the plain had been much greater than the movement at a comparatively shallow depth. Measurements of the motion experienced on the surface and that recorded in pits 10 to 20 feet in depth have already been given . . . The results of these experiments have been practically applied to several buildings in Tokyo by giving them basements and a free area. The Imperial College of Engineering is such a building. It does not show the slightest trace of damage after the last earthquake, whilst at a distance of 20 yards the workshop, which is also a strong brick building but rising from the surface, as already stated, has had to be rebuilt. This is the third time the Engineering College had escaped damage, whilst neighbouring brick buildings have been cracked in almost every room . . . At the bridges, one of which, over the Kisogawa and made up of 200 feet spans, is 1,800 feet in length the destruction was various. In nearly all cases wing walls had given way. At one brick bridge the abutments had been forced backwards and the arch had fallen bodily between them down upon the roadway where it lay in two big segments looking like a gigantic toggle-joint. At the Nagara bridge the piers, each of which consisted of five large iron columns filled with concrete and braced together, had in several instances not simply been broken at their bases, but they were snapped in pieces and thrown out upon the shingle beach of the river where they lay like bits of broken carrot. The bridge was thrown 19 feet out of a straight line and one of the foundations near the centre of the river moved 5 feet 2 inches up-stream. Where the greatest deflections occurred the foundations could not be positively recognised . . .

The questions to which the greatest attention has been given are those of importance to engineers and builders, but inquiries and investigations have been made relating to everything which was thought to be of interest. A few days after the disaster, at the request of Professor D. Kikuchi, I drew up a circular containing some fifty queries. Ten thousand of these documents were issued and now, here and at the Central Observatory, we are surrounded by boxes filled with newspaper cuttings and replies. Five per cent of the whole may be of value but yet it all has to be patiently examined. In addition to this material there is that of our own collecting which includes some hundreds of diagrams taken by seismographs of what seemed to be at one time an unending series of shocks which followed the great disaster. This chaotic mass of material is gradually assuming a form suitable for systematic investigation. Although many of the results may be marked by the magnitude of the phenomena they represent rather than by their novelty, we have already gone sufficiently far to see that certain observations can hardly fail in widening the circle of our present knowledge . . .

When the disaster occurred John Milne and W. K. Burton, who was then Professor of Sanitary Engineering at Tokyo University as well as being a particularly fine photographer, were instructed to produce a permanent pictorial record and left immediately for the striken area. Proceeding with all haste they reached the Neo Valley, centre of the devastation, within two days of the main shock and commenced their comprehensive fact-finding mission.

Nowadays, very few copies of their fine book, *The Great Earthquake of Japan, 1891,* still exist. Well produced, it consists of some thirty pages of excellent illustrations whose printing plates were prepared by F. Ogawa, together with a further forty pages of concise explanatory text. It is a compact yet comprehensive account of the widespread damage which a major earthquake can cause. The photographs of the Neo Fault, showing that in some places the land had subsided more than seven metres, are particularly good. The two professors, who also combined to produce *The Volcanoes of Japan* (Kelly and Walsh, Yokohama), included harrowing scenes of the conditions which bewildered survivors were facing with typical Japanese stoicism, and of the emergency hospital which had been speedily established at Kuroda by the University under whose sponsorship the Milne–Burton report was prepared.

Despite a somewhat limited edition, in its time the book was by far the best of its kind then available to the non-specialist and even today is worth more than a cursory perusal by those able to locate a copy.

Had this great earthquake occurred a short ten years earlier it is certain that the vast amount of vitally important information it yielded to scientists, construction engineers, medical personnel and a host of other experts would not have been so thoroughly investigated. Where there had then been relatively few capable of undertaking such a mammoth task now there were many. In addition to his own part in the affair Milne has described something of the invaluable contributions made by others, mostly Japanese, to ensure that every conceivable factor which could be used to mitigate future disasters was recorded for analysis.

For Japan perhaps the most beneficial result of the calamity — if such a catastrophe could be said to produce something of value — was the immediate creation of the Imperial Earthquake Investigation Committee, (*Shinsai-Yobō Chōsakawai*), by the Emperor. This was sometimes called The Earthquake Hazard Prevention Research Association. It consisted of engineers and architects as well as professors of seismology, geology, mathematics and physics at the University of Tokyo, and was charged with the twofold task of ascertaining if there were means of predicting earthquakes, as well as determining what could be done to minimise the subsequent disasters by the use of more suitable materials in construction and a wider choice of building sites. Many of the members were closely associated with Milne and naturally they sought his advice when establishing working guidelines. He was the only foreigner invited to serve on this committee. Of the sixteen different research headings they finally adopted, most were those on which he had had considerable experience.

By the time this council was established it was clear that the Seismological Society of Japan, founded by Milne and at one time largely dominated by foreigners, had become much less effective as, one by one, the westerners left the country when the various skills they taught had been matched by their former pupils. Moreover, Japanese scientists and other professional experts were now in a position to carry out their own seismic investigations in depth and were anxious to do so.

In all, the Society was in existence for thirteen years during which time sixteen volumes of its journal, the *Transactions of the Seismological Society of Japan*, were published. After it was disbanded in 1892, four new volumes, the *Seismological Journal of Japan*, appeared under the editorship of Milne. These twenty books, now very rare, record the tremendous scope and depth of the work carried out in the Society's name, although Milne himself wrote nearly two-thirds of the contents besides giving advice and encouragement to some of the authors of other papers published. Both the *Transactions* and the *Journal* provide useful material for students researching the history of early seismology and volcanology.

This massive output confirms Milne's dedication to the task which he had now come to regard as his particular mission in life. Few men are able to travel so far towards the achievements of a personal goal in such a short period of time. Driven by tremendous enthusiasm and the strange love he developed for earthquakes, success was inevitable. The young man who, in 1875 had wondered what life had in store for him, by now had no illusions on that score, for a scant fifteen years later he was already recognised as the world's leading authority in the growing world of seismological studies. Thus the note of sadness that is evident in the preface of the first of his *Seismological Journals* in 1893 is understandable:

> The present volume, rather than being regarded as a new publication, may be looked upon as a continuation of a series of volumes published by the Seismological Society of Japan. This society was founded in 1880 and for many years its meetings were frequent and well attended. At one exhibition, which extended over several days, the visitors were so numerous that it became necessary to admit them in detachments. Of late years, however, partly in consequence of those who took an active interest in seismological investigations having left Japan, partly because geological, engineering, and other publications accepted material which formerly found a place in the *Transactions*, and for various other reasons, little by little, interest at last so far flagged that it became difficult to form a quorum sufficient for the transaction of the Society's ordinary business. The result was that in 1892 the Seismological Society ceased to exist.

So for what at this stage was to be purely a detailed inquiry into the nation's own earth disturbances, the formation of the new Imperial Earthquake Investigation Committee was both a logical and sensible extension of the old Society's pioneering work. It also ensured that for the first time full responsibility was placed in Japanese hands.

In the years which followed its inception this committee was to produce extremely valuable work. Even so, most of the fine Japanese seismologists who served on it would have confirmed that, in the main, they built upon and extended the earlier achievements of Milne and his colleagues. But, inevitably, the position had to change. Where with Milne in the early 1880s it was westerners like Ayrton, Chaplin, Ewing, Gray, Knipping, Mendenhall, Perry, Wagener, Verbeck, West, and, later Knott, who had been prominent in Japanese seismology, now it was that country's own experts, some of whom had been founder members of the Seismological Society, such as Kikuchi, Sekiya, Omori, Kato, Mano, Tanabe, Koto, Tatsumo, Nagaska and many others who were as influential. Nor must the pioneering work of Hattori, the first president of the Society, be forgotten.

Despite the undoubted academic accomplishments of two of Milne's colleagues, Baron Dairoku Kikuchi — one of the first members of the Society and instigator of the Imperial Earthquake Investigation Committee — and Seikei Sekiya, first professor of seismology in any university in the world, few would challenge the outstanding contribution made to the science by Milne's protégé, Fusakichi Omori. Both master and pupil embraced the widest range of seismic investigation. Omori was to become noted for his important memoirs on after-shocks, the effects of vibrations in buildings, and the duration of preliminary tremors among other works which, in general, should be considered as important extensions of Milne's own labours. A kindly, courteous gentleman, Omori was the natural successor to the man he looked upon not only as a great friend but also guide and mentor.

Thus, as the science rapidly developed, Japan had the distinction of becoming a leading country in the field of seismic research, partly because of the many opportunities arising from an inherent instability of the earth's crust in that region, but mainly as a result of the widespread and enthusiastic cooperation of her ever-growing number of capable scientists. This position has never been lost.

Yet, although John Milne may have been somewhat dismayed when the Seismological Society ceased to exist he was far from being despondent. While he was willing to give considerable advice and assistance to the new Committee, and, indeed, devoted much time to this purpose, from 1891 onwards he was becoming more and more involved with the problem of recording earthquakes which occurred in countries far distant from Japan. As early as 1883 he had thought this would eventually be possible, for at a meeting of the

Society in that year he had said, 'It is not unlikely that every large earthquake might, with proper instrumental appliances, be recorded at any point on the surface of the globe.' If it could be constructed such an instrument would be of inestimable value in revealing yet more of the subterranean secrets still hidden from man. Yet the problems were immense. Such a seismograph would need to be extremely sensitive since it was known that the amplitude of disturbances were greatly reduced the further they travelled from their epicentre.

In 1889, a young German, Ernst von Rebeur-Paschwitz, was experimenting with a modified form of Zöllner's horizontal pendulums in order to detect and measure the lunar disturbance of gravity when he noticed that a number of distant earthquake traces were being registered by the instruments. Stimulated by these observations Milne began his own investigations and by 1893 had designed, constructed and tested the now famous seismograph which bears his name. It was capable of detecting earthquake waves which had travelled many thousands of miles from their origin.

In design it is typical of Milne's philosophy in that it is basically simple. The instrument itself is placed on a rigid masonry column in firm contact with the ground. A heavy iron plate, with three levelling screws, forms the base. From this a vertical metal rod about 500 mm high supports the horizontal pendulum frequently known as the Boom. This boom, made of aluminium or steel and nearly 1 metre long, has a jewelled cup at one end which pivots about a steel point on the vertical rod. It is held in positon by a fine wire or thread of silk attached to the top of the rod so that the height can be adjusted. On the horizontal pendulum, or boom, two small brass balls, each about 250 g, are placed on a cross piece near the point of suspension by the thread; these weights are necessary on a seismograph of this type to give it inertia. The end of the boom remote from its vertical support has a thin metal plate across it in which is cut a fine slit. Light from an oil lamp is reflected by a mirror through this slit to fall onto a photo-sensitive paper via a second fine slit placed at right angles to the first. Thus a small spot of light is produced and this falls onto the long roll of sensitized paper which is moved below the second slit by clockwork. When developed, the paper shows a straight line until the boom has been disturbed by tremors and a trace is produced. Records of the passage of the waves from the earthquake's source are called seismograms and it is from these that the epicentre, strength and other vital information can be determined.

A time signal is placed on the trace by eclipsing the light beam every hour using a pocket watch fitted with a small extension to the middle hand and which is so sited that this extension passes between the slits every hour, thus acting as a simple shutter and interrupting the record for a few seconds at known intervals.

Friction on the pendulum is removed by the use of the photographic recording and draughts and convection currents are eliminated by covers. The seismograph can be operated in the light provided the sensitive paper is kept in a light-proof box. The roll itself has to be changed once a week.

With this instrument ready for use a whole new concept in earthquake investigation was open to Milne. The scene for those important discoveries which were to lead to the establishment of seismology as a significant international science had now been set.

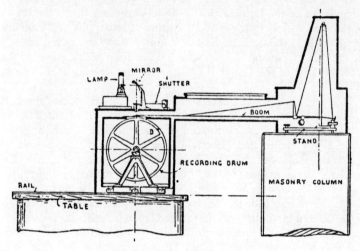

Milne's Horizontal Pendulum Seismograph.

6

Life in Meiji Japan

Even in the late 1860s tales were still being told of the fierce antagonism of the Japanese to foreigners entering their country to work. And widely exaggerated accounts of actual physical violence perpetrated in this strange Asiatic country were still going around the capitals of Europe and elsewhere when John Milne accepted the Professorship at the Imperial College of Engineering at Tokyo in 1875.

That there had initially been some bad feeling cannot be denied. It had begun to generate openly after the two visits of the United States naval forces under the command of Commodore Matthew Perry some years earlier had effectively ended Japan's long period of voluntary isolationism. The American's insistent and somewhat domineering demands, backed by what to all intents and purposes was a considerable show of military might, eventually persuaded the Shoganate to conclude the Treaty of Amity which permitted vessels of the United States to enter designated Japanese ports for provisions and trade. Similar treaties with Britain, Russia and the Netherlands had followed quickly and many Japanese came to feel that their traditional independence was being threatened. Thus a spirit of nationalism was generated and with it came a desire by some to expel the foreigners.

When, after the restoration of power to the 14-year old Emperor Meiji in 1868, his government declared an intention to proceed with the acquisition of European and American technology, the decision did not meet with the whole-hearted approval of every ideological faction in the land. There arose vociferous groups and individuals who strenuously opposed the idea of modernisation, and naturally they objected to the employment of foreign experts. From the outset, therefore, certain tensions existed and on occasion these spilled over into actual aggression against the newcomers although this fell far short of the degree of unpleasantness reported in the horrifying tales reaching the West.

Treaty obligations had stipulated that stringent measures were to be taken to ensure the safety of the new arrivals, and the young Emperor's government swiftly responded by instituting special guards, *bettegumi* who, besides protecting the strangers' com-

pounds where by law they were required to live, accompanied them
whenever they ventured outside. But it was not long before the
active dislike of these 'hairy foreigners' appearing on the streets in
ever-increasing numbers slackened with familiarity. By 1872 the
guards were no longer required and aliens could go about their
business in the capital and treaty ports without undue harassment.
Indeed, when John Milne arrived in Tokyo in 1876 the token force of
British and French troops based on Yokohama had been withdrawn
as the Meiji government was by then in full control of public order in
the city. Several factors had brought about this rapid change of
attitude towards the foreigners, not the least of which was the
intense feeling of loyalty for their Emperor felt by the majority of the
Japanese people in addition to a growing realisation by most of them
that their treasured independence could be retained only by
accepting the modernisation programme advocated by his government.

In the centres of population closest to the treaty ports a growing
enthusiasm for western culture quickly became the accepted mode.
One visual indication of this was the swift adoption of foreign dress
by all classes even though some of the early imitations produced by
local tailors were so outrageous as to defy the keenest imagination.
Individual tastes ranged from those who abandoned their traditional
costume completely and appeared in full European garb down to the
inevitable spats, through to others who scorned the transition
altogether. These latter greeted the pro-westerners with loud cries of
'hairy idiots' or 'foreign fools'. Many tried to mingle the styles and
caused much merriment as well as becoming the recipients of even
more derisive remarks. One would have given much to have seen
the swaggering court official who, although otherwise clad in his
official robes of office, struggled to maintain the dignity his calling
demanded while attempting to restrain the wobbling of an ill-fitting
silk top hat perched precariously on his head!

But the introduction of western clothing had one important
advantage — that of general disarmament. A two-sworded *samurai*
in European garments could no longer wear his murderous swords
with ease, and in any case had by now lost his jealously guarded right
to carve up any peasant who failed to show him proper respect as he
was to lose so many of his ancient privileges in the transition. Others
who customarily had gone about with cumbersome weapons soon
found it incongruous to do so while in Caucasian dress.

The speed with which modern technology was being introduced
surprised the western world and even the Japanese themselves. In
1870 the feudal system of warrior, farmer, artisan and merchant was
abolished. In the same year, in order to raise money to build a
railway, Japan's first public bonds were floated in Britain with a high
rate of interest. A year later came the introduction of a national

postal service and a unified currency. At the same time administrative districts based on the former feudal domains were abolished and the country was divided into prefectures, each with a governor appointed by the central government.

The benefits of telegraphic communication, too, were beginning to be appreciated. One British official wrote:

> The first line of telegraph which, when constructed two years since met with such opposition on the part of certain Japanese has now become so popular that telegraph wires are springing up in all directions within the capital. Already the Mikado's palace, the Foreign Office, the Board of Works and the Tokei-Fu (municipal government) are in telegraphic communication with the Kanagawa Ken, and eight other stations are to be opened to the public in various parts of the town.
>
> The government have engaged Mr George, an English engineer, who, with a staff of English superintendents, is constructing a line to Hiago and Nagasaki whence Yedo (Tokyo) will soon be in direct communication with the whole world.

In 1872 farmers were granted the right to buy or sell land for the first time and could even decide what crops they would grow. The first railway line in the country — it linked Tokyo with the port of Yokohama — was opened. Several trains daily traversed the 18 miles in just under an hour. In the same year the government established four national banks and the country's first modern spinning mill began operating. New primary schools were built, but perhaps equally satisfying to the Japanese was the building of the *Soryu-maru*, the first warship to come from their own shipyards.

A new system of weights and measures to replace local standards was introduced by the Meiji government in 1873 and a year later the first gaslights were installed along the Ginza, Tokyo's main street. Soon afterwards came the establishment of the Supreme Court and the new juridical system.

These were but a few of the major changes taking place in Japan and when John Milne arrived in 1876 the exciting adaptation of western ideas was gaining the impetus of a cultural and technological revolution. He was fortunate enough to be caught up in it and stay long enough to see the country reach the stage where it was both willing and able to accept any challenge to its people's cherished independence.

But in those very early years there was yet much to be done. Among the many problems was that of satisfying the urgent demand for young Japanese engineers to assume responsibility for running the new technology. To this end the Ministry of Public Works, assigned the difficult task of producing engineers in sufficient numbers, gave every possible assistance to the European staff at the Imperial College. To ensure the comfort of the Professors houses were built in the College grounds. One of these was allocated to Milne. Called 'Yama Gouchi' or 'Mouth of the Mountain', it suited him very well as the setting up of the new Mining and Geology Department initially took up much of his time.

Even had he so wished, there was little opportunity for him to join in the whirl of social activities of the foreigners flocking to Tokyo. His academic duties and a growing preoccupation with earthquakes frequently kept him at home so that the early friendships he formed were with staff colleagues and a few others with a similar hobby interest in the curious earth movements. Like most of the foreigners he probably occasionally visited the new Metropole Hotel in Tsuliji which had been recently opened under the sponsorship of some French naval officers and was practically the only western-style club in the area at that time. To go there he would have hired one of the many *jin-riki-shas* which plied the streets. These were two-wheeled carriages, or chairs, the size of which was little larger than a child's perumbulator and just large enough for one man to sit in and be drawn by a coolie instead of a horse. He was always amused that, being a foreigner, he was expected to pay three times the official rate. It was Cairo all over again!

During these excursions he would have seen that as yet relatively few houses of brick had been erected and noted that when fires, which were frequent, destroyed the dwellings, usually the rebuilding was done immediately with the same inflammable materials and style. Even so, local builders were beginning to see the advantage of brick construction and already overseas architects were being employed. Indeed, the Imperial College itself had been designed by two Englishmen.

At first Milne was content with his bachelor life in the College where he could study or carry on his experiments in his spare time without distraction. In point of fact for some time he was scarcely known to most of the foreign community in Tokyo, for as soon as the long summer vacations arrived the young professor would set off on prolonged geological excursions throughout the Japanese islands.

In the early years of the Meiji rule foreigners — other than those consular officials who had already been exempted — were soon offered the opportunity to live outside the settlements in the treaty ports although a licence to do so was required. But if they wished to travel beyond the immediate vicinity of these areas all aliens had to obtain a permit. These were seldom authorised unless it could be shown that the journey was for purely scientific purposes. The restriction was imposed partly for their own safety in rural areas not yet adequately policed, and in part to ensure a measure of control over their movements and activities. Although at the signing of the Treaty of Amity the Japanese government had declared a willingness to open up the country fully, not unnaturally there still lingered an understandable fear of foreign infiltration and extortion. But, as a Japanese government employee with special scientific responsibilities Milne had little difficulty in obtaining the necessary permission to travel extensively about the countryside. Once away from the outskirts of Tokyo, however, he would have encountered the foreigner's ever-present problem in those days of finding satisfactory accommodation. Most often it became necessary to follow the practice of seeking shelter in a large mansion belonging to a Japanese peer or warrior and being prepared to risk the inevitable snub if the owner was anti-alien; of accepting quarters in a temple open to foreigners — which was more usual — or, if lucky, being invited into the house of a resident foreigner.

It must be mentioned at this point that Milne's name has been coupled with that of seismology so often that some less well-informed sources have given the impression it was solely to investigate earthquakes that he went to Japan. The fact that the work which made him famous was incidental to the terms of reference under which he was employed either escaped their notice or was deliberately ignored. In addition to his teaching duties Milne was required to act as a mining consultant and, whenever practical, to advise on the mineral deposits in the country since these were now urgently needed by the Japanese government.

The primitiveness of many of the mines he visited shocked him and he quickly learned that no recognised code of mining practice existed.

But if he was amazed at the general inefficiency of the industry he was appalled at the working conditions he found underground. It appeared to him that site selection was often a particularly haphazard affair. Once the site was decided upon, a diagonal shaft was dug and if the hoped-for mineral was found then work began, otherwise the mine was quickly abandoned. If the required mineral was discovered only a little could be extracted before the drift mine became waterlogged. In those days the Japanese could not sink a deep shaft as they had nothing more than bamboo pumps for lifting the water. Most often Milne found that the underground workings of coal mines were ill-ventilated, lit by coal-oil lamps and had absolutely no precautions against firedamp. The casualty rate among the workers was very high and he never relished descending the narrow, slippery slope to the bottom of a pit and still less crawling along the small galleries which fanned out in all directions from this point even though they seldom penetrated more than 20 metres. Quite often coal seams were less than a metre thick and as there were scarcely any wooden roof supports precautions against collapse of the workings

Images of Japan: 1875–1895

From John Milne's slide collection

were virtually non-existent. When one did occur it was sometimes impossible to mount a rescue operation owing to the workers' fear of offending the gods who had caused the disaster.

The following passage describes the kind of mine he often came across in the less developed areas of Japan:

> It had only one entrance and the ventilation below ground must have been atrocious. A tunnel little more than a metre wide and even less in height had been driven down at an angle of 50° for some 30 metres and then 20 metres horizontally. It produced 240 piculs of coal daily (14½ tonnes). Forty coolies, working in pairs could extract 10 piculs each day for which they were paid a sum of money upon which they could just about keep from starving. In this particular mine water was being extracted but it could scarcely keep pace with the seepage. For the underground workers it was a miserable existence. On the surface women were employed to move the coal to the riverside in small carts capable of carrying 100 or 150 kg. They earned less than the men despite walking more than 30 km a day dragging these loads.

The remarkable inefficiency of the undertaking was emphasised at the pit head where the baskets of coal from the mine were emptied onto the ground from whence it was transferred piece by piece into the carts. It was evident also at the riverside where the carts discharged their loads onto the jetty instead of transferring them directly into the hold of the waiting vessel. Milne was not able to ascertain the reasons for these curious procedures but his many recommendations to both the Japanese government and the various mine owners, together with his insistence that action be taken to remedy the appalling conditions of the work-force so as to improve efficiency, paid dividends to the extent that, in later years, one of his ex-students was to write: 'It would not be too much to say that the present-day mining industry in Japan owes a great deal to Professor John Milne.' In this respect his *Miner's Handbook*, discussed in an earlier chapter, proved a boon to several generations of Japanese mining engineers.

Milne's work in mineral exploration is less well known outside that country since his reports were confidential to the governmental department concerned. He himself did not benefit from his surveys since foreign employees were not allowed to undertake personal business transactions in addition to their specialist occupation and if caught engaging secretly in trade could expect to be disciplined. In the event such was Milne's integrity that it is doubtful that he ever thought for long of yielding to the many temptations despite obvious opportunities in the remoter areas of the country.

Not long after his arrival in Japan he appears to have received a request from the Colonisation Department for help in prospecting for mineral deposits on Hokkaido, the northernmost of the country's four main islands. This department had been established in 1871 and charged with the task not only of developing the resources there and of encouraging the settlement of Japanese immigrants, but also of improving agriculture generally throughout the Japanese empire by the introduction of foreign crops, livestock, implements and fruit trees. Prior to this Hokkaido seems to have been virtually unutilised by the Japanese. Although in area more than 83,000 square kilometres the island had a population of less than 100,000 when Milne first visited it in 1877. He learned that most of these were Ainos, or 'Hairy Men', popularly supposed to be the last remnants of the aborigines of Japan. He found them to be an active, muscular people, quiet and gentle in manner, who lived by hunting and fishing. As was his custom whenever the opportunity arose Milne stayed with them for a while to learn something of their way of life.

To the surprise of many of the resident foreigners in Tokyo who thought that the treaty port of Hakodate would have been a more obvious choice as a capital for the island, the government decided upon Sapporo, a place some distance inland and then consisting of no more than a few buildings. The Colonisation Department was already pushing ahead with its plans and Milne was able to use a road which had been constructed to connect the new capital to Muroran on the southern coast where there was a good anchorage, and in his travels would have observed several others being built.

By the time he was able to visit Sapporo the new Agricultural College had been erected although there was little else to be seen in the area apart from a handful of buildings. The College had been founded for the education and practical training of young Japanese from all parts of the Empire. Like other government-sponsored students of that era, after graduation they were required to remain in its employ for several years. The youngsters were given a good general education. In addition to their agricultural and horticultural studies they were also instructed in civil engineering and chemistry, astronomy, botany, geology, zoology, military science and tactics as well as a certain amount of political economy. It seems certain that Milne would have met the three 'foreign' professors and the Japanese staff. No doubt, too, he was prevailed upon to talk to the young students about life in other parts of the world he had visited, which doubtless broadened their somewhat limited experience.

Although at this time the Colonisation Department had arranged for the building of a silk factory, flour mills, a brewery and a tannery in Hokkaido as well as initiating other worthwhile projects, it was not being particularly successful in establishing permanent settlements. The reason was not hard to find. Despite the largely untapped wealth of the island with its deposits of coal, silver, sulphur and other minerals; its fertile soils capable of producing a variety of crops including cereals and hemp; its large forests of excellent timber; its rivers and surrounding seas teeming with salmon, cod, herring, sardines and other species of edible sea-life, and the considerable quantities of seaweed along the extensive shoreline, it was the climate which deterred many, being much colder than that to which they were accustomed. Of those who went to the island to settle many found the winters unacceptably rigorous and soon returned to their own warmer areas of Japan. Yet the Department sensibly continued its efforts to colonise Hokkaido and in the end achieved a fair measure of success.

Milne and others eventually were to discover that the coal deposits there were the largest in Japan and that Milne himself found other valuable mineral deposits is confirmed in a letter he wrote on 3 September 1878 to His Excellency Toketo Tamemoto, Governor of Hakodate at that time:

> *Dear Sir,*
>   *I beg to thank you very much for the permission you gave me to travel in the* Gimbu Maru *to the Kurile Islands. If these islands were carefully examined I think it would be likely that valuable deposits of Sulphur might be met with, — any other minerals which you would find there would be of interest more from a scientific than a commercial point of view.*

The letter than went on to describe a visit to a lead mine in a valley in Hokkaido with a detailed analysis of samples taken from it; to estimate the percentage of pure lead which could be extracted from the galena; and to note the quantities of lime sulphates as well as the iron and copper present. Giving his opinion that the vein was too thin and contained too much material of no value he added: 'From what I have learnt I should therefore not recommend workings to be carried out upon the present portion of the vein.' He did not mean that the site should be abandoned. He counselled that a search should be made along the possible direction of the lode to establish whether it became thicker. A long and precise description of how this should be done then followed before he went on to discuss other minerals he had found in the Marakawa valley:

> *Of these the barytes were the most interesting as being the first sample of this mineral I have seen in Japan. If large veins of this are found it may be profitably extracted as it is used in the manufacture of white paint. It is also used in sugar refining and in certain chemical manufactures.*

Among his other discoveries was a bed of impure talcose rock and of this he commented: 'Talc when pure is used for several purposes such as the manufacture of utensils, ornaments, etc.'

He reported that in the same valley he had seen many highly metamorphic black slates, traversed with rusty veins of quartz and recommended that specimens of these ought to be collected and analysed for the presence of gold.

Although obviously not the only expert so engaged in this work it is through valuable reports like this that Milne was able to assist the Japanese to determine the nature and extent of their country's mineral deposits. But after imparting such useful information to the Governor he clearly felt no compunction at seeking favours in return! His letter continued:

> Could you assist me in collecting information about the volcanoes and earthquakes in Yezo (Hokkaido)? In Hakodate, Satspiro, Matsumai and other towns I think there are persons to be found who have books or manuscripts relative to such things. If it is possible I should very much like to buy or borrow papers of this description. I want them partly for my own information and partly to place copies in the library of the Kobu-dai Gakko.
>
> When I was in the Kuriles, and also last year when I was in Yezo I collected specimens of various rocks. Do you think I could make arrangements to exchange some of them for duplicate specimens of fossils of which I have seen many in your department? I want them for the purpose of sending them to England where I can get them named and described and thus form a foundation for the working out of the geology of this country and that of Nippon. If you could kindly help me in either of these two undertakings which are both purely of a scientific nature I should esteem it a great favour.
>
> In conclusion I again thank you for the kindness you have already shown me.

When the Professor travelled to Hokkaido he usually established a working base at Hakodate, a port on the south coast of the island which in those days was hardly more than a large fishing village. From there he would set forth in search of those mineral deposits which were large enough to make their extraction a commercially viable proposition. As John liked Hakodate he usually returned again to write his lengthy reports and recommendations. After the noise and bustle of Tokyo he undoubtedly felt able to relax in the relative peace of this little place before undertaking the wearisome journey back to the College.

For him walking was no chore. There was always something new to see there, something new to learn, and few days passed without significant facts and observations being recorded in his copious notebooks. Unspoiled countryside delighted him and he must often have meandered along the rocky promontory that forms the eastern boundary of the vast natural harbour. For a man of John Milne's disposition the place must have been a little paradise. As he carefully

picked his way over the loose boulders, observing the geological
strata and collecting the marine plants and shells at the water's edge,
he would have been able to look across the bay and watch the
incessant coming and going of the many small fishing boats whose
plentiful catches provided the little town with its principal source of
revenue.

In the earliest years of the colonisation of the island almost all
manufactured goods had to be imported and were paid for with fish
or its by-products such as oil and manure. The unmistakable odour
of this piscatorial industry in summer permeated every corner and
when it was particularly vile no doubt Milne, like most visitors as
yet unused to the smell, would have taken the opportunity to escape
by climbing the densely wooded slopes of nearby Hakodateyama.
Rising to some 335 metres, 'Gagyu-san', or 'cow-lying-down' as it
is affectionately called by the local inhabitants because of its peculiar
shape, this hill affords protection to both town and harbour from the
gales which sweep across the Sea of Japan. The reward for such
exertion was not only the pure air to be found there but also a
glorious panoramic view of Hokkaido's unspoiled coastline receding into the far distance on either hand, the grey-blue mountains of
Honshu visible across the Straits of Tsugaru sparkling below in the
summer sunlight, and the tall sailing ships beating slowly up to the
harbour entrance. Doubtless, too, he would have noted with some
satisfaction the ever-increasing number of steamers plying between
the port and the outside world for, despite its remoteness from the
nation's main centres of population, Hakodate, like the rest of Japan,
was being affected by change as the transplantation of modern
institutions and the capitalist way of production crept insidiously,
inexorably, inevitably into the very outposts of the country.

To prevent the spread of the all too frequent fires, wider streets
were now being constructed and oil lamps lighted them by night.
These latter helped to diminish petty crime to the satisfaction of all
law-abiding citizens in general and the newly established police force
in particular. European style bungalows were erected for foreign
officials and businessmen.

Attempts were being made to speed the postal service with
Tokyo. Soon letters were taking only ten days, half the previous
time, to reach the distant capital along nearly 1,000 kilometres of
winding, largely unmade roads across the difficult terrain. Although
telegraphic communication between the two places had been
established in 1875, frequent breakdowns during the first few years
often led to lengthy delays and, initially at least, the postal service
was considered the more reliable method. When Milne made his first
visit to Hokkaido just two years later the centre of attraction in
Hakodate was a newly constructed dry dock, small in size but an
exciting innovation of which the townspeople were justifiably
proud.

Throughout the 1870s and well into the next decade there were very few foreigners actually resident in the vicinity. In a population of some 25,000 their numbers seldom exceeded sixty of whom about a third were Chinese together with a handful of Russians, French, Germans, Danes or Swiss. The rest were British and in the course of his many visits over twenty years Milne must have met most of them. The friendship of two he particularly valued.

The first of these, Thomas Wright Blakiston, was from Lymington in Hampshire, and when Milne came into contact with him in Hakodate the trader was forty-five years old. A veteran of both the Crimea and China wars where he had seen service as a captain in the artillery, the man was cast in the same adventurous mould as Milne. He had explored the Canadian Rockies and the sources of the great Yangtse river in China and had also travelled widely in other parts of the world. He had arrived in Hakodate in 1861 to become a partner in a timber processing firm but, like other foreigners to whom the Japanese government had granted charters at that time, he had extended the business considerably and the firm was soon dealing in several other commodities among which was the selling of salvage from shipwrecks along the coast.

During the years he had lived there Blakiston did much to improve the amenities of the town by planning a water supply, installing much needed harbour facilities and inaugurating a shipping service to Aomori on the northern coast of Honshu. According to one source he was responsible for initiating Japan's first meteorological station and for these and other beneficial acts he was held in high esteem by the community. He kept an open house for travellers, especially those with scientific interests. His knowledge of the island was of tremendous value to Milne during the latter's first tentative sorties into the interior.

But the common factor which drew the two together was Blakiston's skill in classifying the bird-life of northern Japan. As was the custom of ornithologists in those days he had made a personal collection — in his case more than thirteen hundred preserved specimens — and in addition had sent many others to the United States and Europe. As a result of prolonged field observations he developed the theory that the birds of Hokkaido belonged to the Siberian as distinct from the Manchurian sub-region of the Palaearctic region and that the line of demarcation ran through the Straits of Tsugaru which separate the island from that of Honshu to the south. At his request Milne checked the evidence supporting this hypothesis and agreed its accuracy. At a meeting of the Asiatic Society of Japan a few weeks later the Professor explained to Sir Harry Parkes, the British Minister, the importance of his friend's work and suggested that the division be known as the 'Blakiston Line'. The term was eventually adopted.

During his early visits Milne was also genuinely glad to regard the British Consul in Hakodate as a personal friend. Richard Eusden, a man of much charm, was one of the better administrators appointed by the British government in that he was not only interested in his work but, like Blakiston, had developed a great affection for the Japanese and their way of life. Eusden went out of his way to assist the development of the town and in consequence made many friends among the local population. His fluent command of the language smoothed out much of the inevitable day to day irritations which occurred in dealings with the foreigners; indeed, so successful was he that the German, French and Austrian governments were content to leave their affairs in his capable hands. He was quite small in stature and not unnaturally he was referred to as the 'baby' consul and sometimes the 'pea' consul. His wife, too, did much for the women of the little town; among other things she showed them how to wash clothing in the western manner. All were dismayed and saddened when the couple left in 1880.

Both Blakiston and Eusden made a lasting impression on Milne; their knowledge of the island, together with the useful advice they gave him proved invaluable. Encouraged by them, he worked hard to improve his Japanese so as to be able to dispense with the services of an interpreter. They taught him also how best to avoid those European customs which appeared discourteous or even offensive to the Japanese.

There is no firm evidence that Milne visited Hakodate in 1877 although he was certainly at nearby Otaru. But his dislike of sea-travel might well have caused him to proceed overland to Aomori and across the Tsugaru Strait to Hakodate en route even though that relatively short strip of water can also on occasion prove unpleasant enough for those afflicted by sea-sickness. Certainly the land journey would have been a logical decision, and Milne was a logical person. On the other hand it is known that he returned to Tokyo by sea from Otaru — a trip he could scarcely have enjoyed. Did his excavations in Hokkaido delay him to the extent that such a voyage was forced upon him? It will be remembered that on this occasion he arrived at the College two days late.

This seemingly unimportant point could provide the answer to a more serious question as to whether or not Milne actually met the revered Abbot of the Hakodate Temple of Ganjo-ji, Jokyo Horikawa — the relevance of which meeting will become apparent.

Although the Abbot was then fifty-two years old his appearance belied his advancing years and he still retained the build of a Sumo wrestler. Clothed in a Buddhist robe and sitting cross-legged in characteristic Japanese fashion, photographs of him tend to emphasise the Sphinx-like impassiveness of his clean-shaven countenance. To the less discerning he might appear as a stern, unrelenting priest who would have demanded impossibly high standards from his followers. In fact this progressive leader was a man of compassion and much honour whose frequent smile softened the somewhat heavy features. His lively personality at once captivated those with whom he came in contact.

The Abbot was greatly loved by his adherents to whom he imparted the faith through the teachings of Shinran, the great Buddhist priest of the thirteenth century. Jokyo Horikawa — he had changed his name early in the Meiji period — was one of the real pioneers of the colonisation of Hokkaido. He had brought some 370 of his followers to Hakodate where they had established their temple, naming it after the one in which the Abbot's father had been born in Amoriken.

Like Blakiston, Eusden, and several others whose stories lie outside the scope of this biography, the Abbot played a prominent part in the early development of the town. He opened up a stream more than three kilometres long to supply drinking water to the centre of the town, providing places where food and shelter could be offered to the poor and disabled, and by constant endeavour, did much to promote the establishment of a settled community. His pioneering spirit is recalled in modern times at Horikawacho, a district of the port named after him.

If the two had become acquainted that year, the genuine interest Milne would have displayed in this sect's theology undoubtedly would have been matched by the older man's desire to understand the finer concepts of Christian doctrines. Largely as a result of his own theological studies at King's College Milne would have been able to discuss differences between the two religions. But this is mere speculation.

The Abbot's marriage was blessed with children some of whom did not survive childhood. Of those who did there were two sons, Taiei, the elder, who became a priest in his father's temple, and Michizo. There was also a daughter, Toné. Family records show that, at the age of thirteen, she was sent south to the Kaitakushi Girls' School in Tokyo. According to Shindo Akashi, her nephew, a distinguished Professor of Architecture, she was to be educated to become 'a good housewife for a farmer in Hokkaido, but Toné did not greatly care for this idea.' The Professor added that 'she disliked the school intensely. One of the things she resented was having to serve saké to the male teachers.' When the school was transferred to Sapporo she was ill and her name does not appear in the class registers from that time. On recovering, Toné seems to have helped her father in the temple where eventually she was introduced to John Milne by Blakiston.

Many westerners have a stereotyped image of a Japanese girl — petite, almond-eyed and graceful; long black hair as glossy as the wing of a raven; blemish-free skin glowing with health; fragile, delicate hands and long, slender fingers tipped with nails the colour of cherry-blossom. Toné had all of these attributes. She was tiny: although John was below average height for an Englishman, her coiffured head scarcely reached his broad shoulders. Her slim, youthful beauty and his lively personality and irrepressible humour drew them together. Before long they were deeply in love; a warm, tender love that was to last for the rest of their lives.

Inevitably, the two faced many problems. Marriages between the 'foreigners' and Japanese girls did take place, of course, but thus early in the Meiji rule were still infrequent and caused comment which often was far from favourable. Some of the class-conscious Victorians among the British residents considered Milne was marrying beneath him and was, in fact, 'rather letting the side down'. Others would have been churlish enough to wonder why and rudely ask if it was really necessary. Doubtless, too, there would have been Japanese whose upbringing was such that they could only deplore an action which, in their opinion, was likely to demean their cherished racial purity. Even some of Toné's relatives would have opposed the idea. These attitudes may well have influenced Milne in later years to make humorous but wholly improbable comments about his marital state which will be discussed in another chapter.

Such initial disapproval was held in disdain by the pair and there were far more important difficulties to overcome not the least of which were the cultural differences so very much wider than in normal mixed marriages. It will be recalled that Japan had only recently begun to emerge from several centuries of almost total isolation, and some of her people were not finding it easy to comprehend many of the customs and beliefs inherent in the already established industrial societies of the West. There was for them both something of a language barrier. Although the spoken tongue could be mastered with application, the Japanese script was a much more difficult task for a busy man like Milne despite his aptitude for language study. A story is told of how their early efforts at communication involved the use of Toné's simple Anglo-Japanese dictionary. In truth, English was always to prove something of a burden to Toné.

But there was another hurdle which, perhaps, outweighed the others. It was that of contrasting religions. She was not only a devout Buddhist but was also the daughter of an Abbot of high standing in the community and whose family had for long been deeply involved with the priesthood. On the other hand John was a Christian who, through his studies in Divinity during College days, had become an A.K.C. (Associate of King's College). As if these obstacles alone were not enough, the untimely death of Toné's father in 1878 may have added yet another complication for, unless

Milne had met the Abbot the previous summer, and 'spoken' for Toné at that time, there was now no possibility of seeking parental blessing.

Whatever difficulties were encountered they eventually were overcome by the two determined young people. It is now generally agreed that the marriage took place in 1881 at the Rananza-ku church in Tokyo. Obviously there was a mutual agreement between them about the religious rites to be used and as the marriage was a singularly happy one the formalities which preceded their union become of little importance.

As the end of his initial contract with the Japanese government approached Milne was informed it would be extended if he desired. These foreign teaching appointments could be terminated also if a six-month notice was given by either side. His original monthly salary had been 300 yen. In March 1897 this was raised to 350 yen and a few years later to 400 yen, a monthly sum which was then approximately equal to the annual earnings of an average Japanese worker and is an indication of the vast amount of money the government had to pay to attract the talent they needed. Even though Milne's salary was not as high as that paid to some western experts it was still much more than many senior Japanese officials received. The Director of the Meteorological Observatory, for instance, was paid considerably less.

In 1882, after six years absence from Britain, Milne travelled home for a short holiday, crossing America from San Francisco to New York. His first class fare was paid for by the Japanese authorities and it is likely that Toné remained in Tokyo where they were now living as there is no evidence that she accompanied him. Milne visited his mother in Surrey and other relatives in Rochdale before returning to Japan via the Suez Canal and India. On the way he paid a courtesy call at the Italian observatory on Mount Vesuvius which had been established to monitor the ground disturbances caused by volcanic action.

There was a similar round the world trip in 1889 when he took the prototype of the Milne-MacDonald Vibration Recorder to Britain. On the way he demonstrated the instrument to several railway companies in the United States. On this occasion the return journey to Japan was made via Messina so that he could observe the work being done there by Italian seismologists. There was a further, but shorter visit to Britain in 1893. Other working 'holidays' the Professor undertook during his service in the Land of The Rising Sun were to Borneo, the Phillipines, several other islands in the Pacific, and to Australia and New Zealand.

Some of his expeditions involved him in personal danger. According to reports not yet fully substantiated Milne went to Korea when that country was at war with Japan. He seemed to have no conception of fear; it was as if this emotion was absent from his psychological make-up since there were many occasions when the action he took could only have been regarded as foolhardy. Some have already been discussed, such as his ascent of the Oshima volcano when he took appalling risks during a particularly violent eruption to investigate the deposition of red-hot lava at close hand. More than one of his experiments which involved the use of dynamite ended in near disaster, while his intense preoccupation with seismic instruments during earthquakes could have resulted in serious injury if not death.

During the courtship of Toné and even after their marriage Milne still found little opportunity for what he regarded as purely social activities. When not lecturing at the College, acting as a consultant on construction in seismic areas; advising on mining problems; carrying out endless seismological investigations and experiments; or away from home on one of his frequent explorations, he would sit for hours at his desk writing copious notes, drafting articles, correcting manuscripts or compiling those verbose reports which seemed to give him so much pleasure to produce. But although Toné understood the perpetual need within him to continue working long after most men would have tired, in her quiet way she encouraged him to develop his natural interest in the Japanese way of life. Through her guidance he was able to learn much which had once puzzled him as hitherto he had not appreciated the Asiatic way of thinking. The more he delved into the evolution of the indigenous creative arts the greater became his love for those whom some of the resident westerners still regarded as barbarians. To his amusement he found that there were just as many Japanese who considered *their* culture to be far more developed than that of the 'uncivilised' foreigners. But he also knew that it was a lack of real knowledge and understanding on both sides which was the major factor determining these illogical convictions.

The direction in which his interest in Japanese civilisation developed can be gleaned from a perusal of the magic lantern slides he used later in Britain to illustrate his lectures. Part of this once superb collection was found recently mouldering away in a damp outhouse. Unfortunately, many of the unique hand-tinted photographs have been broken or have deteriorated through the years of neglect. Yet enough remain for a viewer to absorb many aspects of the way of life in nineteenth century Meiji Japan.

From some of these slides one can sense the splendour of the ancient temples in whose garden pools flowering water-lilies invite the weary traveller to pause for meditation. In others the towering ginko trees with their green, fan-shaped leaves resembling maidenhair ferns contrast sharply with the glorious reds of autumn maples so subtle in their perfection that they invoke a feeling of *shibui*

— refined elegance — to the Japanese. The gaiety of April festivities in cherry-blossom time is recorded by picnic scenes in the parks and these lovely flowers of spring also provide settings for the aching beauty of the sacred mountain, Fuji, whose symmetrical snow-clad slopes have for centuries provided inspiration for Japanese artists.

Milne captured the spirit of the changing times of that era with his pictorial compositions of people at work; street traders hawk their wares in crowded thoroughfares; craftsmen demonstrate the ancient tools of their trade, while yet others display the product of their labours. The mundane is not missed. There is one delightful study of a coolie struggling to pull a night-soil cart. The look of obvious distaste upon his face remains to this day to affirm his dislike of the work! Even the erection of such things as telegraph poles and brick-built western style factories has not been omitted.

The comprehensiveness of Milne's collection is a further indication of the way he could become absorbed once his interest was aroused. It ranges from photographs of sumo wrestlers who have long since joined their ancestors, depicted in a fierce struggle for physical supremacy, through the devotees of martial arts brandishing weapons in mock conflict, to portraits of be-medalled high-ranking military officers and impeccably dressed political leaders who are in utter variance with other scenes of direst poverty. In one of the latter a tiny child, shoeless and ragged of dress, with dirty thumb in mouth and in sore need of a handkerchief, has a gaze so wistful that an instant feeling of sympathy is invoked before the realisation comes that a century of change has passed since the picture was posed.

Nor did Milne neglect the ancient cultures of Japan. Young girls are shown learning the skills of the geisha, its self-discipline, its perfection of traditional dress and art of conversation, the intricate details of the sophisticated tea-ceremony originally instituted by monks as an adjunct for meditation, the artistic gestures of dance and mime, the skills of traditional music played on the thirteen stringed *koto* or on the *samisen* — which has only three. He has captured them all. His illustrations of the magnificence of Kyoto, the imperial capital for nearly eleven centuries, proclaim the serenity of Buddism and the older, more accommodating Shinto religion.

Those of the even more ancient Nara, where Japanese culture first evolved from that of the Chinese, are represented by Daibutsu, the gigantic bronze statue known to westerners as the Great Buddha, and in whose outstretched palm two or three men can stand with ease.

In another section there is a badly produced court scene of the Emperor Meiji being presented with a pair of hawks. This particular slide was possibly illicitly prepared because for a long period it was forbidden to make a likeness of the Mikado. The prints of his

Empress and the young Crown Prince are of higher quality and a later date.

Coloured sketches typify the bloody but triumphant battles against the Chinese on both land and sea, while gruesome details of political assassinations and pictorial examples of severe methods of punishment outline the continuing struggle to achieve constitutional stability.

That Milne understood something of the mysticism which is an inherent part of the Japanese character is made obvious by the inclusion in his collections of representative examples such as the graphic portrayal of a murdered man's soul hovering above the body after death. Manifestly clear also is the fact that he was conversant with the underlying but fundamental Oriental desire to achieve a spirit of harmony in their lives. Known as *wa*, this is best interpreted as a wish to observe and perfect the agreeable relationship they are convinced exists between people and objects, and between objects themselves.

His involvement with geophysics led Milne to accumulate many scenes of the natural disasters which from time to time had devastated parts of the country. Earthquakes and volcanic activities predominate, but some of his pictures show the destruction inflicted by a *tsunami*, the dreaded wave caused by undersea earthquakes which, when it approaches the shore, can exceed forty feet in height and sweep all before it.

It is indeed fortunate that these fragile glass slides have been recovered as many of them illustrate a way of Japanese life which has long passed into history. Yet Milne's interest did not confine itself merely to acquiring a series of pictorial records. His frequent travelling throughout the country enabled him to obtain an insight into crafts which had continued to flourish for centuries unmodified by outside influences — crafts which demanded skills of the highest order. Of these there were many. He would have discovered, for example, that lacquer wax could be produced in several entirely different ways. In one area it was made from sap taken from lateral cuts in the trunks of Urushi trees, while in others it was the rind of the fruit which was collected, steamed and pounded until the liquid wax exuded and was channelled away.

From his talks with farmers he learnt more than a little of the multifarious techniques used in the production of silk from silkworms. Growers of tea and tobacco, mushrooms, sugar, cotton and the newly introduced cereal, wheat, explained their problems. But it was the traditional methods which fascinated him most; the way hemp was made, for instance. Here a high degree of skill was required in what at first sight appeared to be a particularly simple operation. One man would gather enough of the plant to provide him with a day's work as all the essential processes could be completed in that time. After being soaked the stalks would be broken open to separate the rind from the pith. When the inner white coating had been scraped off the remaining green fibre was dried and woven.

His considerable knowledge of the quality of different kinds of rice grown throughout the Empire probably stemmed from an appreciation of *saké*, the national beverage of Japan. In this he became something of a connoisseur. It is unlikely that he would have drunk *Nigori*, the cheap, milky, sour-tasting spirit of the poor. Only its purified form, the clear *Leishu* or the sweetened liquor, *Mirinshu*, would have been acceptable as both not only had a higher alcoholic content but were far more palatable. He would never have considered drinking *Shiro* since this was thought fit only for women.

As a westerner Milne was intrigued with Toné's use of *oshiroi*, the 'honourable white' cosmetic without which no Japanese women of her day would have felt 'dressed' and also of the rouge *beni* which she and many others used to imitate the beauty of the blush. He accepted the fact that, while in Japan at least, her eyebrows were always being depilated to a willow-leaf shape as after her marriage she was determined to show that she had achieved the dignity and authority of a *femme-en-titre*. Although this latter practice was no longer widespread Toné undoubtedly felt it necessary to indicate she was not a 'secondary wife' or concubine as these had been compelled to display inferiority in rank by leaving their eyebrows unshaven.

After his marriage Milne left his bachelor house in the college grounds and set up home in another part of Tokyo. In common with accepted practice, its dimensions were determined by the number of *tatami* mats which covered the floor area and Toné explained that these woven rushes were of different sizes in other parts of the country. She was much occupied in siting the various articles of furniture so they could achieve the necessary *wa* with each other.

John Milne's involvement with Japan was complete — he interested himself in just about everything that country could offer. As a result he came to feel that he should assist its development towards modernisation in every way possible and this he did. In retrospect it can be stated without fear of contradiction that if he was not the first then he was certainly one of the earliest and most dedicated of British Japanophiles.

It is probable that he would have been content to remain there for the rest of his life even though at times he felt isolated from the main stream of scientific progress taking place in Europe and America. But early in 1895, there was a serious set-back to any plans he may have had in this direction. In what was for him a laconic comment tucked away in his annual report to the British Association he reported:

It is with regret that I have to announce that on February 17th my house and observatory were entirely destroyed by fire. The losses consisted of books, instruments and other things accumulated during the last twenty years, the stock of the *Transactions of the Seismological Society* which at that time were packed ready for shipment to Europe, and about 1,500 books and pamphlets relating to earthquake and volcanic phenomena. All I saved was the clockwork of a new seismograph and a bundle of photograms. The analysis of the later form the chief portion of this report.

He was to describe later how, clad only in his nightgown and clutching a few charred but cherished personal papers, he watched the flames, fanned by a rising wind, envelop his house in a matter of minutes.

Fortunately, the new seismograph which could detect major earthquakes wherever they occurred was not affected, but the loss of his valuable reference library, perhaps the most important collection of works on seismology and related subjects then in existence, was a bitter blow. Copies of his latest publication, the *Catalogue of 8,831 earthquakes* were still with the printers and he offered these to his scientist friends in many countries in exchange for surplus works. Soon he had assembled another library, but many irreplaceable texts had been destroyed and he mourned their loss for years.

The cause of the fire has never been established. It could have been an accident and most probably was, although doubts on this were cast by some of his friends who pointed out that the recent resurgence of Japanese nationalism had already led to further unpleasant incidents. The Sino-Japanese war which had recently ended had proved to the world that Japan had become a military power to be reckoned with; her army had captured Korea and invaded Manchuria, while at sea the numerically superior Chinese fleet had been crushed by the Emperor's modern navy. After China had sued for peace, Russia, France and Germany began to put pressure upon the Japanese to relinquish most of their territorial gains. Because of this there was an understandable reaction from a section of the public, not only against the nationals of those three countries, but against other Caucasians then in Japan. Some were manhandled in the streets or had their houses burned in the general protest.

The fire at Milne's house may not have been the outcome of this unrest, of course, yet why did it occur? The lamps in the observatory where the fire started were of the type which extinguished automatically when overturned. On the other hand the fact that Milne was a prolific smoker of cigarettes and might carelessly have left one alight when he had finished work that evening cannot be overlooked. In none of his personal statements however does he hint that the fire was not an accident.

This incident may well have been the factor which made Milne decide finally that the time had come to leave Japan, but there could well have been another reason why he resigned his Professorship. By now there were very few foreign lecturers at the University; the years of absorbing western technology had more than brought Japan to the stage where her people felt themselves competent to manage their own affairs. In the specialised skills for which he had been employed there were men he had helped teach already well qualified to take his place and even in seismology his Japanese colleagues were now considered experts in their own right. In fact, Milne was no longer 'Mr Irreplaceable Person'. He realised that for him the exciting Japanese experiment was at an end and, although saddened at the thought of leaving the University after nearly twenty years, was consoled by the knowledge that he had done his job well and had made major contributions beneficial to the people of Japan.

He made up his mind to return to England, but first there was one thing he had to do. At the British consulate in Tokyo on 12 June 1895 he was married to Toné again — this time according to British law. The ceremony was obviously to ensure she would legally become his next-of-kin. He did not want there to be the slightest misunderstanding about this.

Early in June also his resignation from the University was accepted. He was given a farewell party by his colleagues who presented him with a pair of beautiful cloisonné vases as a token of his long and valued service.

Towards the end of the month he was received in audience by the Emperor. This was a great compliment: in the early days of his reign he had seen all foreigners when they left as a matter of courtesy but before long, through force of numbers, it was decided to limit these audiences to a selected few. On this particular occasion it is understood His Imperial Majesty himself commanded Milne's presence. After his return to Britain he was to learn that the Emperor had conferred upon him the Third Grade of the Order of the Rising Sun — a rare distinction, rarely awarded. Additionally, he was also the recipient of a life pension of 1,000 yen.

So yet another chapter in the lives of John and Toné Milne ended. As the ship which was taking them on the first stage of their journey to England cleared Yokohama Bay no doubt they would have watched the country they both loved receding slowly in the distance. Perhaps, too, they caught a brief glimpse of sunlight reflecting from Fuji's snow-capped cone. Yet for Milne, the sadness of leaving behind so many of his dearest friends would have been ameliorated to some extent in the pleasurable thoughts of a permanent home in England after an exile which had lasted so long.

For Toné, too, sadness would surely have been mixed with excitement and even a little apprehension at the thought of life in a foreign country. One wonders what her feeling would have been could she have known that twenty-five years were to pass before she would return to her native land.

See notes to illustrations on page 197ff.

7

The Master of Seismology

John Milne arrived in England with his wife during July 1895 to establish an observatory at a permanent home where he could set up the new seismograph. For this he needed the best possible site if he were to be able to record earthquake movements from the other side of the world. Although other factors must have helped determine the final choice, he found Shide Hill House in the Isle of Wight suitable for his purpose.

The rock formation underlying the observatory was of major importance and in making his choice of site he would doubtless have been aware of the work of other geologists who had already closely studied this particular area, including that of G.A. Mantell who had written that hereabouts there was a transverse dislocation, or rent, across the range of chalk hills, produced by the tension of the strata during their elevation from the horizontal to their present nearly vertical position.

In more general terms Shide was, in those days, a quiet, restful spot, hardly more than a scattering of cottages sheltering in the lee of a grassy down a mile or so outside Newport, the Island's principal town.

The house suited Milne well and in a report to the British Association later that year he recalled some of the problems encountered in setting up his instruments:

> I reached Shide on July 30 and on the following day a pit was excavated in a dry stable, about 3ft 6in in depth, down to the upper surface of the disintegrated chalk. On August 6th and 7th a brick pier, 6 feet in height and 1ft 6in square was built on a concrete bed to rise freely in the pit. The necessary wooden covering for this was completed at noon on the 16th, and that evening an extremely light horizontal pendulum was installed and set to work. This instrument, which I call 'T', gave a beautifully defined two-line diagram until the 21st when the clock ceased to drive the film which had become damp and sticky.

This temporary set-back was overcome by drying the air inside the case, and by the 25th of the month he was recording what at first appeared to be a violent tremor storm. Several experiments showed however that the movement was caused by the rapid dessication due to the action of the drying agent. This was quickly corrected and the work of the station began in earnest.

In his next report Milne added more geological detail about the site he had selected for his observatory:

> The position of Shide Hill House, where instrument 'T' is installed, is approximately 50° 14' 18" N. Lat., and 1° 17' 10" W. Long. It is near to the Shide railway station, at the foot of the western side of Pan Down, which is a portion of the chalk backbone of the Isle of Wight.
>
> Up on the Down the chalk reaches to within a few inches of the surface. At Shide Hill House disintegrated chalk, which may have a thickness of about 6 feet, is met with at a depth of 3 feet. In front of the house, or towards the west, at a distance of about 150 yards on the other side of a small stream (the River Medina), there is a railway. In a N.E. direction, at a distance of 242 yards, there is a chalk quarry, where at certain fixed times blasting takes place.
>
> At the back of the house within a few yards of the buildings in which the instrument is placed there is a lane down which on week days carts heavily laden with gravel pass.

He went on to report that he was able to establish a second instrument, 'U', within the grounds of Carisbrooke Castle just over a mile away. The foundation was similar to that at Shide, being a brick column built up from the chalk and it stood in a small room, one wall of which was the western wall of the castle. This instrument gave its first records about 22 June 1896, but it was not in proper working order until the middle of July.

So within a year he had two stations operating in close proximity. The Shide observatory itself was to grow both in size and importance during the next few years. In 1900, with financial help from Matthew H. Gray, a fellow seismologist, an experimental laboratory was constructed at one end of the main house, although the principal seismographs continued to be sited in their own building in the grounds well clear of disturbances.

Describing the observatory some years later, Mrs Lou Henry Hoover, a visitor from the United States, wrote in the *Bulletin of the American Seismological Society*:

> The two seismographs that are in active service at Shide are installed in a little building of their own, with a wonderful old door, far out in the garden, where there is no chance of their being disturbed. The experimental laboratory is separate from the house, but is approached from the study by a sheltered verandah. All is methodical within, and as spotless as though a

speck of chalk from the overhanging downs might disturb one of those glass-encased horizontal pendulums. The writing table stands in the centre; by the door is a great black globe, with the earth's surface scantily outlined in white, all the stations having Milne seismographs marked, and cryptic characters scattered over it; nearby are shelves full of files of station registers, all neatly jacketed; windows face both north and south, with shelves of books between, and the walls are hung with prints of unusual seismograms and earthquake pictures . . . Off in one corner stands a relic of early days, one of the first seismographs made at Shide. The pillar going down into the chalk is larger than those used now; the mast is a lamp post of the day, brought up from Newport town; the six-foot booms are made of bicycle tubing, — a north-south, and an east-west one. But the indicators are the modern grass-straw ones, grown in the pasture one sees from the south window; and they register on a roll of smoked paper. All the other seismographs record photographically . . . On the other side of the room is a later instrument, but with the mast but a couple of feet high, and a corresponding short boom. A push of one's thumb against the stone pedestal on which it stands causes the indicator to swing the full amplitude of its case.

From Milne's regular reports to the British Association it is clear that his experimental seismographs were continually being modified. In 1902, for instance, the lamp-post instrument had an 80lb mass and a boom of just over 3ft, while a year later both its mass and boom were greater.

In the same report he listed the various seismographs regularly in use at Shide:

1. A photographic recording horizontal pendulum orientated North and South. This is the type of instrument similar to those at other stations.
2. A pair of pendulums similar to the above orientated North-South and East-West. This instrument was kindly presented to your Secretary by Mr A.F. Yarrow.
3. A pair of horizontal pendulums writing on smoked paper. These have arms 14 inches in length, and each carry a 10lb weight.
4. A pair of horizontal pendulums also writing on smoked paper. The arms are 9 feet in length, and each weighs about 100lb. This and instrument No. 3 give open diagrams.
5. A simple spiral spring seismograph for vertical motion. Record photographic.
6. A large balance arranged to show tilting.

More and more stations were being established both at home and overseas and all used the Milne horizontal pendulum seismograph. Their recordings were sent to Shide, and Mrs Hoover commented that over six thousand were filed in the laboratory building alone, adding:

> It is a quaint conceit that to the utter quiet of this pretty, tree-encircled old house, with its grassy stone-stepped terraces leading down towards the little valley, with the great peaceful downs rising at its back, should come the earthquakes of the world to be classified and studied. But come they do, and a vast amount of work they make for Professor Milne and his clever Japanese assistant, Mr Hirota. There are about sixty stations whose reports come, some monthly, some twice yearly and some when a chance boat may bring them. These must all be carefully correlated and filed away, and every six months a circular containing all the recent registers is sent out to all the stations. This is practically a labour of love on Professor Milne's part. He holds no official position.

By this she meant, of course, that the observatory was not a government establishment.

The *Shide Circulars* were to become famous in the world of seismology and the village of Shide of premier importance to earthquake investigators in many parts of the globe. But not all of them wanted to acknowledge British prominence in the developing science or Milne as the focal point of their joint efforts and cooperation. The stimulus given by Milne's team working in Japan had helped the spread of er.thusiasm for seismology to many other countries. Scientists of note throughout the world were turning more of their attention to this particular field and there were challenges to his supremacy brought about, curiously enough, by Milne's own repeated calls for full international cooperation.

As has already been mentioned, as early as 1883 he had realised and stated publicly that, with proper instruments, it might well be possible for large earthquakes to be recorded at any point on the land surface of the planet. Consequently it was of no real surprise to him when, a few years later, a young seismologist, Dr E. von Rebeur-Pashwitz, confirmed this theory by recording in Germany earthquakes which had occurred in Japan. He and Milne communicated frequently, comparing notes and ideas and Milne himself was soon reporting long-distance earthquakes recorded in Tokyo. Before von Rebeur-Pashwitz died in 1895 at the early age of thirty-four he had suggested the foundation of an international organisation of seismic observatories. The idea was supported wholeheartedly by Milne and others, but excellent though the idea was, nothing came of it. Milne obviously gave the matter deep thought and after experiments had shown him he was right stated that, unless the seismographs to be employed internationally were standard in design, then unacceptable anomalies would exist. In this theory he had the backing of the British Association.

As one of the joint secretaries of the Seismological Committee of the British Association, Milne once again drew attention to von Rebeur-Paschwitz's suggestions and pointed out that Dr G. Gerland, of Strasburg, had translated them into French and published them on his own initiative — apparently without result. As Milne was later to write:

> For this reason, but more especially because individual efforts have not led to any definite results, the Committee have issued a letter to a number of observatories requesting cooperation in the observation of earthquakes which are propagated round and possibly through the earth.

In all, some forty countries were invited to establish between them a chain of nearly sixty observatories capable of carrying out continuous seismic surveillance of the world, and many of them willingly cooperated. But in 1902, when Milne already had more than thirty stations in operation based mainly in Commonwealth countries, the British Government received an official invitation from Germany to take part in a congress the object of which was to establish an international enquiry into earthquake phenomena. Milne was one of the two men who went to this congress in 1903 where he observed that, of the one hundred delegates who represented twenty-five countries, sixty-two were Germans, although Germany, like Great Britain, had only one vote.

The congress decided that a central organisation would be formed with its headquarters in Strasburg. Each contributing country would have one member on the governing committee which in turn would elect a president, a chief for the central office and a general secretary. The chief would reside in Strasburg but the president and secretary should be elected from outside Germany.

The proposals were clearly not to Milne's liking. Yet the work of this new association was to be almost exactly that which he knew to be essential, namely, to carry out observations to a common plan, to carry out world-wide experiments on important seismic matters, to establish and support observatories and to collect, study, and publish reports from them. Milne referred back to the British Seismological Committee and the implications of the proposals were discussed at length. Eventually its conclusions were published:

1. This Committee is of the opinion that any moderate subsidy would be most profitably expended in support of the seismological work inaugurated by the British Association, and that

there is urgent need of such help, which should be a first call on any such funds.

2. Assuming this need supplied, the Committee would approve the further co-ordination of the work by joining the proposed Association.

Even with this edict it was not entirely satisfied and in 1904 proposed changes which included the condition that the choice of a central station be decided by the General Assembly. Nor was it felt necessary for the locality to be named in the Convention. Furthermore, even if these changes were implemented, Britain would consider joining only if France and the United States were also willing to cooperate and that British seismology received state aid.

Obviously, Milne's influence on the Seismological Committee and elsewhere explains the position then taken. His views were well known and in 1908 at a Friday evening meeting of the Royal Institution he explained them in detail:

> So far as I am aware all foreign stations are subsidised by their respective governments. Great Britain enjoys the cooperation of 45 stations provided with similar instruments which are distributed fairly evenly over the four quarters of the world. The home stations are supported by the British Association, the Royal Society, the *Daily Mail*, Mr M. H. Gray and other individuals.

He made no mention of his own substantial financial contribution and the point he was stressing was that his organisation at Shide was not directly financed by the British government and would benefit from a state subsidy. He continued:

> So far as the recording of world-shaking earthquakes is concerned, I believe the British cooperation to be, at the present time, quite equal to a combination of the stations of all other countries. The last outcome in connection with observational seismology has been the establishment of an International Seismological Association. The central bureau is in Strasburg, its president is Professor A. Shuster, and its general meetings take place once every *four* years. I am not aware that France has' formally announced its adherence. The British Government, by subscribing £160 to the central bureau, has accepted a shelter from a Continental Aegis. For nearly fifty years the British Association has encouraged seismological research but whatever prestige it may have gained, together with its attendant commercial and other advantages, these are passing under a new *regime* across the Channel.

In those days cables were the only speedy and secure means of communication and their protection was of paramount importance. Emphasising this point, Milne went on:

A government of a country does not wish to seek abroad for an explanation why telegraphic messages have ceased to flow. To confirm, extend or disprove a cablegram, a government, a business house or the public of a given country would like to obtain information within its own boundaries. When a country or a colony finds itself cut off from the outside world[1] in consequence of cable interruption, that country or colony together with other countries would like to have a ready means of saying whether the interruption had been due to submarine disturbance or to some other operation, for example, war. Those who lay cables would prefer to have information as to positions of sub-oceanic sites of seismic activity from records made in their own country rather than those which had been made abroad.

On the other hand, he did suggest two occasions when he thought international cooperation would be of use:

When after great convulsions cities have to be re-built, and there are many at the moment, it is natural that information bearing upon reconstruction to reduce earthquake effects would be sought for at the world's central office, and those who supply information would in all probability supply engineers and material. Insurance companies who wish to apportion rates to risks when insuring against earthquake effects, might also think it best to seek their information at a central bureau.

But he was obviously against the kind of international co-operation being proposed at that time:

After an earthquake when such companies are called upon to pay the insured, many difficult questions arise which can only be answered by seismograms. Millions of pounds sterling are dependent upon these records, and it is important that the same should be readily accessible. A seismogram which travels quicker than a telegram may affect the stock exchange. We no more require a central bureau to discuss applied seismology than we do to discuss the construction of torpedoes or flying machines.

This almost complete *volte face* from his enthusiastic agreement with the original suggestion of von Rebeur-Paschwitz was in part

1. In 1888 the simultaneous fractures of three submarine cables between Australia and Java by an earthquake caused Australia to mobilise its naval and military forces — *Seismology* (John Milne)

Illustration from the Milne-Burton book, The Great Earthquake of Japan, *published by Stamford Press, London & Yokohama, 1892.*

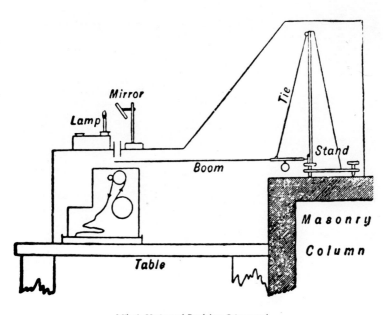

Milne's Horizontal Pendulum Seismograph.

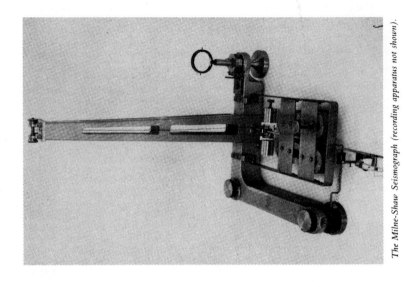

The Milne-Shaw Seismograph (recording apparatus not shown).

The Gray-Milne Seismograph (also featured on book jacket).

logical, yet there were undisclosed personal reasons which bear consideration. Milne was against full continental cooperation because he had become aware of the growing anti-German feeling in this country and feared disruption of the service if war came. It has also been suggested that this reluctance to take part was a smoke-screen put up in order to get more research money from direct government services. These are but contributory factors. The real reasons were more basic; not only was he guarding his own interests — and after all, much of his own money had been ploughed into the organisation he was now expected to hand over — but also he might no longer have an important role to play in the new organisation. Moreover, after being on his own for so long the thought of working with others again was repugnant. This latter point of view has been hinted at on several occasions. For instance, there is the significant little phrase which the scientist J. W. Judd was later to write in *Nature*:

> Some, perhaps, may suggest that Milne was wanting in sympathy with the work of co-ordinating the results of other organisations than his own; and it may be admitted that his Pegasus did not run well in harness. But it must be remembered how, from the first, he had been accustomed to bear all the weight and responsibility of great enterprises on his own broad shoulders.

★   ★   ★

Just as the good engineer knows that simplicity in design and manufacture means reliability in operation, so a good scientist expects greater accuracy from instruments of sound design and construction. Because the Professor could appreciate both aspects it was inevitable that the Milne seismograph was a tremendous advance upon those then in use for the detection of earthquakes. But never satisfied and always seeking perfection, Milne made many modifications to his original design. In this he was much helped by the firm of Messrs R. W. Munro, engineers and instrument makers, which is still in existence, and their drawings show the many changes made over the years. One of the more significant was the replacement of the long roll of photosensitive paper by a single large sheet wrapped round the recording drum which was about one metre in circumference and some 200 mm wide. The latter could be set to make one revolution every four hours and at the same time to move 6 mm laterally along its axis. Each sheet lasted up to four days and gave an open trace of 4 mm per minute. Although this innovation meant that the paper now had to be changed twice a week, it was cheaper and much easier to process than the long strip used earlier. Another improvement he made was to use two pendulums placed at right-angles yet recording on the same drum. Later he introduced an electromagnetic shutter to eclipse the light, this being a more convenient method of placing time marks on the bromide film. In addition repeated modifications were made to both the suspension and the mass.

In all, some eighty seismographs of this type were manufactured and used by more than sixty nations mainly in the British Empire and so sited that they monitored most of the world. It is of interest that one of them, number 37, made in 1901, is listed in the Munro Order Book for despatch to the 'National Antarctic Expedition'. This was taken to the South Polar regions in the *Discovery* by the explorer, Captain Robert Scott and was set up at the base camp.

For all the Professor's strivings to improve the instrument's performance there remained two major defects — the magnification factor of the pendulum was not as high as he desired nor could it be satisfactorily damped to provide better resolution. Even so, the machine worked quite well and from 1895 onwards the earthquake seismograms from the observatories cooperating with Milne were forwarded to him at Shide where they were correlated and re-issued in tabulated form in what became known as the *Shide Circulars*.

The effort required in preparation of these lists from the many stations' registers must have been prodigious. The various seismograms of each earthquake had first to be analysed and compared. As these arrived at Shide from many parts of the world at irregular intervals there was always some delay before the essential mathematical calculations could be applied and overall conclusions reached. Major task though it undoubtedly was, Milne and his small staff worked enthusiastically and the prophecy he had made many years earlier, that

> A ring of 12 to 24 stations situated round our globe would in a short time give us valuable information, not simply about its crust, but possibly about its interior,

was more than justified.

That they might better understand the phenomena, a number of the great early seismologists devoted many years to the compilation of earthquake catalogues. Inevitably, these were tasks of infinite labour and patience requiring intensive research. Milne's catalogues were no exception and followed a predictable pattern. Initially, there were his numerous lists published in the *Transactions of the Seismological Society of Japan* and elsewhere, of which mention has been made earlier, and culminating in his *Catalogue of 8,831 earthquakes recorded in Japan between 1885 and 1892*. The completion of this latter work enabled him to produce a map of Japan which established once and for all the areas of that country where the greatest seismic activity could be expected, and also to propound his theory of the relationship between seismicity and terrestrial relief.

After his return to England the most important list he produced in what is now regarded as the third period of his life, was the *Catalogue of Destructive Earthquakes, A.D.7 to A.D.1899*. It was an important document as it contained information of some 4,136 disturbances which had occurred throughout the world during these years. Necessarily incomplete, it was still as informative as the paucity of many of the records permitted. In it he classified destructive earthquakes by three degrees of intensity with a scale of measurement which the Comte de Montessus de Ballore, without doubt one of the greatest compilers of earthquake catalogues the world has ever known, considered to be eminently practical. Methods of assessing earthquake intensity are today much more precise, of course, but the one Milne employed is interesting in that it is easily understood by the layman:

1. It means that an earthquake has an intensity sufficient to crack walls, break chimneys, to shatter old buildings or to produce slight cracks in the ground . . . destructiveness is usually confined to a town or village, and the radius of the area affected will not exceed five miles.
2. With earthquakes of this intensity . . . its effect will have a radius of twenty miles. Buildings may by unroofed or shattered and some may fall, the ground may be badly cracked in places and small landslips occur.
3. Earthquakes with this intensity are those which destroyed towns and devastated districts. The ground has been faulted and fissured, whilst from these openings water, mud and sand may issue. In hilly country landslips will be common. . . . Beyond the mesoseismic area up to distance of 100 miles the effects produced may be similar to those of class 1.

For each class he quoted a numerical value for the accelerations of the ground that could be expected.

To some of his contemporaries, who were ever ready to criticise what they did not fully understand, it was puzzling that Milne seldom attempted to draw conclusions from his own catalogues, for, they reasoned, with the knowledge he must have gained from their compilation, he must also have formulated theories he did not pursue. Notes which perhaps he ought to have made would have been of value to others if only to save them time and labour in arriving at conclusions which, by familiarity with the lists, he himself must have already reached. But Milne was primarily interested in the phenomena of earthquakes and most often offered theories and facts for others to follow while he himself continually opened up new lines of research with his wide-ranging investigations which probed ever deeper into the many unsolved mysteries.

On settling in England, Milne found that the pressure of work at the observatory and his continuous investigations into the phenomena of the earthquake gave him less time to contribute as much written work to the scientific journals as had been his custom, but he still spent a fair amount of time with his pen. After revising *Earthquakes* for yet another edition, he wrote his second major textbook, *Seismology*, which was published by Kegan, Paul, Trench, Trübner and Co. Ltd., of London, in 1898.

Perhaps the best method of summarising this latter work is to use part of the review John Perry wrote for *Nature:*

> He has a pleasant style, and knows from experience as a popular lecturer how his subject may be made interesting to the general reader, and the result is a very readable book which probably contains all that is worth knowing on this subject at the present period of its development . . . Every sentence in the book contains the result of much thought and observation, and yet it is a book which is just as easy to read as the report of a popular lecture. One has the feeling that the writer is appealing for sympathy and cooperation of all kinds without which his great work in the establishment of observatories cannot go on; it is the kind of appeal that one reads between the lines of a traveller's book sometimes, an appeal that the author does not know that he is making. It certainly adds to the interest of an already interesting subject.

One of Milne's unpublished manuscripts which recently came to light, and to which further reference will be made, demonstrates his desire to write serious instruction in such a way that the intelligent layman would enjoy it. For instance, although mainly of a technical nature, in the section on the economics of an earthquake he introduced the subject with a light-hearted story as follows:

> One day I was called from my laboratory to see a lady visitor. I thought it would simply be the old story, and I was in for a lot of reiteration which, in order to save time, might well be sent round on a phonograph. Seismographs and seismograms must be explained, after which I will give illustrations of the benefits seismology conferred on mankind, and finally listen to the usual stereotyped expressions of gratitude. 'Oh, how interesting', 'Thank you so much', 'Hope I haven't wasted your time', 'Goodbye, so very amusing', 'Goodbye'. The parting guest has always failed to catch what I have had to say in reply! On this occasion, however, I was quickly undeceived. My fair visitor had no particular desire to see either seismograms or seismographs. She had come on a question of economics. 'I do love

earthquakes,' she commenced, 'not little ones, but great big ones.' I looked at my visitor with alarm, and thinking it might be necessary for me to fly, I also looked at the door. Before I could reply she continued, 'Let me tell you, most of my capital is invested in cement mills, and when cities go down cement goes up.' I will not say what my suspicions were, but they disappeared, and I felt that I was face to face with a very practical-minded person. With a big earthquake we know that things go down, the value of private dwellings, public works, stocks of various descriptions suffer a marked depreciation, while labour and materials necessary for re-construction go up. Earthquakes create a lot of business.

His chapter on this subject goes on to develop the theme that, destructive though they be, and perhaps bringing ruin to many, earthquakes can make others rich.

The many stories Milne told in his lectures and writings, and the frequent analogies he used drove home his message and made clear the more technical content. His aim was always to popularise seismology and in letters and articles to newspapers and periodicals, particularly the *Daily Mail* group, he went some way towards achieving this object in Britain.

Just as it has been impractical to deal at length with every one of the many investigations which the Professor carried out in Japan within the confines of a single chapter, so it is that nearly two decades of his work in Britain must of necessity undergo a similar restriction. It is also impractical to determine a chronological order as his probings into individual problems in both countries often lasted many years. These were periodically shelved while research into other aspects of seismology was in progress, and were recommenced only when fresh ideas or a new impetus once again stimulated his interest. Some of the topics which will not be discussed at length in this book include the study Milne made into the possibility that earthquakes occur in groups and also their possible relationship with the erratic transit of the magnetic poles. Neither will further mention be made of Milne's many attempts to solve the problem of drawing time-curves of earthquake motion, while his most important contribution to seismology at this time, the resolution of a satisfactory method of locating the epicentres of distant earthquakes, is possibly too mathematical in content to be developed here.

Once again he reveals his intense involvement and the persistent nature of his character through his investigations of diurnal waves and earth tremors which he studied over the years. Although they were not wholly connected with earth movements, he knew it was necessary to understand them as fully as possible, not only because they might well advance the knowledge of seismology but so that their frequent appearance on seismograms could be identified.

These diurnal waves cause the slow tilting that takes place in columns and buildings, especially upon sunny days, first in one direction, then in the other. Milne also showed the depth of his thinking by the many questions he posed as to why this happened, such as: Have changes in the vertical been most pronounced in regions where it may be supposed that orogenic changes are yet in progress? How far are changes from the vertical affected by seasonal and daily changes in temperture, by fluctuations in barometric pressure, by the rise and fall of tide upon a coast line, and by lunar attractions? What tilting effects would result if the seasonal growth and partial removal of foliage and herbage on one side of an observing station were greater than those upon the opposite side? Is the amount of moisture transpired by various plants per day, per month, per season known? What is the transpiration of plants at night as compared with that during the day? Can there be such a thing as sub-surface dew, and if so what is its effect? Do we know anything respecting diurnal flow in rivers, and the semi-diurnal rise and fall in certain wells? Will a load equal to the weight of an average man at the base of a column produce any appreciable change of level on the top? In mine workings beneath the sea what data do we possess respecting deflections in the roof due to the rise and fall of tides?

'These are examples of the varied questions which have been placed before the seismologist,' he would say modestly, knowing full well that many of them were the product of his own reasoning, 'and to most of which, as the result of experiment and observation, he is able to give fairly definite replies.'

The studies which Milne fostered in some of these problems were very extensive. For example, he wanted to discover if valleys always retained the same form or if they opened and shut daily, and, if the latter was the case, to establish the cause of these alternations. He had already carried out some experiments in Japan which had a bearing on this particular enigma and these were continued at Shide.

He set up on both sides of a valley horizontal pendulums of the kind used to record teleseismic motion since they were sensitive to small changes in level. He found that on fine days the booms of these instruments moved in opposite directions, each away from the bed of the valley. So diurnal movements were evident and, however small they might be, fluctuations in seismic strain were confirmed.

Summarising these experiments, he wrote:

> During the day the records indicated that the sides of the valley opened and at night they closed. The two valleys I worked upon behaved like ordinary flowers, they opened when the sun was

shining and closed at night. The best explanation I can offer is that the phenomenon is largely dependent upon the transpiration of plants. This is marked during the day, but not at night. On a bright day a sunflower or a cabbage may discharge 2 lb of aqueous vapour; a square yard of grass will give off 10 or 12 lb. The result of this is that during the day underground drainage has not received its full supply of water to load the bottom of a valley. At night time when plants' transpiration is reduced, subsurface drainage is increased, and the load at the bottom of the valley is also increased. Therefore, at night the bottom of the valley, in consequence of its increased water load, is depressed, and this is accompanied by a closing of its sides. During the day the load runs off, and the valley opens. This may explain why soak-wells in valleys and streams carry less water during the day than they do at night, and at the same time it suggests that the side of a valley is a bad place for an observatory. Every day as the world turns before the sun, lamp-posts and tall structures salute the same, whilst many valleys open. At night these movements are reversed.

In addition to his theory that the transpiration of plants altered soil weight, he thought it was quite possible that the considerable load represented by a shower of rain or snow, or a heavy fall of dew, might be capable of bending the surface of the ground to such a degree as to affect the stability of any instrument not having very deep foundations. In looking for these effects, it might be expected that tilting due to rainfall, though irregular, would show some evidence of annual periodicity, while those produced by dew would show a diurnal variation. Naturally, Milne had to test these ideas. To the British Association he reported:

> The University Observatory at Oxford was chosen as being particularly suitable, standing alone in a grassy park. Two instruments for detecting and recording any difference of level consisted of one of my horizontal pendulums and the level of the Barclay transit circle. The effect of a sudden shower was imitated by securing the services of seventy-six people, who were marched, in various degrees of compactness, up to and away from the slate slab supporting the registering apparatus. The result of these experiments was that a small depression was observed, always towards the crowd, the maximum value, however, being only 0.5 inches when the load was concentrated and close to the instrument. The load employed being estimated greater than is likely ever to be produced by rain, etc., it is concluded that on that particular site at least no distrubance due to meteorological causes need be feared.

In his investigations of minor terrestrial disturbances carried out in the Isle of Wight he found evidence that they originated from several sources. A number were due to real earthquakes on a small scale, or to faint echoes of very distant earthquakes, while some may have had their origin in the various states produced on the surface of the ground by other agencies.

Compared with diurnal movement, other tremors which distorted his seismograms were more serious.

> Sometimes the apparatus will swing, and perform for hours or days, various irregular, and sometimes marvellously regular back and forth movements, with the result that all traces of important phenomena have been eclipsed. Not only do 'tremors' affect finely constructed horizontal pendulums, but in all probability they affect magnetographs, the delicate balance of the assayer, and accelerate or retard the swing of pendulums. They are frequent in winter, at night, and when the observatory in which they are recorded is crossed by a steep barometric gradient. They are particularly noticeable with a frost and a falling barometer. With a howling gale, and even during a typhoon, when buildings shake and shudder, they are as likely to be absent as present. They could affect a pendulum situated a yard or two away from another of similar design which remained astatic.

By patient elimination of the most likely factors he was eventually able to deduce that the trouble was due to air currents rather than ground movements, although these occurred as well. He found that these air tremors were reduced if he covered his instruments in cases through which air could freely circulate, but above all by working in a room that was almost draughty with ventilation.

'Whether this is a true explanation of the seismic bogey remains for more careful demonstraion,' he commented wryly, 'but already I have learned that with draughty surroundings an instrument will remain at rest, whilst when this condition is neglected, what is apparently a slow and steady circulation of the atmosphere will cause motion.' He added that he still wished to know why the troublesome visitor appeared with such regularity at certain hours and seasons.

Another series of his microseismic experiments concerned the effects of tidal loading on the shore line. This had interested geophysicists for years and much was already known. Milne's approach was that of the seismologist whose instruments could be affected by this stress. Therefore it had to be investigated fully, as in so doing there might be a chance that something new would emerge that could further the understanding of earth movement.

In 1905 he obtained permission to install one of his seismographs in a cellar at the Royal Victoria Yacht Club's premises at Ryde, a town on the north coast of the Isle of Wight. This instrument required special modification before it could be used, and it was 'Snowy' Hirota who adapted the boom to give a much greater magnification than was necessary for ordinary earthquake detection. When ready it was attached to the top of an upright glazed earthenware drainpipe cemented to the concrete floor.

To the north of the cellar was a sea-wall against which a spring tide rose to a height of 5½ feet. Such a tide meant that there was a considerable extra weight of water on the sea-bed in the vicinity. Milne was extremely puzzled to find that, contrary to his expectations, when the tide rose the shoreline rose also! This he attributed the banking up of drainage water from the land. Sir George Darwin, who had been studying this type of problem for many years, offered another solution, suggesting that the greater quantity of water in the English Channel might more than counterbalance the effect of the smaller volume of water in the Solent. The experiments were by no means conclusive and were repeated in 1909, this time at Bidston, near Liverpool. Milne commented on their completion that, although it was too soon to draw reliable conclusions, the deflections accompanying tidal loads indicated that there was a measurable relationship between the yielding of the rocks and loads placed upon them, adding:

> This yielding may be truly elastic, or it may possibly be due to the sagging of a surface like that of a raft under the influence of a load. This latter idea falls in line with seismological observations, which show day by day that the large waves of earthquakes, whether passing beneath the alluvial plains of Siberia or beneath the crystalline rocks of North America, do so at a uniform speed. Seismology suggests that we live on a congealed surface, which, whether it is thick or thin, light or dense, apparently responds in a uniform manner to undulations which pass beneath it.

*　　*　　*

Dictionaries define the noun 'pioneer' as 'an original investigator, explorer or worker; an initiator'. On many occasions throughout his life Milne was a pioneer in the true sense of the word, observing, investigating, formulating theories from his ideas, making further observations and probing deeper and yet deeper into some subterranean mystery to wrest from it secrets which might be of benefit to mankind. Although he was sometimes unsuccessful in his quest, any riddle of the unknown would present a challenge he could not resist if it had a possible relationship with his beloved earthquakes. A case in point was the strange lights sometimes observed during large earthquakes.

In 1903 he noticed that, from time to time the huge chalk quarry cut into Pan Down towering behind his home at Shide appeared to be luminous. For this condition he had no explanation other than there was a possibility of hypogenic activities giving evidence of their existence in the form of light. Pan Pit faces north, and in the winter its depths are not reached by the sun. He observed that its glowings apparently rose and fell in intensity and were most noticeable after a dull, damp day. What was causing this erratic flowing? Did it occur only where the chalk was exposed to the surface, or could it be traced throughout the whole strata? Was it found only in chalk or were all rocks similarly affected? Could it be visible evidence of some earth-moving activity? To a man with the curiosity and seismic dedication as Milne this was a challenge which had to be accepted. So began the first series of experiments which lasted some four months.

In several articles and lectures Milne described his initial experiments:

> At the end of a chamber twenty yards from the mouth of a tunnel driven into the chalk, a hole about two feet square was excavated. Into this a box with a light-proof door was cemented. The back of the box, which touched the chalk, was made of zinc. In the zinc three holes of different sizes were made along a vertical line. A cylindrical drum, covered with bromide paper and driven by clockwork, was brought up to within one-eighth of an inch of these holes. Neither the drum or the paper touched the zinc plate or the chalk.

He also arranged for a similar piece of apparatus to be installed in the King Edward's Mine at Cambourne in Cornwall. In each place a self-recording thermometer and hygrometer were used to show that temperature and moisture in the chamber were practically constant. The results of the twin investigations were collated, put on one side, and almost forgotten.

Then, in 1906, after reading a report from the captain of the RMS Orissa written at the time of the Valparaiso earthquake which noted that lights had been seen which were similar to chain lightning, his interest in the Shide chalk-pit luminosity was again aroused. He considered that a possible explanation of the curious emissions was the discharge of static electricity caused by the rubbing together or rocks under stress. As well as the geophysical disturbances in a megaseismic collapse, he wondered if part of the initial energy generated was converted into some other form which could travel with the velocity of light and produce a response at distant places. If this actually happened, he reasoned, then seismologists would be able to record earthquakes as they took place. He knew that such a theory was suspect but, because it was a possibility, even if remote, it could not be ignored and he engaged himself for the next eight months in further extensive experiments in the chalk-pit. At the end of this period he wrote:

> A sheet of bromide paper on development was frequently quite clear, but at times it was partly or entirely marked with dark bands, black lines, round black spots, or semi-circular spots along the lower edges. Some of the black spots varied from a fraction of a millimetre to 8 mm. In the centres of some of these is a small white or brownish spot.

A close friend pointed out that these resembled spots which can be produced on bromide paper by a tiny electric spark. More of these bands, lines and spots appeared on the sheets from the Cambourne mine than there were on those at Shide, and Milne came to the conclusion that, as the marks did not always occur at the same time as large earthquakes, their appearance when they did must have been coincidental. He also decided that there was no connection with either radioactivity or any particular meteorological condition. He continued:

> With the object of determining whether micro-organisms played any part in the phenomena, a friend made cultures from scrapings from the surface of the chalk before which my cylinder was exposed. Cultures were also made from scrapings taken from the open chalk. Micro-organisms were found in both. These have been exposed to a moving photographic surface similar to that used in the pit, but they gave no evidence of luminosity.
>
> The conclusion for the present is that the luminosity occasionally seen at Pan Pit may result from a very feeble brush or glow-like electrical discharge. If this be the case it would also account for the bands on the photographic paper, the other markings being due to minute sparks.

In a lecture at the Royal Institution in 1908 he went further and considered a possible outcome from these small electrical discharges, making what now seems to be an astonishing statement.

> It is difficult to escape the conclusion that these must have an effect on what we call 'climate', and hence upon everything that lives on the surface of the globe. We have many instances of places separated by a few miles, as for example, Newport and Sandown in the Isle of Wight, or Bournemouth and Swanage, the climates of which are said to be very different. The thermometer, barometer, and hygrometer do not explain these differences; the only apparent differences between such places

appears to be one of soil and the moisture in the same. Inasmuch as we find great differences in the emanations from granite, clayslate, and chalk, it would seem extremely probable that we should find differences in the relative electrical conditions of different soils.

He felt that there was little point in pursuing the problems of rock luminosity further at this stage. Others could take up the matter if they so desired and the project was again shelved. Milne had satisfied himself that it had little direct connection with earthquake activity and so, with much other seismic investigation demanding attention, it was time to move on to something else. He never re-opened his studies in this fascinating little curiosity of nature which is recalled here mainly to emphasise once again the great lengths to which he was prepared to go if he could lay bare the secrets of nature. Even if the yielding-up of them did not directly advance the knowledge of earthquakes, the smallest possibility that they might have done so was sufficient incentive for him to look at them very closely indeed.

Viewed in retrospect, John Milne's work in England, although important, produced no really major advance that was not predictable. There were no successes of the kind which, in Japan, had won him his international fame. It is true that he established the first world-wide system of earthquake recording stations whose reports made the *Shide Circulars* the valuable publications they were. This is also clear from the majority of reports he wrote in this country for the British Association, for they consist mainly of organisational details of his observatory and out-stations; facts and figures deduced from the incoming seismograms; modifications to the horizonal pendulums, and reports of the macro- and microseismic investigations he carried out in conjunction with others. Although he pioneered work in some of the microseismic phenomena it cannot be said that the results were of major importance to seismology.

The deep interest — almost fanaticism — he had for earthquakes was still there, and he was never happier than when interpreting the wavy lines of a trace which indicated a massive seismic upheaval in some far distant land, determining its origin, assessing the probable damage it had occasioned, and considering the possible post-motion effects. Although his observatory at Shide could now be run competently by his staff and friends he seldom left it for long.

In truth, the 'highflyer' who, between 1875 and 1900 had raised the science to great new heights; who had stimulated the world-wide interest which has never since diminished; who was widely recognised throughout the world as the 'father' of modern seismology, was now past his best. Where there had been but few interested in this developing branch of geophysics, now there were many. New men were taking over; fresh fields of investigation were opened and improved recording instruments were under development. Advancements were now so fast and numerous that there was never a hope he could keep abreast of them.

Milne admitted it to none but, for students who examine his seismological achievements at this time there are signs that, during the last few years of his life, he was desperately anxious to produce something really new, some startling breakthrough that would restore his faith in himself. But the inspiration never came. No longer young, by 1912 he was beginning to lose touch and he knew it.

8

Life at Shide

After so much time spent abroad John Milne was almost a foreigner in his own country. Since both he and his work were virtually unknown in England his arrival in the Isle of Wight was unannounced in the newspapers and Toné and he were left very much to their own devices. He was thankful for this being much preoccupied with establishing his observatory at Shide. Those of the villagers who showed curiosity found he had little inclination to indulge in more than the briefest of courtesies with them at that time. Toné, too, was involved in mastering the Victorian etiquette necessary for the smooth running of their spacious house which had been designed by John Pennethorne, a pupil of the famous British architect, John Nash.

So, initially, a little coolness towards the newcomers arose as the natural reserve of the local people prevented them from imposing unduly either on the Professor, who was clearly too busy, or upon his wife whose spoken English was so different from their own Island dialect. But such a situation could not last. Although Milne's now elderly mother and step-father were both living in the house, of his other relatives and friends none was close enough to make frequent visits and for a man so extrovert as he the need to extend his interests soon forced him to seek other social contacts.

By a fortunate coincidence a group of residents in nearby Newport, eager for intellectual stimulus, had decided to join the Oxford University Extension Movement then gaining ground in the provinces, and a month after Milne's arrival at Shide organised a public meeting to discuss the feasibility of a season of lectures. It was at this meeting that the Professor made his first public appearance since his return to England and, invited to speak, commented upon the need for higher education for the masses. He told how, in the twenty years he had lived in Japan, he had watched the tremendous development resulting from the large amount of money spent on education. 'If lectures were offered there,' he continued amidst laughter as he pointedly gazed around the almost empty hall, 'people would engage seats for many weeks ahead or they would not get in!'

He made friends at these meetings and also at the other clubs and organisations he joined and before long Toné and he began to integrate into the life of the community. Of those people he met locally, four men were to become immensely valuable and their visits to Shide Hill House particularly welcome. Each was able to offer skills Milne did not possess.

William H. Bullock, a builder, was employed initially to undertake most of the construction work at the observatory. He became so inspired by Milne's work that he set up his own seismic station in Newport. The two men also had a mutual interest in photography.

Sam L. Pring was a quiet, studious man whose delicate health in childhood had prevented him being sent away to boarding school. But he read widely and had an instinctive interest in everything around him; science, nature and music were among his studies as were languages including Russian. It was a need for help with the translation of papers which first brought Milne into closer contact with him but the two men soon found they had much else in common, particularly a deep love of music. Pring was an expert on Slavonic music, translating a number of books on it and acting as a liaison between English and Russian musicologists. As both Milne and he had travelled widely they enjoyed comparing experiences of journeys each had made in Australia and Africa.

The third friend was J. Howard Burgess who undertook the printing of the *Shide Circulars*. He, too, fell under the spell of Milne's enthusiasm and spent long hours at the observatory as one of the amateur assistants. A keen golfer, the pair played many a round on the Island courses.

Finally, there was F. M. 'Johnny' Walker, a schoolmaster with unusual talents. He had a wide grasp of mathematics and natural philosophy, and it was for assistance with the former that he was originally sought out by Milne who discovered to his delight that Walker not only loved music deeply but was also a skilled instrumentalist. A fine geologist, he shared with Milne an inquisitiveness into the inner secrets of the earth.

Obviously, there were other local friends and acquaintances but it was these four who appear to have given most of the practical help John needed at Shide. Although he used their expertise for his own ends it was through this willing collaboration that true bonds of friendship were forged and strengthened by the development of their mutual cultural interests, a point brought out later by Sam Pring's daughter, Lady Maybury, who wrote:

> He (Milne) was a very genial, kindly man, immensely popular because of his humour and *joie de vivre* which he had the gift of communicating to other people. Anyone who worked with him became his devoted slave and was rewarded by a real friendship.

There were mainland based professional associates who were also close friends, of course, among them Professor John Perry to whom reference has already been made. He would come to the Island as often as his work permitted as would Professor H. H. Turner, the eminent astronomer who was later to play a part in the history of seismology, J. J. Shaw, of whom more later, and M. H. Gray[1], a businessman who was keenly interested in seismology. He it was who, besides providing financial assistance for the construction of an earthquake laboratory at Shide Hill House in 1900, unconditionally offered Milne the then large sum of £1,000 for research. At first the Professor felt obliged to refuse this very generous gift but eventually was prevailed upon to place it in trust and use only the interest to supplement his own large personal contributions.

In the eighteen years Milne was at Shide experts from all over the world went to see and discuss current developments, among them Prince Boris Galitzin, the Russian seismologist who had developed the first electro-magnetic instrument. The two men had many stimulating discussions on the merits of their respective earthquake measuring techniques.

Travellers from Japan were always made welcome, particularly by Toné since they brought news from her own country so far away. Some of these, like Baron Dairoku Kikuchi, went to renew their acquaintanceship with the man who had so inspired them in their own country. The visits of Fusakichi Omori, one of Milne's protégés, for instance, were eagerly awaited by both John and his wife. Many other Japanese, including students studying in Britain, found their way to Shide, but all callers, no matter what their nationality or eminence were accorded the same pleasant hospitality for which the house became known, and it was Toné who ensured that this was so. Lady Maybury, recalling visits she had made as a young girl with her father, Sam Pring, has commented:

> Mrs Milne was a tiny lady, dressed in European costume, usually black, who presided over the tea parties with gaiety and charm, chattering all the time in almost unintelligible English, and laughing at jokes we could not quite understand, but which caused much hilarity. We would pool our impressions afterwards and try to form an idea of what she had intended to convey. She was fond of enlarging upon symptoms of the Professor's illnesses, to his great embarrassment, and on one occasion she was describing an attack of bronchitis when she said, 'Cough, cough, like an oyster coming' and the Professor walked out of the room. He treated her with amused indulgence

1. This was not Thomas Gray who some twenty years earlier in Japan had cooperated on the Gray-Milne seismograph.

Professor H.H. Turner (left) who assumed responsibility for the observatory after Milne's death, Professor John Perry — Milne's friend of many years and colleague in Japan, with John and Tone Milne and dog Billie.

John Milne in the garden of Shide Hill House, Newport, Isle of Wight, with his mother, wife and stepfather.

Captain Robert Scott of Antarctic fame at Shide Hill House with John Milne, Tone, and Arnott, Milne's stepfather.

In 1926 a memorial was raised to John and Tone Milne in Hakodate where Tone is buried.

as one would a favourite child. She must have been altogether delightful in her prime.

Even now, isolated snippets of information about Toné's life at Shide come to light from time to time. A very old lady recently explained that her most vivid recollections of Mrs Milne were the soft rustle of her silken dresses and the unforgettable perfume she wore which seemed to linger long after she had passed by. An equally aged man recalled a childhood memory of being repri-manded by her for 'scrumping' apples from the orchard and forced to relinquish his ill-gotten gain. Then, her brief anger having subsided, of being presented with one tiny apple to appease the dire warning against future trespass. 'Not that it stopped us,' the unrepentant old reprobate went on, 'if caught we knew we'd always come away with at least one apple!' Although generous to a fault Toné did not allow her tolerance of children stealing fruit to extend to the house servants. Food and commodity cupboards were kept locked when not in use and the ring of keys jangled from a belt she wore at her waist.

In an article on Milne for the *Bulletin of the Seismological Society of America*, Mrs Lou Henry Hoover touched briefly on the numbers of people who made long journeys to meet him:

> From the leaves of his visitors' book, turned over during his few minutes absence, one cannot but be interested in the dozens of names in the past few weeks, which appear but an average sample. From all parts of England these pilgrim questioners come; from Scotland and Ireland; all the great universities are represented — Edinburgh and Glasgow, Cambridge and Oxford, Sheffield University, University College of London, and Bristol University, Corfu in Greece, Bermuda, Milan, Japan, Paris, Pennsylvania, and Greenwich Observatory; jostling one another are the names from all the pages of one's geography, come to do homage to a man who is interested in all of them.

Had Mrs Hoover been able to delve more deeply into this fascinating document doubtless she would have observed that among those who recorded their visit was Edward, Prince of Wales, then a naval cadet. Another was Baron Ryochi Kujo, a brother-in-law of the Emperor of Japan of whom it is said that on one occasion he refused to record his visit by conventional means but scratched his name with a diamond ring on one of the windows of the drawing-room instead. She would also have been able to confirm that several of her own country's scientists had been to the observatory, including Professor Harry Fielding Reid of Stanford University who played an important role on the State of California's

Earthquake Investigation Commission set up after the great earthquake of 18 April 1906 and on which Milne's expertise was sought. Not all the guests were interested in Milne solely for his seismology. The visit of Prince Peter Kropotkin is a case in point. Like his host, the Russian had explored extensively in Eastern Siberia including part of the route Milne would have taken on his way to Japan via Vladivostok had not unacceptable winter weather conditions forced him to make the dangerous diversion through Mongolia and China. In a life of considerable adventure the Prince himself had been confined for political activities in both Russia and France and was now studying prison conditions in England. One evening Milne invited the governor of Parkhurst prison to join them at dinner and a somewhat acrimonious argument developed between his guests which threatened to get out of hand with the Prince's daughter, Sasha, shouting at intervals, 'You mustn't contradict my papa. He knows what he's talking about as he's been in prison!' So angry did they become that Milne said later he thought they were going to throw things at one another!

Other visitors went mainly to appreciate the fine music to be heard when the Milnes were 'at home' and joined by Sam Pring and 'Johnny' Walker. The latter wrote in a biographical sketch that Milne was 'a keen musical critic . . . particularly of Japanese music with its weird, quarter-tone intervals and its quaint Dorian-like cadences', a point also made by Professor Akashi, who recalled that when his brother, Norimichi, stayed with his aunt at Shide, Milne often asked him to play the piano and would listen appreciatively to Japanese classics like *Rokudan* and *Chidori*. These arrangements by the blind composer Yatsuhashi Kengyo were among the Professor's favourites. The haunting melody of the *Chidori* particularly enthralled him. On warm evenings this delightful interpretation of plovers could often be heard stealing through the open windows of Shide Hill House and across the gardens bathed in silver moonlight. Yatsuhashi Kengyo, who had died in 1872, surely would have been moved could he have heard his music in such a perfect setting in this far distant land.

It is not known if Toné herself was able to play the 13 stringed *koto* with its moveable bridges but, skilled as she was on the *samisen*, it is reasonable to assume she had had some experience Whether she owned one of these more sophisticated zither-like instruments while in England is another matter. When, in later years, most of the contents of the house at Shide were auctioned prior to her return to her own country, no Japanese musical instruments were among the items listed for sale although, of course, she may have taken them with her.

Professor Akashi commented:

When Mr Milne listened to my elder brother's music it seemed that he felt rather nostalgic and remembered the happy times when he was doing his research at the Imperial College of Engineering in Japan.

Walker had another anecdote about Milne's musical interests:

A few years ago another distinguished Newportonian, Mackenzie Rogan, then a bandmaster of the Coldstream Guards, came to Shide, ostensibly to see how earthquakes were managed. The conversation by some chance turned upon music, and the Professor, unaware of his visitor's eminence in the musical world, ventured to regale him with specimens of the sailors' shanties which he had collected in his various travels by sea. Dr Rogan also chanced to be an ardent admirer of the fast-decaying sailor-music and promptly retaliated with other choice examples; so together they kept the ball rolling and it was not until the visitor rose to depart that they both realised it was too late to think of inspecting seismographs and the like.

Editors of national newspapers would send reporters hurrying to see Milne when news of a major earthquake came in. One reporter wrote, 'He usually corrects their information — as in June, 1896, when Shide was beseiged by newspapermen. "This earthquake happened on the 17th," they told him, "and the whole eastern coast of Japan was overwhelmed with tidal waves and 30,000 lives were lost."

"That last is very probable," answered the Professor, "but the earthquake happened on the 15th, not the 17th," and thereupon gave them the exact hour and minute when the shocks began and ended.

"But our cables put it on the 17th!"

"Your cables are mistaken."'

And, sure enough, news came later with the information that the destructive earthquake had occurred on the 15th within half a minute of the time Professor Milne had specified. There had been some error in transmission of the earlier despatches.

Again, a few months later, the newspapers published cablegrams to the effect that there had been a severe earthquake at Kobe with great injury to life and property.

'That is not true,' said the Professor, 'there may have been a slight earthquake in Kobe, but nothing that need cause alarm.' And the mail reports arriving later confirmed his reassuring statement and showed that the previous sensational despatches had been grossly exaggerated.

Bearing in mind that in those days the quickest and safest means of communication with other countries was by cable, Milne's comment that fifteen breaks in Atlantic cables alone between 1884 and 1894 had cost the companies £600,000 emphasised the importance placed on the information he was able to give them about the possible location of the faults. For instance, early in 1898 it was officially reported that two West Indian cables had broken on 31 December.

'That is very unlikely,' the Professor told the Company who queried this with him, 'but I have a seismogram showing that these cables may have been broken at 11.30 a.m. on December 29.' Then he located the position for them as being off the coast of Haiti. Incidents like these were frequent and the saving in costs to the cable companies alone must have been enormous.

Enquiries would come from reporters who wished to assure their readers that earthquakes could not happen in Britain. To these Milne had a standard reply:

> The fact that any region of the earth has been long free from these movements of re-adjustment and from seismic disturbance is no reason for thinking that it will enjoy such immunity in the future. In the cooling of our planet (which has been going on for a hundred million years) a few centuries are but as an hour, so that countries about the Atlantic will doubtless have many more periods of earthquake activity just as they have had many in the past.

He also had mixed feelings about some journalists. Although always anxious to obtain publicity that would help people appreciate the value of seismology, he found to his cost that, in the scramble to meet deadlines, their copy often contained inaccuracies that infuriated him.

Occasionally, too, he would become tired of beng pestered, especially after his instruments indicated that a large earthquake had occurred. Knowing from previous experience that the Press would be arriving post-haste and clamouring for information, Milne would feel an urgent need to escape their attentions. When such a mood was upon him he would hurriedly find 'Snowy' Hirota or another of his companions and together they would disappear 'to the woods' — his own pun for a round or two of golf. A pony-trap would be ordered and driven along the quiet country lanes to the village of Chale where there was then a course Milne particularly favoured. On return he usually found the reporters waiting on his doorstep and, now relaxed, would greet them affably, inviting them into the observatory for the story they needed while Toné, as always, offered refreshments.

Although he sometimes played croquet on the lawns of the house with his wife and guests, golf was Milne's chief recreation, a game at which he was more enthusiastic than successful. A short walk up the steep hill from his home brought him to the first tee of the Newport club, a small but pleasantly sited course on the crest of the nearby

Down with its superb views of the surrounding countryside. Here and at Chale he became a familiar figure and was accompanied for many years by his small white fox-terrier.

Billy was no ordinary dog. His ability to retrieve lost golf balls from hidden recesses and impossibly thick hedgerows and gorse was little short of marvellous. When the dog died in 1904 Milne was distressed and wrote an obituary which appeared in *Golf Illustrated*. It included a poem by a fellow club member, Dr Cunningham-Brown, of which the following verses are extracted:

> *But O, most excellent caddie ever born,*
> *Endowed with smell so wondrous keen*
> *That ne'er a ball was lost; we stand forlorn*
> *And miss thee most upon the green.*
>
> *Groping, where once thy black unerring snout*
> *Revealed what's hid from purblind men.*
> *Nay! often with four balls you've led us out*
> *And gaily brought us back with ten!*

Milne had trained Billy to find his lost golf balls by the simple device of coating them with aniseed or a substance similarly attractive to the canine world and the intelligent animal, having received fulsome praise for retrieving them, soon took to collecting every one he found in the undergrowth! Those which did not belong to the Professor were stored until the end of the year when they were auctioned for charity.

Several men have told how, as young boys, they used to go to Shide Hill House, collect Billy, and search among the gorse for lost balls. When they returned, the Professor would pay them a small sum for each one found and Toné would reward them with a glass of milk and a biscuit.

Milne's generosity to his caddies is recalled by one who said that, at the end of the game, he was always tipped with a silver sixpence — in those days quite a useful sum.

As the editor of *Fore*, a local golfing magazine, Howard Burgess published an article on Milne by 'Johnny' Walker which contained the following anecdote:

> On the occasion of the British Association's meeting in South Africa in 1905, Professor Milne achieved what was for him a novel distinction. A party of these distinguished men of science went away up country in the neighbourhood of the Victoria Falls on a sight-seeing excursion, and it was here that the Professor conceived the brilliant idea of driving a golf ball from one side of the Falls to the other; this he successfully did and to this day is proud of the fact that he was the first man to do so.

It was also alleged that the telegraphed phrase 'Milne drove across the Victoria Falls' had been so garbled by the time it reached England that it read 'Milne drowned in the Victoria Falls' and caused much consternation until corrected.

Milne loved his golf. For six or seven years he captained the Newport club and on retirement from active play continued his association.

Although a tennis court existed in the grounds of Shide Hill House Milne had little time for the game and it was used for some of his experiments. On one occasion a pit was dug there for the installation of a tiltmeter and tarpaulins were spread over it for long periods while he was observing changes in ground levels due to precipitation and evaporation.

Milne frequently mixed business with pleasure. During the time he was carrying out his investigations into the effects of tidal loading at the Royal Victoria Yacht Club at Ryde, he spent many a convivial session playing billiards and drinking whisky with fellow club members. A story is told that when the seismograph had been set up in the cellar Milne visited it often but nothing much ever seemed to happen until one day he was excited but extremely puzzled to find a series of enormous swings on the trace for which he could not account the reason. A week later and at the same time of the day they appeared again. Milne eventually deduced that the records were made when the butler and the housekeeper were both off duty together!

The Professor's instruments were able to tell him many things unconnected with seismology. They indicated when trains arrived and left Shide station, registered when blasting was taking place in the chalk quarry, and noted when the gravel carts trundled down the lane behind his house. He joked that he knew how long the drivers of these carts stayed inside the 'Barley Mow' at the bottom of the hill while they refreshed themselves before continuing their journey. Even so, these seismograms from the Yacht Club must have been the strangest he ever recorded!

In the early years at his Island observatory he had difficulty in obtaining the accurate time checks which were so important for his records. In Japan he had been provided with telegraphic time signals by the Japanese government for many years. In England, however, the red tape of officialdom denied him this facility, to his intense chagrin. Bullock's version of the farcical position in which Milne was thus placed is interesting:

> John applied to the local Post Office in Newport for permission to see the electric signal drop there so that he might have the time true to a second. For some reason or other this was refused and in John's own words: 'After the signal arrived I could hear the girl upstairs walk *slowly* across the room and shout down the tube, "It's eleven o'clock sir" — many seconds late!'

Milne tried to persuade the Postmaster-General to have the time signal telegraphed direct to his observatory at Shide. His several requests were backed by both the Council of the British Association and the Astronomer-Royal. The Council emphasised the importance of the Professor's work to various government departments while the Astronomer-Royal pointed out that Greenwich and other British observatories consulted Milne on earthquake phenonema. Both authorities stressed the urgent need for him to have accurate time for the precise rectification of his seismic observations. The Postmaster-General referred the matter to the Lords Commissioners of the Treasury. When Milne was informed that the only condition under which the time signal could be obtained was 'the usual rental terms', this being the huge sum of £22 per annum, with the agreement to last five years and he was required to pay for the costly installation, the correspondence closed. No wonder the British Association and the Royal Society thought the government should support British seismology before committing themselves to Strasburg!

But the ever-practical scientist in him soon produced a temporary answer to this set-back. He modified a method which the ancients had used long before the advent of clocks. At best it was but a gesture of defiance against the stupidity of officialdom. Perhaps so many important visitors came to see him that he hoped one or more would put a quiet word in the right ear. The method he adopted was described by Mrs Hoover:

> High up on the south wall is a queer vertical slit in the thick wall, looking like an archer's window in an old castle. A question reveals a mark slanting across the floor and ascending the opposite wall. At noon the line of sunshine coincides with this mark and from it Professor Milne gets Greenwich time within one second.

William Bullock explained how the problem eventually was overcome:

> Early in the twentieth century the Eiffel Tower in Paris started sending out time signals by radio and almost immediately Mr Shaw of West Bromwich offered to make a crystal receiver and aerial so that Milne could tune to the signal in his own home. This he did and the apparatus duly arrived at the observatory. They decided to erect the aerial on the morning of Boxing Day. It was a cumbersome six-strand affair, 7 feet wide and about 40 feet long, one end of which was to be fitted to the observatory roof and the other to a chimney of the main house.
>
> Boxing Day arrived, blowing a gale and raining heavily. The Professor suggested we should put it off but Mr Shaw would

not hear of it. 'We can get it up in five minutes,' he insisted. So we made a start and secured the observatory end before we realised that there was an intervening chimney on the main house that had not been allowed for and while we were discussing this the wind took charge and wrapped the six strands in a glorious tangle around it. After working for nearly an hour to free this aerial, soaked to the skin and not helped particularly by John's humorous remarks, we found that the whole thing was 10 feet too long anyway and then he decided not to have it fixed to the house at all. A few days later it was erected between two elm trees and the Eiffel Tower signal came through very well on the crystal set so that the problem of the correct Greenwich time was solved to John's satisfaction at last. After that episode, however, I often heard the Prof. remind Shaw slyly about 'one of his five minute jobs'!

Although not involved to any great extent in politics Milne supported the Unionist Party, and it is known that in at least one election he spoke on behalf of its Island candidate. Occasionally, too, he would make casual reference to the current political situation in his lectures and some of his magic lantern slides are cartoons depicting local electioneering propaganda. In general, though, he had neither the time nor interest to participate more fully. But he was a firm believer in maintaining the status quo of the British Empire which accounts in part for his militant stand against the proposed German-based international seismic centre.

Thus, irrespective of the political party in power at the time he was always prepared to oppose strongly any act he thought might lessen the power of the Empire or, indeed, any policy advocated in Parliament which he considered too reactionary. In 1911, for instance, he became highly critical of the Daylight Saving Bill then being discussed in the House and wrote an article for *Nature* which, although light-hearted, made clear his strong disapproval of the whole idea. After deriding it in general terms he continued:

Next, where does the happiness come in if on a cold spring morning you have to get up one hour earlier? What will the wife and children say to the arrangement? Turning out too soon on frosty mornings, groping about at 4 a.m. to find a box of matches to light a fire, may give rise to domestic irritation, bronchial catarrhs and other illnesses. Thousands and thousands of workmen in the north of England, to be at work at 6 a.m. when it is really 5 a.m., will have to disturb households at the time specified. At the commencement of April a man will get up in the dark, walk to his factory in the dark, and commence work by artificial light. Whatever light and fuel has been saved on the previous evening in the house or workshop

will be spent in the dark hours of the early morning . . . There
is not so much daylight saving in the Bill as may popularly be
supposed. It gives an hour in the evening but cuts off an hour in
the morning. Will a darkness creating Bill please the British
workmen?

After drawing attention to the confusion which could arise if the
proposed exemptions for certain occupations were enforced he
concluded:

> The simplest solution to the whole question would be to
> commence work one hour earlier in the morning and not
> confuse ourselves and others by altering the clock. In Japan
> thousands of schools open in the summer time at 7 a.m.,
> Government offices open at eight and close at two, and what is
> done in Japan is done in other countries. Surely it is possible for
> business houses in this country to do something similar?

Milne was by no means alone in opposition to this Bill but
daylight saving eventually became law and has been with us ever
since.

In those Victorian days superstition was rife in small, closely-knit
communities like Shide and speculation on the powers of the
supernatural was frequently a matter for earnest discussion. Much
folklore was invoked to ward off evil of all kinds. It was not unusual
for some people, while indignantly declaring disbelief in the
existence of ghosts, to cross their fingers for divine protection in case
a harmful materialisation occurred. Milne was interested in the
subject from a scientific point of view and, as such, always tried to
find a logical explanation for any strange happening which took
place in connection with his work, as in the weird behaviour of one
of his seismographs. His own account reads:

> With the permission of Her Royal Highness, Princes Henry of
> Battenburg, I was allowed to duplicate my instruments by
> installing one in a hut on the western wall of Carisbrooke Castle.
> From it I obtained records which correspond to those obtained
> at my own observatory about a mile and a half distant. A very
> odd thing, however, was that frequently I found that during the
> night the little lamp which was used to obtain photographic
> records at the castle had been extinguished. One of the ladies
> then living in the castle seemed to be anxious about this strange
> occurrence and enquired why a lamp should be blown out at
> one station and not at another. I told her so solemnly as I was
> able that perhaps King Charles I[2] did not approve of modern

2. This was the English king, Charles I (1600–49), whose conflict with
Parliament led to the Civil War and his imprisonment in the Castle
(1647–48) before execution in London.

researches, thus starting a ghost story which went the rounds quickly. I really believe the cause of the trouble was due to little black beetles which from time to time fell down the chimney of the lamp.

Elsewhere in his unpublished writings is a personal version of the story of the local Island ghost, 'Springheel Jack', an apparition alleged to have been seen in many parts of the district at that time:

A few years ago my own house got a bad reputation. It is situated beneath one of Tennyson's noble Downs in a little grove of trees a short way off the high road. In certain rooms lights are burned all night for the purpose of obtaining continuous photographic records of earth movements. Now and then, no doubt, the midnight traveller picks up a twinkling through the trees. As he passes along, stimulating his nerves by whistling, he speculates about the occupation of those who burn lights all night. The village of Shide, which is at the bottom of my garden, consists of two or three cottages, a shop and post-office combined, and the 'Barley Mow'. Every night at the 'Barley Mow' the elders assemble where they discuss root crops, foxes and seismometry, but they all retire quite early. They do not burn lights all night.

One evening it was announced that Mrs Bartlett and her children returning from Newport market met a ghost. Another and another had seen the ghost and Shide was quickly feverish with excitement. Farmer Burt 'wer'n't going to have his wife and kids' (he meant himself), 'scared to death by ghosts. Joke or no joke they would duck the man who made it.' News spread. The local papers took the matter up and accounts of the Shide ghost soon reached London journals. To see the ghost, people flocked to little Shide to line the lanes between it and Newport. One or two had shotguns. The railway company did well and the 'Barley Mow' a roaring trade.

Unfortunately for myself, one intelligent person looking up at the lights twinkling through the trees remarked that 'if that there Professor can catch earthquakes when there aren't any, perhaps he could make ghosts — some sort of magic lantern picture, you know.' When I saw this in the Island press and at the same time received a warning from the police to lock up my observatory at night, particularly as it might be difficult to control a crowd when the 'Barley Mow' had reached bed rock, I thought of 1066 and the Norman invasion.

At last I met the ghost. What I saw as something like a white table cloth at a height about that of a lamp-post and it was about 20 yards distant. For a few seconds it advanced and retreated in a most threatening manner. It disappeared, reappeared, and then vanished. Above my head at the time there was a layer of fog which I know from looking down on such fogs from the top of a hill could not have been very thick. At the same time flash lights in connection I believe with the visit of the Emperor of Germany were assisting in illuminations at Portsmouth, some 8 miles distant. I concluded that the beams from these lights had been refracted downwards on the upper surface of the fog and I was therefore, so to speak, at the back of a curtain at a lantern show.

I gave an explanation for the Shide ghost on these lines at a large meeting in Newport but it was received by jeers. I knew how the ghost had been made and they would like it stopped. Fortunately for myself, His Imperial Highness the Emperor of Germany left, flash lights became less frequent, November fogs disappeared and there was no more ghost. To settle the matter thoroughly an effigy of the ghost was made, carried in procession to the top of Pan Down behind my house, and there burned.

The lights through the trees at Shide again twinkled through the wood and seismological observations go on in peace!

Despite Milne's attempts to explain ghosts he obviously had certain reservations and was not prepared to reject outright the possibility of the existence of supernatural phenomena for still later he wrote:

Many places I have had to visit for the purpose of attending the little lamps made me feel creepy. I never actually saw a ghost but I was always full of expectation.

The feelings of the impassive-faced Japanese 'Snowy' Hirota, as he went stumbling through the stygian blackness of a wet November night and on through the wind-swept tunnel leading to the bottom of the towering chalk cliff-face of Pan Down known locally as 'Dead Man's Drop' in order to check instruments, are not recorded.

Both 'Snowy' and Milne were keen on photography, not only for its value to seismology but as an art form in its own right. The Professor became the president of the Isle of Wight Photographic Society where he learned from William Bullock whose skilful compositions of Island scenes are still occasionally found. Resulting from this Milne reported to the British Association an easier method he had developed for processing seismograms — yet another example of his ability to simplify unnecessarily elaborate procedures.

So, over the years following his arrival at Shide, Milne became closely integrated into the life of the local community, continually widening his circle of friends and acquaintances, absorbed with the ever-increasing work in his observatory and, in the main, content with life. Academic recognition came his way with awards such as the coveted Royal Medal of the Royal Society and an honorary D.Sc. from Oxford University, conferred on him at the same Encaenia that Alexander Graham Bell was similarly honoured. In 1902 the University of Tokyo made him an Emeritus Professor.

Like many intellectuals, however, as he grew older Milne seemed on occasion to become a little eccentric with harmless oddities of behaviour which were quite out of character. A frequently authenticated example will suffice. In those distant Victorian days it was customary for men to wear hats. Consequently he seldom left the house without donning his favourite wide-brimmed trilby which, through constant usage, inevitably became the worse for wear and eventually developed a hole in the crown. This increased in size to the extent that it was quite noticeable — particularly by sharp-eyed small boys some of whom took to following him for the childish glee of watching as he politely raised this head-gear in a mark of respect to ladies he encountered on his way. As he then returned it to his head without, apparently, observing anything amiss, they would laugh uproariously. This occurred on so many occasions it is unlikely Milne could not be aware of the situation but he chose to ignore it, wearing the same battered hat for years.

John's lively sense of fun never deserted him even when asked probing personal questions such as why he should have wanted to marry a Japanese girl. With a straight face he told at least one man that he had to — because Toné had been given to him by the Emperor for services rendered. To another he confided with an equally serious mien that she was, in fact, a Japanese princess who had fallen in love with him and, fearing death, they had both fled the country of her birth. Surprisingly, perhaps, this latter story was until recently still thought to be true in some quarters. With its shades of Gilbert and Sullivan's *Mikado* it is with some regret that its accuracy must be denied!

In her own way Toné was also happy. If she was not able to extend her social contacts quite as much as her husband did her consolation came from the love and consideration she received from John at all times. Her life revolved around him and she was always talking about 'my Plofessor'. It is certain she loved him dearly.

Like any wife, however, she could become angry. On one occasion when he left her guests suddenly during a meal to attend to his instruments she became furious, shouted 'Seismology, seismography!' and snapped shut her elegant fan.

This idyllic situation could not last indefinitely. Of all Milne's many friends perhaps his assistant Shinobu ('Snowy') Hirota, was his closest. Not only was he a constant companion in the observatory but John had a high regard for the skill the quiet

Japanese had developed in maintaining the earthquake instruments and interpreting the seismograms during the many years the two lived and worked in daily contact. 'Snowy' was a dedicated man who enjoyed working long hours in the laboratory. The first major blow was when he became seriously ill. The Professor tried to cheer him up by sitting on the end of his bed and singing sea-shanties! But with the typical stoicism of his race 'Snowy' accepted that death was near and knew that he must return to Japan if he was to be buried near his ancestors. On 16 December 1912, after seventeen years together at Shide the two friends parted sadly, each knowing that they would not meet again. 'Snowy' died almost immediately after his return home and Milne was deeply distressed. So moved was he that he took the unusual step of writing an obituary in the British Association's annual report in which he gave credit for the work they had done together in England. One passage reads:

> Directly it was shown that certain sub-oceanic disturbances had interrupted cables, Colonies desirous of knowing the cause of these sudden isolations from the rest of the world set up seismographs. This was the commencement of the Association's cooperation on seismological stations. To bring this into being Hirota played an active part . . . In practical seismology he made many innovations some of which rendered instruments more sensitive . . . I feel it my duty to give recognition to an assistant pioneer.

Milne missed his hard-working Japanese friend sorely. For some time he, too, had not enjoyed the best of health, occasionally suffering from mysterious high temperatures and blinding headaches which confined him to bed for a few days. The kidney disease he did not realise he had was beginning to weaken and depress him. Although fond of a glass of whisky he had never drunk to excess but as the frequency of the attacks increased he resorted more and more to its pain-killing effects. The periods of depression lengthened. During these he sometimes expressed to close friends a wish to die: once he was discovered semi-conscious and with a raging temperature sitting in front of an open window. Yet it seems he never confided this desire for death to Toné. On recovering he would jokingly refer to his illness as 'just another attack of the feebles'.

Then a whole year passed when he seemed to be free of the symptoms of what eventually was diagnosed as Bright's disease and he became once more like his usual cheery self although noticeably less active physically.

In mid-July 1913 there was another attack but as he had been affected similarly before no particular apprehension was felt. At Shide, Howard Burgess, who had now taken over 'Snowy' Hirota's place in the daily running of the observatory, merely hinted in a letter to J.J. Shaw in West Bromwich, Birmingham, that the Professor was not very well. Toné, however, was always agitated at these times. She herself was confined to bed with what appeared to be an arthritic hip and became more and more uneasy about her husband as the days went by without visible improvement in his condition.

On 21 July Burgess again wrote to Shaw:

> My Dear Shaw,
>   The maid has just handed me your letter with a request from the Professor that I should answer it. He, i.e. the Professor is in bed with a temperature of 102F. I have not been able to see him and talk over your letter with him so I do not quite know what to say to you. Mrs Milne is far from well also.
>   I am afraid Professor's condition is more serious than it appears. For sometime past he has been failing and it has been borne in upon me that his work is nearly done. For the last fortnight he has not been able to do any work at all, suffering from violent headaches which commence about 9 a.m. and do not leave him until 3 p.m. The report from a specialist he went to see sometime ago was not very comforting. Of course, he treated the whole thing as a joke as he treats everything but I was much concerned about him and I am afraid he is not in a condition to stand a serious illness.
>   Please treat what I have said as strictly confidential and do not refer to it in any way.
>   Now, with reference to the machine.[3] I am delighted to hear such a good account of it and I know the Prof. is very anxious to see it and I need not say I am. Bullock is here today getting the column ready for it. There will not be much alteration required . . .

Two days later Milne was able to dictate a note to Shaw suggesting that because of this illness the latter's visit to Shide be postponed temporarily.

The new instrument which became well known as the Milne-Shaw Horizontal Pendulum seismograph arrived at Shide, was set up in the observatory and immediately began to produce excellent earthquake traces. This news was kept from John so that he should not become over-excited in his weakened condition. He seemed to be making some improvement but on 30 July Burgess' now almost daily letter to Shaw was foreboding:

> The report of Prof. this afternoon is not at all good and I am doubtful as

---

3. This instrument, upon which Milne and Shaw cooperated, was designed to overcome the difficulty experienced in the Milne seismograph of damping the pendulum and to improve the magnification factor. Unfortunately, Milne did not live to see the machine established in his observatory or to learn of its success.

to the issue. Two doctors are coming again this afternoon and I will not post this until I have their report.

I am having a very lively time hanging on to the telephone all day and trying to get things in some sort of order. The people in the house seem to have completely lost their heads. It is a very sorry household.

The doctors have just had a consultation and have not given up all hope. Am broken-hearted . . .

Shortly after this had been despatched John Milne, the master of seismology, lapsed into a deep coma and it was a deeply distressed Howard Burgess who awaited the opening of the local post office next day to send the telegram he knew in his heart had been inevitable.

July 31

Shaw , Sunnyside, West Bromwich.
Milne died early this morning.   Burgess.

Not yet sixty-three years old and at the climax of an illustrious career, the suddenness of his death stunned those who knew and revered him.

The funeral took place five days later. From near and far the mourners came; men of science from the Royal Society, the British Association, the Royal Geographical Society and the Geological Society; many university and government establishments sent representatives who mingled with local dignitaries and the people who had known and loved him. His Imperial Highness, the Emperor of Japan was personally represented by Baron Kujo, his brother-in-law. An impressive service was held in the parish church of St Thomas à Becket in Newport where copies of a tribute to the life and work of the Professor were distributed. This was a reprint of the *Eminent Living Geologist* article first published in 1912. The interment took place in the nearby tiny churchyard of St Paul's, Barton, next to that of his mother and step-father.

The plain oak coffin with its heavy brass mounts bore the simple inscription he would have approved:

JOHN MILNE
BORN
DECEMBER 30, 1850
DIED
JULY 31, 1913

The very many floral tributes were exquisite with summer chrysanthemums, the flower of Japan, prominent, and the national red and white colours of that country conspicuous both in the flowers and the ribbons that adorned them. Toné's last gift was a bunch of white blossoms from the gardens of Shide Hill House the Professor had loved so much. From Howard Burgess there was a wreath of red and white flowers skilfully arranged in the form of a seismograph's horizontal pendulum while a small bouquet from a little girl in London was simply inscribed, 'For Dear Uncle John Earthquakes'.

Among the hundreds of letters and telegrams of condolence received by Toné was the message from the Japanese Ambassador, Mr K. Inouye:

> *Please accept my deepest sympathy on the great calamity which has befallen you. It is not only an irreparable loss to this country and to the scientific world but also to Japan where his name will never be forgotten.*

9

Post Milne

The unexpected death of the world's foremost seismologist caused dismay among those of Milne's fellow scientists who understood the full significance of the work being done at Shide and knew that without expert guidance it could not continue. Tributes to the man and his work began to flow in as the news spread. Leading newspapers and journals of many countries printed obituary notices which revealed to many for the first time something of the tremendous scope of the work the Professor had been doing and emphasised its importance to mankind.

Quotations from two eminent men of the science of seismology will illustrate the importance of Milne's life and achievements. Of Milne's work, Prince Galitzin, then President of the International Seismological Association, commented:

> Seismology, this new and promising branch of physical science, will deplore the death of one of its most distinguished and valiant pioneers who, through his remarkable activity and energy, had covered the earth's surface with a whole net of seismic observatories and who, through his important investigations, set seismology on a firm scientific basis, founded upon instrumental observations. Nearly all the problems of modern seismology have been considered by Milne and he can duly be considered as a real founder and promoter of this new and important branch of geophysics. I entertain the most sincere hope that the great work of Milne will be continued, taken up by others, and developed in accordance with the necessities of modern investigation. This would be the best monument to his memory.

But it was Professor John Perry, friend and confident of Milne since those early days in Japan who, reviewing nearly forty years of cooperation, best summed up the man himself:

> Milne's success was greatly due to his power to interest all sorts of people in his work. But it was something much deeper which gave him the help of scientific men. He took an interest in all scientific work and perhaps he thought too highly of the work of other men. He was very modest as to the value of his own

services to the world. He grudged no time or trouble spent in helping other people when his help, scientific, social or pecuniary, could be of value. Both in Japan and at Shide he was very hospitable. As one who lived with him in great intimacy in Japan for nearly four years I put it on record that Milne never talked scandal or detraction, and hated to listen to such things and I cannot remember one expressed thought or action of Milne which was ungenerous or mean. Many people gave him admiration but his intimate friends gave him affection also.

It was apparent immediately that the work at Shide had to go on and appeals for its continuance were made by leading geophysicists among whom were Professors J.W. Judd and A. Geikie and, of course, Prince Galitzin. The man eventually persuaded to fill the gap was the Savilian Professor of Astronomy at Oxford University and chairman of the British Association Seismological Committee, H.H. Turner. He had for years been a personal friend of John Milne and had made many visits to the Shide observatory. Yet because of his commitments he could travel to the Island only occasionally and so, under his general direction, the day-to-day running of the observatory was undertaken by Howard Burgess who, assisted by Sam Pring, carried on throughout the long years of World War I. Even so, other help was needed as both these local men had their own business interests to consider and some of the administrative duties were undertaken at various times by the Misses Caws and Pring and later by Miss Bellamy transferred from astronomical work at Oxford.

Milne's own money no longer being available for the purpose, Turner had considerable difficulty in obtaining sufficient financial help to keep the observatory open and it was to his credit that he was able to do so. For example, the total income in 1915, almost wholly from grants, just balanced expenditure of £470. Work which had been done and financed by Milne for the sheer love of the subject now had to be paid for officially and salaries bit deeply into the slender purse. It was as much for reasons of economy as for convenience that the observatory was transferred to Oxford in 1919.

The move coincided with Toné's decision to return to her own country. She had been very lonely since John's death six years earlier. Although the observatory was always occupied during the day and often late into the evening, fewer and fewer visitors called at the house as the war dragged on though they were welcomed as warmly as ever. Her incomplete command of English made it difficult to cope with everyday affairs and she herself was often ailing. She became very frail and much dependent upon her nephew, Jodo Horikawa, a Buddhist priest who had come to England to stay with his aunt both for companionship and for her spiritual comfort.

In his will, revised just two months before his death, John Milne made adequate provision for Toné by a generous guaranteed income for life. His trustees arranged for the money to be deposited in a Daiichi Bank in Japan so that it could be withdrawn without difficulty. Milne's thoughtfulness for his wife's welfare was of continual comfort to her and a relative has recorded that she told him how happy this made her, 'especially when she heard that some Japanese ladies who married foreigners in Japan had gone abroad and come back without anything.'

Toné Milne took most of her husband's personal possessions with her when she returned to Japan and over the years many have been dispersed or lost. She gave his favourite Waltham watch to one of her nephews who recalled: 'My aunt told me to keep it because it kept very accurate time. The thickness of the glass was approximately 6 mm. Mr Milne was always breaking watches and it was the only one left when he died.'

By coincidence the watch itself was eventually destroyed in an earthquake.

His prized Royal Medal, of gold and over 70 mm in diameter with a weight of some 350g has been lost forever. In World War II it was apparently surrendered to the Japanese government which, like those of other countries, including Britain, was forced to collect metals from the public to further their war efforts.

Milne bequeathed all instruments and books relating to his work to the British Association, 'in the hope that they may be used in one or more of the stations erected or maintained under the control of the Seismological Investigation Committee if they so desired.' Some of these are now housed in the Science Museum, London. The few personal possessions left in Britain were dispersed when Shide Hill House was sold and its contents auctioned. A number of his papers, however, some of which had survived the disasterous fire in Tokyo and bear the scorchmarks of that conflagration, were given to friends who many years later donated them to local archives.

John Milne left a legacy to the world far greater than mere possessions. He fostered seismology until it could achieve the international importance it commands today — a service of incalculable value to mankind. But its tremendous post-Milne development is another story, fascinating, but outside the scope of this biography since detailed study of it would fill many volumes.

Milne was saddened that in his lifetime seismology did not achieve the importance he was convinced it deserved and late in his career often commented on this fact. In an article published in *Nature* in 1911, for instance, he wrote:

> The popularity of the seismologist would be enhanced if, like the astronomer, he had the power to predict. The latter tells us

exactly when we shall see the next eclipse of the moon. We stand outside our door at the appointed time; the eclipse takes place, and we are again reminded of the accuracy of astronomical calculations. Whether the eclipse did or did not occur at the minute specified, so far as the general public are concerned might not matter very much. But it would matter if the eclipse really meant, as it was supposed to mean in the Middle Ages, a portent of great disaster. What the public imagine they would like to know about an earthquake is the time at which it might occur. It this could be stated, and at the same time something about the character of the expected disturbance in earthquake districts revealed, seismology would be liberally supported. Astronomers have received the support of nations since the days of astrology, while seismology is in its childhood seeking for more extended recognition.

Just how far from such accurate predictions are today's geophysicists? Are they close to solving the enigma? Many are working on the problem at the extreme frontiers of technology using computer studies of sophisticated records from modern seismic stations around the world. The results obtained contribute towards the creation of a reliable early-warning system.

In Japan, the home of Milne's early pioneering work, the Meteorological Agency now has, perhaps, the world's most well-equipped seismological observatory at Matsushiro. There are also more than one hundred stations with seismographs which can provide immediate information at the occurence of an earthquake and six forecast centres which can estimate epicentres in order to issue tsunami warnings. Of the seventy volcanoes recognised as active, sixteen, including Mt Asama, are under constant watch. During a visit to the Meterological Agency in connection with the preparation of this biography the Director of Observations appropriately commented:

How we wish John Milne could be with us today!

The direction and intensity of current investigations aimed at the prediction and control of earthquake activity could not have been visualised by Milne but the pioneering work to which he devoted his life has truly earned for him the right to be called the 'Father of Modern Seismology'.

10

Forgotten yet Remembered

It is a fact that most people alive today have never heard of John Milne. The story of his life and work is unknown to them: as far as they are concerned he might never have existed. There are many reasons for this and a few are offered here to illustrate how fate determines which pioneer will be remembered and which is forgotten.

Milne's major work was accomplished in Japan, a country where earthquakes are a frequent occurrence and in consequence a regular subject of conversation, but when he returned to the British Isles he came to an area almost completely free from seismic activity. As human experience is an essential stimulant to both interest and memory this can be considered the major reason for his great contribution to science being generally undervalued in his own country. He was well aware of this and at one of the Royal Institution's Friday lectures in 1908 he told his audience somewhat firmly:

> Until recent years the attitude of the ordinary Englishman with regard to earthquakes has been one of apathy. He would argue that although every year 30,000 earthquakes might occur in the world, his country only contributed about half a dozen, and because they were so small did more to excite curiosity than to create alarm. Although Colchester in 1883 and Hereford in 1896 lost a few chimney pots, and buildings were unroofed, and although at intervals, reckoned by one or two hundred years, London has been shaken, still England could not be regarded as an earthquake country. British-made earthquakes may be of rare occurrence but should there be any relief of seismic strain similar to that of 1883 or 1896 in the synclinal on which our great metropolis stands, we might find as many chimney-pots in the streets as there are inhabitants. A suggestion of this kind, however, does not disturb the mind of our ordinary Englishman. Hints respecting the instability of his country produce no effect and he fails to see why he or his government should be called upon to support seismological investigations.

Thus ignorance through lack of experience produced public indifference to his work in Britain. His was not an everyday science as little ever happened to bring it to notice. Such a situation still exists in the minds of the majority of people there today who are firmly convinced that earthquakes will never happen! While he was in Japan everyone — the people, the government, even the Emperor himself — had a natural interest in them and many enthusiasts were working on the problems posed by the phenomenon, aided by the financial and material support that was frequently forthcoming from a number of sources. Milne was able to take advantage of many opportunities for close cooperation with numerous deeply interested persons — so much so that Charles Davison in his book, *Founders of Seismology* (Cambridge University Press 1927) wrote:

> Milne differed from Perry and Mallet in the preference for working with others. He was not a solitary student.

But things changed drastically on his return to Great Britain. There were no seismologists of his calibre close at hand with whom he could consult. He was very much on his own. Also, although he still received some financial help from the British Association and an occasional grant from other bodies, their purses were not bottomless and had to be shared with other worthwhile projects. The money he received from time to time was never sufficient for his needs. Neither did he have the continuous support from a British university such as he had received at the University of Tokyo and no large commercial organisation offered sponsorship. Yet, although adequate finance was not forthcoming, he chose to continue his research which had reached a crucial stage.

Now that it was possible for him to record earthquakes wherever they occurred in the world, he considered it essential not only to set up his own observatory designed for the purpose, but to encourage Commonwealth and other countries to cooperate by establishing similar centres from which records could be forwarded to him at Shide for classification and subsequent publication. To do this he was forced to supplement the small financial help he received with his Japanese pension and a large part of his other income. He was by no means the only scientist in Britain to be inadequately supported nor will he be the last. As it was, he was probably one of the few remaining Victorian pioneers who could personally afford to sponsor research on such a scale, although to do so he was forced to rely upon the services of a very small professional staff augmented by a number of enthusiastic amateurs. The drain on Milne's resources is reflected in his will.

Thus he became a lone worker in what was to the British an obscure field. Such a man tends to be forgotten quickly when his personal involvement has ended. It is interesting to note that while Milne was working in the Isle of Wight, Guglielmo Marconi also conducted a series of relatively short experiments there. His work has for long been commemorated on the Island by a monument and plaque but until 1974 there was no such recognition for Milne. This statement is not intended to denigrate the work of the Italian. For the enormous benefit his pioneering work in radio communication fostered, such honours and more are his by indisputable right. Nor is the comparison made as a measure of the relative worth of either man's contribution to society. That of Marconi, however, is immediately apparent while Milne's is much less tangible.

Other circumstances leading to the almost total public unawareness of the seismologist's work are less striking when considered individually but the cumulative effect is decisive. The choice of Shide, near Newport in the Isle of Wight, for instance, although possibly technically correct, was also indirectly a contributory factor as the little village in those days was a quiet and somewhat isolated spot. Although Milne desired most of the conditions it offered for his research, because of its relative remoteness from the main areas of scientific activity it was less frequently visited by those influential persons who could possibly have been of use to him. Few other than those engaged in similar or allied projects could comprehend fully what he was trying to achieve. To many, far from the epicentres of most earthquakes, the squiggly lines which represented the end product of his instruments were incomprehensible. It is not easy for an untrained eye to understand the significance of the minute variations on a seismogram trace.

There were other factors, too. After the First World War had ended, economic reasons decreed that the observatory was transferred to Oxford, and at the same time Mrs Milne, now an ailing old lady, returned to Japan, the two moves breaking a connection with the Island which had lasted for twenty-four years. Toné and John Milne had no children. Milne was an only child and, with Mrs Milne's family living in Japan, only distant relatives of the seismologist were left in Britain. Before he went to Japan neither he nor his parents remained in one locality for any great length of time and, not unnaturally, none of these places has accorded him local recognition. It seems that every home in which he lived in Britain has suffered at the hands of progress and time. His birthplace in the Vernon Court area of Liverpool has been re-developed; Tunshill House was demolished during the construction of the Lancashire-Yorkshire motorway and his homes at Hounslow and Richmond have proved impossible to trace. The original part of Shide Hill House has been pulled down, the observatory converted into private dwellings and the beautiful gardens, once the pride and joy of Toné have been built upon. The one exception is 147 Drake Street, Rochdale, scene of the seismologist's early childhood which still stands but has not as yet, any indication of a connection with its famous citizen.

After the eulogistic obituaries, all factually incorrect in some detail or other, had been written by various contemporaries, none of those who knew him well seem to have had the time or inclination to record in full his life and work for posterity and therefore important material has been lost for ever.

When the individual facts mentioned above are considered as a whole it is little wonder that the mention of John Milne's name today almost invariably is met with a stare of total incomprehension.

On the other hand, the man has not been completely forgotten in the United Kingdom. Thousands of visitors to the Geophysics section of the Science Museum in London have been able to see some of his horizontal pendulum seismographs on display in the permanent exhibition. Earth movement recorders of other early seismologists are exhibited, too, and one wonders how many of those who pause to examine them can relate the instruments to the men who invented them or how few realise that Milne was by far the most important. Only a few of his seismographs exist today and it is surprising to learn that at least one of them is still in use. Although now modified to act as a tiltmeter, this is quietly continuing to record earth movements in the power-station at Arapuni, New Zealand.

In 1927 there was a revival of interest in the Professor's work when Charles Davison wrote *Founders of Seismology* and devoted some thirty pages to it. In 1939, A. W. Lee, then Superintendent of the Eskdalemuir Observatory near Edinburgh and one of the world's leading authorities on microseisms, was invited by Milne's publishers, Kegan Paul, Trench, Trubner and Co., to re-write *Earthquakes and Other Earth Movements* to bring it up to date. In the preface of the book Lee paid tribute to Milne:

> The great progress which has been made in the scientific study of earthquakes during the last sixty years is largely due to the pioneer work of John Milne . . . and the recognition of earthquake study as a quantitative physical science is due, in no small measure, to the investigations which he carried out in Japan and after when he returned to England.

Milne's *Earthquakes*, written in 1883, had passed through six editions with only minor alterations, the last being as late as 1913, the year of his death. But, as further rapid advances in the science had been made, the seventh edition was so much altered by Lee that little of the original remained. Although it is an excellent book it might have been more honest of him to have used his own name instead of coupling it with that of Milne.

Apart from the permanent display of his seismic instruments in the Science Museum, London, very few efforts have been made in Britain to arouse nationwide public interest in Milne's work although an occasional local interest has emerged briefly. E. W. Pollard, a pharmacist in the Isle of Wight, for instance, inspired by the Professor's pioneering work became a keen amateur seismologist and operated his own simple horizontal pendulum instrument. In the 1950s he began to collect material in the hope of establishing a permanent Milne exhibition in the County museum at Carisbrooke Castle. For various reasons he was unsuccessful and although an exhibition was staged and reported in the national press as 'permanent' it did not become the continuous display he desired.

During the 1960s John Wartnaby chose the work of the great seismologist as a subject for his M.Sc. dissertation and later gave him further attention in his doctorate thesis which examined the seismology of the nineteenth century.

Some years ago a few houses which form a pleasant cul-de-sac were built at Shide in a quiet area on the opposite side of the river to the chalk down on which Shide Hill House stood and was given the name of Milne Way. Although the developers have confirmed that it was so named because of the association of the Professor with Shide, as it now exists there is no indication that this was so and for those who do not know of Milne it conveys nothing. Recently some twenty people chosen at random in the vicinity were asked the question, 'Who was Milne?'. None knew the answer but the comment of one youngster would have vastly amused the seismologist.

'Well,' said the boy confidently, 'he played for Arsenal, didn't he?'

There is little else except for one or two articles which have appeared in English and foreign newspapers in which his name has been mentioned. One of these published in the *Rochdale Observer* some years ago covered the demolition of Tunshill House during the construction of the M62 motorway.

In this brief summary of how Milne has been remembered it would be wrong to omit mention of his trophy at the local golf club which is still played for annually at Newport — even if the man who donated it is less well-known, there perhaps, than he should be. It is also right to state that there are still a few people alive who remember him personally. Of these, now also decreasing in numbers as time takes its inevitable toll, the views of Lady Maybury, daughter of Sam Pring, who herself worked for a while at the Shide observatory, must be respected. In answer to the question 'Do you think Professor Milne should have been forgotten?' she replied:

> I shouldn't have said so because he was one of the originators of seismology — he was the father of it. I would have thought that in his age and his generation he was one of the great men. And he certainly was a great man in character. He dominated any assembly that he was in. He was very natural and charming

with everybody. He never asserted himself, but he had the
character, he had that personality. He had one manner for
everybody.

Agreeing that Milne should never have been forgotten, an old
man living on the island remarked:

> I can remember him as if it were yesterday and it was all of sixty
> years ago. I still have in my mind the squat figure of the old
> gentleman standing up there on the golf house behind his
> house, with that broad-brimmed hat of his, and his slight stoop,
> pointing out the houses on the other side of the valley, and
> making us laugh at the jokes he made as he explained their
> bowing movement. He always spoke with a quiet Lancastrian
> accent which fascinated us lads, as did his nicotine-stained
> moustache with a gap burned in it by numerous cigarettes.

As the years go by and the memory of John Milne fades still
further, as new generations are born and benefit from his
achievements without being aware of the man who made it possible,
it is as well to reflect briefly upon some of the outstanding
contributions he made. There was his drive and dedication which
caused the sudden great leap forward in the science of seismology
and the prominent part he played in the construction of seismographs, as well as the irrefutable evidence that the extent of our
present knowledge of earthquake motion owes much to the
development of the ideas he propounded. Additionally, he was one
of the earliest to realise that the vibrations of great earthquakes may
be recorded anywhere on the land surface of the world and the first
man to carry out a world-wide seismic survey the result of which
helped significantly to unravel the mysteries of the earth's interior.
The practical side of his nature enabled him to turn theories to the
immediate benefit of mankind as in the case of the Milne-
MacDonald vibration recorder which made rail travel safer,
smoother and more economical, while his design of houses, bridges,
and other buildings which could withstand much of the destructive
effects of earthquake shocks should for ever earn him the gratitude of
present and future generations in those countries where such
disasters occur. Even his experiments with the crude microphones
he used in Japan have their counterparts in the geophones used in
modern seismic surveys, and if he were alive today how interested
he would be to learn that, within a very short distance of his Shide
observatory, they were used to help determine the site of a recent
drilling for oil and natural gas at Merstone.

In Japan, as one would expect, Milne is still remembered for there
schoolchildren learn of his work. Moreover, in 1926 a memorial to
the memory of John and Toné Milne was raised in Hakodate and in

1963, fifty years after he had died, a commemorative exhibition was staged. In 1974, the University of Tokyo donated a number of cherry tree saplings to be planted at Shide and at the Isle of Wight College of Arts and Technology as 'a living memorial' to the great seismologist. This was duly carried out by the Japanese Ambassador to Great Britain, Mr Haruki Mori, who also laid a wreath on Milne's grave as had his predecessor at the funeral ceremony some sixty years earlier.

It can only be hoped that, with the present and ever-growing interest in the life and work of the great pioneers of the past, the name of John Milne, Father of Modern Seismology, will be accorded its rightful place in the history of science.

Appendix 1

The Storyteller

The recent discovery that John Milne wrote fiction using psuedonyms means that no biography of him would be complete without a clear appraisal of that facet of his extrovert personality which declared itself as an urgent need to communicate. An ability to entertain in this way can be traced from his early travel journals through to the science-based fiction to which he later aspired.

One of his unpublished works which survived the disasterous fire at his home in Japan is the story of his youthful wanderings in Iceland. The scorched pages of the notebooks in which he recorded impressions in his atrocious handwriting bear witness that several attempts were made to bring the manuscript to a point where perhaps it could be offered to a publisher. There are also two amusing bids to illustrate the title which itself seems to have been changed several times; *Wanderings in known and unknown Iceland*, was replaced by *Iceland, or the scramblings of a lunatic*, and then, with a view to possible publication, *Fireland*. Written in verbose style it is an immature, rambling account of what to the young man was evidently an exciting journey. Marred by frequent lapses into unintelligible scrawl and often displaying a fine disregard for both spelling and grammar, his developing humour is already discernable as the following extract from the first few pages shows:

> Delay! Delay! Delay! It must be part of travel's nature to beget innumerable delays. Travellers such as we were travelled for pleasure, but delays beget vexation which by no means tends in any way to add to the enjoyment of a pilgrimage. All had been confusion, packages here, packages there, boxes without hinges, locks without keys, saddles lost, bridles broken and, as a surmounting difficulty, our steeds had been missing. 'But time works wonders', at least, so says the proverb and it was certainly a wonder that all went well and on the morning of Tuesday, 28 July, 1871 we were roused by the clatter of our train of well-shod hoofs stamping in the yard below.
>
> The missing steeds were found, the packages were stored in the packboxes, the locks had keys, hinges were on the boxes, in fact, to make a long matter short, that chaotic litter of boots, bacon, biscuits and bundles of all descriptions had been reduced

by the aid of scientific packing into the interior of four highly coloured packboxes and we were ready for the journey.

Tumbling out of bed, dressing, rushing down stairs and bolting our breakfast was a matter of a few minutes — a hop, skip and jump into our saddles and with a parting 'Hurrah' at last we were off. But stay, there is a little something to be done before leaving your Danish or Icelandic hostess. I declare I never thought of it, filthy lucre is as great an object up North as it is with us and our continental neighbours — there is yet a bill to settle. To read it there is no difficulty, all written in neat, well formed characters, both figures and letters, evidently summed up, signed and dated, but to understand the details of your small account is another matter, ours being about as intelligible to us as Chinese to an Irishman. Our only alternative was to refer to our interpreter, presume all to be right, push our hands into our pockets and at once dub up thirty two dollars Danish or three pounds twelve English for three days board and lodging for two.

Your Icelandic hostess, although she charges first class hotel prices for accommodation not better than you would have expected had you lived in medieval times, having bagged the needful, now intends pouring oil into your wounds. There is yet a parting stirrup cup to drink, one of these old customs of bye-gone days which with us is almost obsolete; a pleasing little ceremony which when practiced often helps in smoothing over much ill humour and bad feeling towards your hosts which may previously have existed, and in sending you on your journey light-hearted and with kindly feelings towards those whom you leave behind. Such, I presume, is the object. At all events I am certain it was the effect of Iceland's sch . . . (schnaps?). What a happy combination of Samaritan and Robber! Seeing there was a chance of a little more delay we sent our packhorses on the road in charge of a boy whilst we ourselves stayed behind to gulp down a libation called brandy wine and take farewell of our friends who had collected to see us start.

Hands had been shaken all round, our guide, an Icelander, had kissed both great and small, women and children indiscriminately, for such is the custom of Icelanders and a custom which I will broach upon in another chapter. We were almost off when, to our annoyance, up comes a youth blowing and puffing, the perspiration streaming from his face, carrying an immense bundle of bread which we supposed to be safely stowed and on its journey in the packboxes. Disagreeable as it was we felt we could not lose the staff of life, for once away from Rekyjavik our hopes of seeing more were nil; so, dividing the bundle in two, we each took half and tied it to our saddles.

A few more jokes were passed between the English colony, with nods and grins from the Icelanders, the parting (one missing word) and we were off. Waving adieu as we turned into the main street we lashed our ponies to a trot, the fastest recognisable pace in town, soon leaving our friends behind and we were started on our travels.

Although the quality of his youthful writing leaves much to be desired a would-be author must be allowed time to learn his trade. It is obvious he felt more confident when recording in copious detail those scientific observations which form the larger part of this particular piece of work. It was the preparation of material for descriptive journals recording his extensive travels that eventually helped Milne to write in an entertaining manner, but at no time would his style achieve the best literary standards.

His first extended narrative, *Across Europe and Asia — Travelling Notes*, was published in 1877. This consisted mainly of geological data gleaned from personal observation of the terrain along which he travelled but, in the paper entitled *Across Europe and Asia* read to the Asiatic Society of Japan a year later, he described his epic journey in more personal terms. Extracts from these two accounts appear in the chapter *The Long Journey* in this book.

The intervening years between the Icelandic trip and the commencement of his Professorship at the Imperial College brought some measure of maturity to his writing. While still including trivia on occasion, it is generally less effervescent and the descriptive phrasing is far more precise.

His preoccupation in Japan with geophysical investigations, all of which were additional to his College duties, meant he did not find time to write pure fiction for some years. Eventually, encouraged by the editor of the English language newspaper, *Japan Mail*, with whom Milne had become friendly, he wrote a series of short stories about a character called John Henry Fizzles, a somewhat mad scientist. Each is about 7,000 words — far too long to reproduce in full but the following is a shortened version of one of them. *The Chemical Experiments of John Henry Fizzles*, although interesting, would appear to indicate he was more interested in telling the tale than considering the adequacy of his writing!

'John Henry', said Mrs Fizzles to her husband, 'what did you have to drink with Mr Rivets on your way home?'. 'A little warm whisky and water' was the mild reply. 'I thought so' said Mrs F. 'If Mr Rivets had given you some of your coal tar you are raving about, you would have been at least more sensible.'

Little did Mrs F. think of the results which were to flow from her last remark. Mr Fizzles seized the idea it suggested in a moment. In ordinary food there is carbon, hydrogen, oxygen and nitrogen, and the same elements exist in coal, in coal tar, in the refuse of gas works and in a thousand other places. 'Why should not these substances be used as food,' said Mr Fizzles to himself, 'If I can make steak out of coal or the refuse from gas works, the whole of the civilised world will be at my feet. It must be tried. There may be many failures and I may fail, but come what may, like Bruce's spider I will try again.' That night Mr Fizzles dreamt that he was standing on a pedestal near a large machine, into one end of which coal was being tipped. At the other end of the machine which had many mouths, extending over a large plain, beefsteaks, apple pies, bananas and food of all descriptions was being rapidly discharged. Round these different mouths, groups of people from all quarters of the globe were assembled to receive food, while at his feet were representatives of all nations presenting him with addresses. He had just stretched out his hands to pronounce a benediction on the assembled multitude when he was suddenly awakened by the partner of his joys and sorrows, who sharply said, 'don't paw my face in that way, Mr Fizzles.'

His experiments continued until one day:

At 6 o'clock Mr F. mounted on a chair and in a few choice expressions in which he wished his friends a hearty welcome he invited them to be seated. The operation of seating 500 guests took a little time and it wasn't until a few minutes had passed, that it was observed that Mr Fizzles had disappeared. When soup came in it was noticed that it was accompanied by an unusually strong smell of petroleum, and when the guests dipped their spoons into it, it seemed to be petroleum.

Mrs Fizzles hurried towards the kitchen at a rate which did not add to the graceful appearance of her black silk gown. She arrived too late, nearly every dish, pudding, tarts, entremets had been filled up with tar, while in the middle of the fire stood the fish kettle filled with boiling sulphuric acid. Before Mr Fizzles could remonstrate, Mrs Fizzles had emptied three pans of tar and petroleum, the frying pan of soda cake and the fish kettle of sulphuric acid down the sink. Little did she anticipate the effects. It was not long before the disturbances had transversed the whole length of Muddleton and the invited and the uninvited inhabitants of that quiet town were demoralised with fear. Next Sunday when the parson preached from a text which referred to the destruction of Babylon, Mr Fizzles gave a gentle sigh.

As is well known, science fiction dreams often become fact. A hundred years after Milne wrote this story protein is being produced from petroleum.

It was not until his return from an extended trip to Australia, Tasmania and New Zealand that Milne wrote *Colonial Facts and Fictions: Humorous Sketches* (Chatto and Windus, London, 1886), under the psuedonym 'Mark Kershaw'. Professor John Perry recalled that this story of Milne's travels in the then pioneering countries of Australia sold quite well, particularly at railway bookstalls in Britain. It was the kind of reading material which could be enjoyed on a long journey; light-hearted and, as the title suggested, full of amusing anecdotes about our 'cousins' down-under and their way of life — it was a book which could be laid aside for a while without serious loss of continuity.

An accurate description of Milne's style of writing in this book is not easy to convey but the suggestion by one of his friends that there is a marked similarity between the writing of 'Mark Kershaw' (John Milne) and those of the contemporary great American humorist 'Mark Twain' (Samuel Clemens) should be disregarded. By 1886 Twain had already published many of his major works and had become successful because, among other things, he had adapted his writing to encompass a type of humour then current along the eastern coast of the United States. Moreover, he skilfully interspersed descriptive passages with satirical stories of the people and places in that part of the country. It is reasonably safe to assume that Milne, avid reader that he was, would have been familiar with some of these works and while it can be argued that he appears to have written *Facts and Fictions* in a similar formula, the suggestion that it, too, was successful because of this has no supporting evidence. In perspective, it is as well to remember that 'Twain' achieved international fame as a writer of several volumes of classical humour while 'Kershaw' was the author of a single successful travelogue.

Be that as it may, Milne's book had a kind of humorous appeal that readers of his day enjoyed. Even though now dated, the stories in it are interesting enough as the following extracts reveal. The first is a story of the Chinaman, Ah Foo, a gardener on Thursday Island. The narrator begins:

> Pearls and pearl shells are now getting scarce at and about Thursday Island. In early days pearls were common enough to be had for the asking. There are some of my mates here that have had pearls given to them by the handful. They would get a few set in rings for their sweethearts, the balance they would pass on to their friends. The first who discovered this El Dorado was an Israelite from Vienna. He came and bought up all he could, and then he went, and we have never heard of him since. After the first Oriental there came a second Oriental. This was a

Chinaman. He called himself Ah Foo, and told us that his home was in Shantung or Shanshi. I forget which. In big colonial towns Chinamen are usually washermen. In the suburbs, and in the country, they are gardeners. About half Australia depends upon Chinamen for their vegetable diet. As Chinamen supply it, the profession of a gardener has come to be regarded as an occupation by no means comparable with true manhood.

You point to the only fertile spot in a barren burnt up township, and before you can ask what it is, you are told that it is one of those gardens made by Chinamen. They are always making gardens. With the manure they use they will poison some of us yet. Would you believe it, they only use night soil. They are such a dirty lot.

This is all the thanks a Chinaman gets for making a pleasant little green oasis and feeding the whites on cabbages and peas. To be a gardener is looked upon as a Chinaman's profession. In fact pottering about with a watering pot, and hawking vegetables, is the greatest height to which a Chinaman's soul is supposed to rise.

Ah Foo, when he came to Thursday Island started a garden. How things were to be induced to grow, nobody could conceive. That was the Chinaman's business. If there is a second Aden in the world, it must be remembered that it is well represented by Thursday Island. It seldom rains on Thursday Island, but yet Ah Foo kept digging away at his ground, expecting that some day or other it might produce a crop, and the harvest he would get, for cabbages were worth five shillings each, would well repay him for his labours. But weeks passed, and no rain came, and the Chinaman for a month or so paused in his labours. From time to time during this period of melancholy, he would descend from his hut up the gully, and take a seat upon a bench within the little Public.

'Well, John, and how's the garden?' the landlord would ask.

'Me loose plenty money. No catchee lain, water melons and cabbages no makee glow,' replied John; — and he looked sad enough for the first mourner at a funeral. Several of the residents on Thursday Island, who had travelled, knew that Chinamen succeeded in growing vegetables in places where even a Mormon would fail.

'Just let John alone, we'll have our cabbages yet. Why, Chinamen can raise peas out of a bed of salt in a baker's oven.' So John was encouraged by a smile and toleration. Many of the older hands on the Island hadn't tasted fresh vegetables for three years and they regarded John's efforts with great interest. Now and then a resident who had taken an evening stroll past Ah Foo's patch, would, whilst taking his tot of 'Square Face,' casually refer to what he had observed. 'That garden up there ain't doing much,' one would remark. 'Exactly as I was saying to Smith, here,' was the reply. 'Plenty of stones and dirt; I reckon he's waiting for the rain.' By and bye John's garden became a joke — in fact a sort of by-word for a bad spec. Still John pegged along. Now and then he could be seen toiling up the hill with two baskets filled with sea-weed suspended at the end of a stick. This was manure for the garden.

Six months passed and still there had not been a sprinkle, and John had never produced a single vegetable. Thursday Island was as brown as a baked apple. 'Curious folks these Chinese,' said the old resident, 'always industrious. Why if we had their perseverance we'd been millionaires by this time.'

People next began to speculate as to what would be the price of John's cabbages when they did grow.

'I wonder how he lives? Why it's half a year since Ah Foo came, and he hasn't sold a copper's worth of stuff as yet. I suppose the other Chinamen help him along.' We heard that they are terribly clannish in their country. In the midst of all the speculations as to the source of Ah Foo's income, there was a clap of thunder, and the rain fell in buckets' full. Everybody looked up towards the Chinaman's cabin as if they expected to see cabbages rising like the magic mango.

A week or so after this down came Ah Foo from his patch boiling over with tribulation. He said, the birds had taken his seeds, and, while all Thursday Island was putting on a coat of green, Ah Foo's patch remained as brown as a saddle. 'No makee garden up that side any more, more better look see nother place. My flend talkee that island overside can catchee number one land. I make look see.' For two months after Ah Foo was heard of cruising round about the Islands. And as there were a good lot of shellers knocking about it was surmised that John got his tucker free. At last he returned still looking fat and healthy let it be remarked, with but an expression more woebegone than ever. 'More better my go away. Spose flend pay my money I go China side. No catchee chancee this side.' The rumour that Ah Foo was busted, quickly spread, and a good deal of sympathy prevailed. Hadn't he tried to benefit them, and, in the endeavour, been ruined. The argument appealed to the feelings of Ah Foo's sensitive sympathizers and, as most of the residents on Thursday Island are generous and tender hearted, a subscription was raised to send Ah Foo back to his fatherland. And he left us.

Two months afterwards what do you think we discovered. Why we discovered that Ah Foo had never had a garden at all, and he never intended to have one. All the time he was here he was buying up pearls from the black divers which ought to have come to us. If Ah Foo took a penny out of Thursday Island he took at least £30,000, and we raised a subscription to get him carried off.

John Milne's deep interest in natural history is evident in much of his writing. To shorten the account of his long journey across Europe and Asia it has been necessary to eliminate much detail, including many of the references to the flora and fauna he saw during this time. A large number of the magic lantern slides he used to illustrate lectures concern the subject while his paper on the Great Auk, for instance, could have been written only by someone with a deep interest in ornithology.

As would be expected, such a man as he could not tolerate cruelty to animals lightly and some of the brutality he saw in his wanderings about the world sickened him. On several occasions in *Facts and Fictions* he used the weapon of satire to protest against such barbarity as, for example, in the story of the loading of live sheep he had viewed with such horror in a New Zealand port. He also used the same story to attack directors of the shipping company concerned for the indifferent food they provided for their passengers:

> While lying at Gisborne, we saw a sight to which colonials are probably accustomed. This was a shipment of about 400 sheep. They came alongside in barges. At first the sheep were put in iron cages six or seven together and, by means of a steam-winch, hoisted up to the deck. This, however, was not quick enough, so a number of thin pieces of cord, very like log-line, were arranged with slip-knots. Each sheep to be lifted was secured by fastening the slip-knot round its stomach. Six or seven cords, each with its sheep, were then taken and fastened to the hook which before had raised the cages. As the chain with its hook tightened by the lifting of the winch, the six or seven sheep were dragged sprawling across the deck until they were suspended — then up they went, heads and tails, a living, swinging, twirling mass, bumping against the side of the ship until they reached the deck. Here they were released, and kicked and thumped until they moved to their proper quarters.
>
> The whole performance was sickening, and all of us, who were not accustomed to see the handling of sheep, regarded it as brutal. Several of them died after this.

Milne then goes on to stress the point by recounting a dream which followed this incident. In this he was on a large ship and all the officers on board were sheep with gilt buttons and that there were little sailor sheep with blue shirts. Presently a load of stout old gentlemen, some of whom seemed as if they enjoyed a glass of port

wine and an easy-chair after their dinner, came alongside. These
were the directors of the steamship company. The dream continues
with them being hoisted on board like the sheep and one or two of
them died.

> These proceedings, which caused a great deal of merriment
> amongst the crew, were hardly over, when there was a fearful
> squealing and clawing heard at the back of the ship, and all the
> sheep ran aft to see what was the matter.
> 'Why, it's only a lot of molly-hawks and albatrosses crying,'
> said the captain. 'Let us ask them why they are so sad. Where is
> my speaking-trumpet?'
> The trumpet was brought, and a big sheep, holding it up to
> his face, after several preliminary 'Baas', shouted out 'Ahoy,
> my feathered friends! why these drippings?'
> 'You've killed our friends, our best friends, our very dear
> friends!' replied the sobbing molly-hawks; 'we can never fly
> after your ships anymore.' At this point the tears came pattering
> down like rain, as if there had been a thunder storm.
> 'Be more explicit, companions of the pastures,' yelled the big
> sheep through the trumpet, 'we do not wish to loose your
> pleasant company.'
> 'Why,' said the molly-hawks, 'the gentlemen you have been
> stringing up practiced economy. They allowed the cooks to
> buy bad butter, so that the passengers would not eat the
> beefsteak-pies and pastry they made, which were therefore all
> thrown overboard to us. All the birds in the South Pacific knew
> this, and it can't happen any more.'
> Then they wept until the sheep had to put on their oilskin
> coats for fear of spoiling their uniforms.

Milne's unpleasant childhood experience with the showerbath
more than a quarter of a century earlier must have been a traumatic
experience for one so young and it seems to have remained with him
throughout his lifetime as baths are mentioned several times in his
manuscripts. No doubt the swift punishment meted out on that
occasion underlined the memory! In *Colonial Facts and Fictions*, for
instance, he describes an unusual bath at Victoria, Australia:

> . . . At one club, the internal arrangements of which were quite
> palatial, I saw a bath which would excite the wonder of a
> Barnum. It ought to be exhibited. The performances that this
> wonderful piece of machinery could go through were perfectly
> astounding. If I were rich, I would have a bath of that
> description for the amusement of my friends. It was situated in a
> little room provided with sliding doors in the walls, and electric
> bells. Visitors were told that these doors were for attendants to

pass in towels and cups of coffee. I heard privately that they were really for attendants to see that the bath did not get loose and damage strangers who were unacquainted with its mechanism. When I first saw this marvellous piece of mechanism, I thought it was a new form of organ, and that all the labelled handles were the stops. The music it played was, however, different from that of an ordinary organ. Pull one handle and you might be boiled. Pull another, and you might be annihilated with jets of water, which would simultaneously hit you in all directions, pounding you to pieces like a fragment of quartz beneath a battery. Pull a third handle, and you would be frizzled to a cinder with hot air. To avoid accidents, there were innumerable notices pasted on walls and on handles of the various taps. I only remember a few of them. One said 'Be careful and see that the arrow points to the left.' Another ran, 'Three turns to the right will give you a douche.' This was a thing that flattened you out on the bottom of the bath. A sort of aqueous thunderbolt. 'Mind and turn off number three before entering the bath.' 'See that hot is off before turning right hand number two.' 'Turn on the acquatic gymnasium gently.' This notice applied to an innocent-looking silver knob which, when moved, set free a jet of water, which carried the bather up towards the ceiling. Many visitors had been found clawing and reaching and swearing on the top of this jet, where they were being revolved, and tumbled about like a pithball on the fountains which some fishmongers exhibit. Two hours of this was said to be capital exercise for the muscles and the lungs. There were a whole lot of other notices, but I forget them. A portion of the apparatus was like an ordinary bath; at the end of it, however, there was a thing like a second bath reared on end. The resemblance of this to a sarcophagus was quite appropriate. It was painted blue, and had aureoles and stars as decorations for its dome-like roof. Standing in this you might pose as a saint, or one of the images so common in the niches of large cathedrals. This was also appropriate, for, after having met your death, you might remain standing as a martyr to cleanliness, and as a warning to future bathers.

I got my companion, who described the above, to turn on some of the fireworks while I looked through one of the holes for cups of coffee. First there was a hiss, as of escaping steam, then the sullen roar of a fall like the great Niagara. Sometimes it was hot, at other times it was cold. Oh, conflagrations and volcanoes, where would you be beneath jets like this? Now and then I could catch a view of my companion through clouds of spray and steam. At one moment he was like a deity surrounded by rainbows. At another moment he was like an imp of darkness working the machinery of the infernal regions. The thunder of the douche was appalling. I shrieked to him to retire. The roaring of the waters prevented his hearing my warning cries. Suddenly the deluge ceased. He had turned another tap and produced a gentle spray, like that which water budding plants in spring. The exhibition was marvellous, and it made me change my opinion about Australians being non-inventive. My friends asked me, when all was over, to have a bath. I felt the satire, and did not answer. The volcanic energy pent up behind the silver taps of that establishment have produced too deep an impression ever to be forgotten. To have a bath which will wash your friends, stretch your muscles, give flexibility and tone to your larynx, extinguish volcanoes, put out fires, kill your enemies, create a nervous excitement sufficient to turn black hairs grey, alarm intruders, amuse the children, flood the streets, is a luxury denied to all but those living in the state of Victoria.

Even if writers make serious efforts to avoid doing so all reveal something of their own personality. John Milne was no exception. Though he disclosed the 'Mark Kershaw' psuedonym of *Facts and Fictions* to only a few of his closest friends, by his inability to refrain from relating in the book incidents which were known by many to have happened to him personally, the identity of the author was soon established, for the intensity of his preoccupation with earthquakes inevitably led him to refer to them in his book on many occasions.

One story, for instance, is told as though it had occurred to an acquaintance in Wellington, N.Z. Answering the question as to what he had done when the ground commenced shaking this person replied:

Oh, I — well — I bolted through the front parlour window and landed on my stomach on a flower-bed. It is as true as I am here that I could feel the flower-bed palpitating as if it were alive. Oh, there were many things happened that night! The old man who is supposed to study these things up at the observatory was found by his wife standing in his nightshirt out in the snow with the window-sash around his neck. You know, the old ass had bolted head first through his window without stopping to open it. When his wife asked him what he was doing, he told her that he had just stepped out to make an outside observation.

'I wanted to see if the chimneys moved very much, my dear,' he stammered.

Whether fact of fiction, 'Kershaw' described the various reactions of a group of people when an earthquake began:

Down at the club there were a lot of our boys and some naval officers playing poker. You don't know the game, I suppose? It is a game where they have a pool, and this keeps getting bigger and bigger as the game goes on. They call this pool the jackpot. Well, when the shake came on, the pot was reckoned to be worth about £25. People never thought about money when they felt the movement and heard the timbers creaking; they just looked at each other and stampeded. Some went for the windows, some for the doors, and others, who did not know the place, got jammed in the kitchen and the ends of blank passages. One man landed in the bathroom, another found himself a prisoner in the lavatory.

When the thing was over, one of the party was missing. Now just guess where they found him. Why, shaking and shivering in a cupboard. Well, after a laugh and a drink — for it needs something to square your nerves after a good earthquake — they sat down to finish their game. But do you think they found the jackpot on the table? No sir, not a bit of it; and what is more, they never did find it. It was observed, however, that the man that was shaking in the cupboard, and at whom they had laughed for being such a funk, bought himself a new watch that week. General opinion held that he had never been a funk at all, but had just stayed behind until his friends had cleared and then nobbled the pool, after which he walked quietly into the cupboard!

Yet another of the examples where Milne used fiction to illustrate known fact is found in the story he called *Soft Sammy:*

In many countries when an earthquake takes place the land goes down. At Lisbon it went down so suddenly that it buried a whole lot of people. In our country, so far as I can make out, (the story is being told by a New Zealander), the land appears to have a habit of going up. In 1855 about 4,600 square miles of land rose in some places nine feet, and the breadth of the beach increased more than 100 feet . . . One day as we were walking along the new beach we observed that here and there some pegs had been driven in, just as if someone was staking out a claim; and when we came to enquire we found that somebody had been staking out a claim. 'The fellow who did it was a man who lives up there,' and our acquaintance pointed up the hill to one of the biggest houses in the town. 'At that time he was a new chum and, because we thought he was bit soft, we called him "Soft Sammy". Sammy, however, took the wind out of our sails this time. Instead of pottering around his ruins like the rest of us had been doing, he had quietly staked the new ground which had been lifted up.'

The story goes on to explain that at first the land was thought to be Queen's property, but after Sammy had pointed out to the judge that a ship was stranded on a bit of the land the judge owned, the latter decided in Sammy's favour. Then Sammy sent a note round to the captains of the ships stranded on his land politely informing them that unless they moved their ships within twenty-four hours he would be compelled to take action against them for trespass. As there was no way of moving the ships they were put up for auction and Sammy pocketed half the proceeds. Everybody hoped for more jump-ups and when the cold weather came on — for that is the time that earthquakes are frequent — the excitement was pretty great.

> 'Well, and was there never any more jump-ups after the one when Sammy made his money?'
>
> 'Oh yes, there was one a bit down the bay a few years ago!'
>
> 'And was there a scramble for it?'
>
> 'My word there was! If you had seen the cartloads of pegs and people in buggies all crowding along, each trying to get ahead of his neighbour then you would have thought Wellington was mad. When they got there what do you think they found? Well, they found it had been staked out by Sammy!'
>
> 'What, Sammy again?'
>
> 'Yes, it was Sammy again and as far as we could make out he had pegged out the ground before the earthquake came, and, as his pegs were below water we could not see them. We don't call him "Soft Sammy" any more. We now call him "Seismic Sammy"!'

It would be wrong to give the impression that the fiction of Milne is just an extension of his classroom teaching or lectures to one or other of the many societies to which he belonged. Much of his work is straightforward story telling; often with tongue in cheek when he had a sly dig at something with which he did not agree. For example, he enjoyed his smoke and was seldom seen without either a pipe or cigarette in his mouth. When he learned that smokers in the city of Melbourne at that time were not particularly welcome he commented upon the fact, not without obvious embellishment:

> On the suburban lines between the hours of four and eight in the afternoon you get a sort of smoking-box to sit in. It almost seems to have been intentional to make the smoking compartment as filthy as possible. Nowhere in the world — and I have been round and round it in many directions — did I ever meet with smoking carriages in such a dirty condition as those near Melbourne. If you go in quickly you might possibly get a seat. If you were late you had to stand in the middle of the van (for the carriages are more like vans with seats round them than

carriages). There is a mat, which I always saw in a state of sop: this was produced by saliva. To drop a parcel would be to leave it, for it would be too soiled to pick up.

After 1886 Milne appears to have published very little fiction. His increasing involvement with seismological investigations and social interests left him with but little time since the former included the compilation of the great earthquake catalogues which bear his name and the latter have been discussed elsewhere in this book. On return to England his major work was the textbook *Seismology* but he also began an untitled manuscript: regrettably this was incomplete at the time of his death. It would have been a book popularising seismology, then a little known science in Britain. Amusing stories were included as a relief from the more serious passages: one of these was his explanation for the appearance of the Isle of Wight ghost, 'Springheel Jack'.

Facts and Fiction is not itself a great travel book but, when placed in its correct literary period and making allowance for the penny-a-lining style, it is entertaining enough. One is forced to reflect upon the success he might have achieved had he directed all his energy to the writing of popular fiction. John Milne might now be remembered by the many instead of the few: how often the successful entertainer takes pride of place over the innovator in the esteem of the public! Fortunately for the world his first love was seismology and if at times there is a suspicion that he might have been something of a bore on the subject — albeit a charming one — it must never be forgotten that much of the foundations of present day knowledge of the science stems directly from his tremendous enthusiasm and drive.

It has already been mentioned that John Milne was a splendid conversationalist and those who knew him recall how he was full of entertaining stories which he told superbly. The apparently serious demeanour he would adopt on such occasions was always belied by the twinkle his eyes could not conceal. Many experienced pleasure because of this gift; not only his close friends, his colleagues and his students, but also those he encountered casually as he went about his everyday business. He would enjoy a chat with total strangers and most were happy to be stopped by him, for he cut across the narrow-minded Victorian etiquette which required that a formal introduction should precede discussion — a social attitude he despised. In the predominantly rural community such as that on the Isle of Wight during the closing years of the nineteenth century, movement by the majority of the population was of a fairly local nature. A person as widely travelled as Milne was something of a rarity and his tales of far away places were listened to with a deeper respect than could be commanded today, when earth-shrinking jets carry millions about the world, and coloured television brings news of distant lands and peoples into living rooms at the turn of a switch.

However, this vast experience of life sometimes led him to exercise the imperious side of his character. One old gentleman who remembers John's visits to the Isle of Wight County Club said that, when he entered, books and papers were laid aside, for Milne had declared that 'the clubroom is a place for conversation, not reading,' and soon he would be prevailed upon to embark upon tales of things which had happened to him, or he had heard or seen in some outlandish place whose very name was unknown to most of his audience.

Usually, he was prepared to talk at length to visiting reporters and writers seeking copy. One of the latter was Cleveland Moffett, whose long article, *The Man who measures earthquakes* was published in *Pearson's Weekly*. In it Moffett retells some of the yarns Milne spun to him one evening at Shide, 'which is a real corner of Japan, with a Japanese servant salaaming about, and bringing in pleasant things to drink, and the Professor's wife, a Japanese lady, doing the honours with all the grace of her country.' Milne told him some of the interesting series of experiments he had carried out in Japan and interspersed them with stories about the funnier things that had happened both there and in this country, such as the time when he had an English skipper as his guest and put him in a room where a quantity of dynamite was stored for earthquake experiments. For some reason or other Milne did not think to tell the skipper about this until his guest was in bed. As it was evidently best to let him understand the situation, writes Moffet, Milne went to his guest's door some time later and knocked. The skipper presently appeared in slippers and dressing-gown, his bald head shining in the light of the candle he carried.

'Hullo!' he said, 'what's up?'

'Oh, nothing,' said the Professor, 'only there's some dynamite under your bed. I forgot to tell you. You don't mind, I hope?'

'How much is there?' asked the skipper.

'About ten pounds.'

'Ten pound. Oh, no, I don't mind that. Good night!'

Milne said he regarded that skipper as one of the coolest men he ever met.

He was not averse to telling stories against himself such as the occasion when at the command of the Emperor a seismic exhibition was organised in the Palace yard where a number of miniature towns and villages had been laid out neatly for the purpose of being blown up and shaken down when his Majesty should touch the button. Everything went off perfectly and the courtiers were delighted.

'That, sire, is exactly the way an earthquake does its work,' Milne explained as they looked upon the torn-up ground and the wreck of buildings.

'Really!' said the Emperor, his voice devoid of all expression and without further comment departed with his courtiers. For once the Professor was completely deflated!

Elsewhere he explained some of his troubles in setting up the instruments. Initially there were imperceptible air currents that would start the seismograph booms swinging in a most perplexing way, and when these were eliminated at his Carisbrooke Castle station the little lamp frequently blew out. After much conjecture 'Snowy' Hirota, Milne's assistant, finally discovered that it was caused by small beetles, which managed to drop from the roof and get themselves burned to ashes while extinguishing the flame.

Milne wrote:

> Next there appeared on the scene — or rather made itself felt — a little grey money-spider that managed to hide inside the box and would come out at night for its own experiments. This little spider knew nothing about earthquakes but took the greatest interest in the swinging of the boom and soon began to join in the game itself, catching one end of the boom with its legs to tug it over to one side as far as possible. The spider would then anchor itself, hold on like grim death until the boom finally slipped away, run after it again and tug it to the other side holding on tightly until forced to let go once more. It would go on for an hour or two like this until quite exhausted, apparently enjoying the fun immensely, and never dreaming that it was manufacturing wonderful seismograms to upset the scientific world, since they seemed to indicate shocking earthquake disasters in all directions. This was a bad business and went on for some weeks, some of these seismograms being published and puzzled over. What made the matter worse was the behaviour of a certain woodlouse which began the habit of crouching under the little lamp on cold winter nights for warmth. There it would sit in comfort directly over the slit through which the ray of light was supposed to pass through, and, of course, this stopped all records.
>
> One night the louse discovered the spider playing with the boom, and from that moment became an absorbed spectator of the fun. Unable to join in the game because the slit was too small to enter it encouraged the spider on all occasions and at last is believed to have urged the latter to tie the boom fast with its thread! One morning 'Snowy' found the boom lashed firmly to the side of the box, so that all Japan might have been shaking and it would not have swung from its anchorage. This, of course, led to discovery and the prompt banishing of both louse

and spider from the premises; but while the mystery lasted it
was a good one.

The great seismologist had a host of fascinating experiences to
draw upon, the result of extensive travel and a lifetime of personal
endeavour. It is obvious that he enjoyed recounting them, much as
many who listened have recalled how well they had been
entertained. When, told by such an ebullient, effervescent extrovert
as John Milne they could scarcely have been otherwise.

Appendix 2

BIBLIOGRAPHY

Milne J. *Notes on Crystallography and Crystallo Physics* (London: Trübner and Co, 1879)
Earthquakes and Other Earth Movements (London: Kegan Paul and Trench, 1886)
with Burton W.K. *The Great Earthquake in Japan 1891* (London and Yokohama: Standford, 1892)
with Burton W.K. *The Volcanoes of Japan (Yokohama: Kelly and Walsh, 1892)*
The Miners Handbook (London: Crosby and Lockwood, 1893)
Catalogue of 8331 Earthquakes in Japan 1885-1892 (Tokyo: Seis. *Journal Japan*, 1895)
Seismology (London: International Science Series, 1898)
Catalogue of Destructive Earthquakes AD 7 - AD 1899 (British Association, 1912)
Kershaw M. (pen-name of John Milne) *Colonial Facts and Fictions* (London: Chatto and Windus, 1886)

TRANSACTIONS OF THE SEISMOLOGICAL SOCIETY OF JAPAN

Vol. 1 April-June 1880   *Seismic science in Japan* Part 1 pp 3-37.   *The earthquake in Japan 1880 Feb. 22* Part 2 pp 1-116.   **Vol. 2** July-December 1880   *Notes of the recent earthquakes of Yedo plains and their effects on certain buildings* pp 1-38.   *The Peruvian earthquake 1877 May 9* pp 50-96.   **Vol. 3** January-December 1881   *Experiments in observational seismology* pp 12-64.   *Notes on the great earthquakes of Japan* pp 65-102.   *Notes on the horizontal and vertical motion of the earthquake 1881 March 8* pp 129-136.   **Vol. 4** January-June 1882   *The distribution of seismic activity in Japan* pp 1-30.   *Utilisation of the earth's internal heat* pp 61-72.   *Suggestions for the systematic observations of earthquakes* pp 85-117.   **Vol. 6** January-June 1883   *Earth pulsations* pp 1-12.   *Catalogue of earthquakes felt in Tokyo 1882 January-1883 March* pp 32-35.   **Vol. 7** 1883-1884   *Earth tremors* Part 1 pp 1-15.   *Catalogue of earthquakes felt in Japan 1883 July-1884 May* pp 43-45.   *Secretary's report* pp 46-47.   *On 387 earthquakes observed during two years in North Japan* Part 2 pp 1-87.   **Vol. 8 1885**   *Seismic experiments* pp 1-82.   *Catalogue of earthquakes for Tokyo 1883 July-1885 February* pp 100-108.   **Vol. 9** 1886   *The volcanoes of Japan* Part 2 pp 1-186.   **Vol. 10** 1887   *On a seismic survey made in Tokyo 1884-1885* pp 1-36.   *Earthquake catalogue for 1881-1885* pp 83-96.   *Catalogue of earthquakes 1885 February-1887 January* pp 97-99.   **Vol. 11** 1887   *Earth tremors in Central Japan* pp 1-78.   *Earthquake effects, emotional and moral* pp 91-113.   *On construction in earthquake countries* pp 115-174.   **Vol. 12** 1888   *Note on effects produced by earthquakes upon the lower animals* pp 1-4.   *The Gray-Milne seismograph and other instruments in the seismology laboratory at Imperial College of Engineering Tokyo* pp 33-48.   *Instructions for setting up the Gray-Milne seismograph* pp 49-52.   *Note on the sound phenomena of earthquakes* pp 53-62.   *Relative motion of neighbouring parts of ground* pp 63-66.   *The movement produced in certain buildings by earthquakes* pp 67-75.   *On certain seismic problems demanding solution* pp 107-113.   **Vol. 13** 1890   *Earth tremors in Central Japan* Part 1 pp 7-19.   *On the distribution of earthquake motion within a small area* pp 41-89.   *Report on observations made in Japan 1886* pp 91-131.   **Vol. 14** 1890   *Construction in earthquake countries. Preliminary report on earthquake motion* pp 1-42.   *Effects produced by earthquakes on buildings* pp 43-83.   *An epitome of information and remarks* pp 229-246.   **Vol. 15** 1890   *Seismology as applied to railway trains* pp 23-29.   *Earthquakes recorded at the Chiri-kyoku, Tokyo* pp 93-97.   *Reports on earthquake recorded at Chiri-kyoku* pp 99-126.   *Catalogue of earthquakes 1887 February-1890 April* pp 127-

134.   *Earthquakes in connection with electric and magnetic phenomena*   pp 135–162.   *Construction in earthquake countries*   Supplement   pp   163–169.   **Vol. 16**   1892   *A mantel-piece seismometer*   pp 47–48.   *Report of Chiri-kyoku in Tokyo 1888*   pp 55–80.   *Report of Chiri-kyoku 1889*   pp 81–117.

THE SEISMOLOGICAL JOURNAL OF JAPAN

Vol. 1   1893   (Corresponding to Vol. 17 of the Transactions of the Seismological Society of Japan)   *On the migration of earthquake effects and certain experiments in earth physics*   pp 1–19.   *Seismometrical observations for 1890*   pp 31–57.   *On the overturning and fracturing of brick and other columns by horizontally applied motion* (with Omori F.)   pp 59–86.   *Earth pulsations in relation to certain natural phenomena*   pp 87–112.   *On the movement of horizontal pendulums*   pp 113–118.   *Note on the great earthquake 1891 October 28*   pp 127–151.   **Vol. 2**   1893   *Abstract of a report to the British Association*   pp 93–109.   **Vol. 3**   1894   *Seismic, magnetic and electrical phenomena*   pp 23–33.   *A note on horizontal pendulums*   pp 55–60.   *A note on earth pulsations and mine gas*   pp 65–69.   *Velocities of the earth waves*   pp 87–89.   **Vol. 4**   1895   *A catalogue of 8,331 earthquakes recorded in Japan 1885–1892 by John Milne*   pp 1–367.

REPORTS OF THE BRITISH ASSOCIATION FOR THE ADVANCEMENT OF SCIENCE SUB-COMMITTEE FOR THE PURPOSE OF INVESTIGATING THE EARTHQUAKE PHENOMENA OF JAPAN.

York   1881   pp 200–204   *An attempt to determine the area from which the shakings are so often felt in Tokyo and Yokohama.   Observations to determine the nature of earthquake-motion.   The recording of earth-tremors.   Experiments with artifical earthquakes.*   **Southampton**   1882   pp 205–212   *Sources of Tokyo and Yokohama shakings.   Velocity of propagation of an earthquake wave.   The nature of earthquake motion.   Extent of variation in duration of motion at neighbouring points. Experiments on artificially produced earthquakes.   Relative motion of two neighbouring points of ground.   Production of earth currents.*   **Southport**   1883   pp 211–215   *The Gray-Milne seismograph.   Earth pulsations*   **Montreal**   1884   pp 241–252   *Areas from which the shakings felt in North Japan emanate.   Experiments on the direction of motion of a point.   Simultaneous observations of earthquakes at three stations in telegraphic connection.   Observations with the Gray-Milne seismograph.   Experiments with buildings to resist earthquake motion.   Establishment of an underground observatory.   Earth-tremors and earth-pulsations.   Observation of earth currents.   Tidal observations.*   **Aberdeen**   1885   pp 362–379   *Seismic experiments using several stations in electrical contact.   Motion and velocity of waves.   Experiments on buildings to resist earthquake motion.   Observations in a pit 10 feet deep.   Building in earthquake countries.   Earth-tremors and earth-pulsations.   Earth temperatures.*   **Birmingham**   1886   pp 413–431   *Records from the Gray-Milne seismograph.   Frequency and character of recent earthquakes.   Earthquakes of 1885-1886.   The volcanoes of Japan.   The forms of volcanoes.*   **Manchester**   1887   pp 212–226   *Records from the Gray-Milne seismograph of earthquakes 1886-1887.   Sounding Asamayama.   Earth-tremors.*   **Bath**   1888   pp 422–437   *Earthquakes in 1886.   Earthquakes recorded in Tokyo.   Earth-tremors.   Records from the Gray-Milne seismograph of earthquakes 1887-1888.*   **Newcastle-upon-Tyne**   1889   pp 295–314   *Records from the Gray-Milne seismograph of earthquakes 1888-1889.   On the distribution of earthquake motion in a small area.   The eruption of Bandaisan.   The vibration of locomotives, rolling stock and structures.   Buildings in earthquake countries.*   **Leeds**   1890   pp 160–172   *Records from the Gray-Milne seismograph of earthquakes 1889-1890.   Frequency of earthquakes.   On the distribution of seismic energy.   Earthquakes in connection with magnetic and electric phenomena.   Comparison of Tokyo and Yokohama earthquakes.   Velocity of earthquake propagation.*   **Cardiff**   1891   pp 123–129   *Records from the Gray-Milne seismograph of earthquakes 1890-1891.   Observations in a pit.   The overturning and fracturing of brick and other columns.   Earthquakes in connection with electric and magnetic phenomena.*   **Edinburgh**   1892   pp 93–129   *Records from the Gray-Milne seismograph of earthquakes 1891-1892.   Earthquakes of 1888 and 1889.   On a new method which may be employed for investigating earth tremors or earth-tips.   Earth-tremors and firedamp.   On the overturning and fracturing of columns.   The great earthquake of 1891 October 28.*   **Nottingham**   1893   pp 214–

226   *Records from the Gray-Milne seismograph of earthquakes 1892-1893.   On the movements of horizontal pendulums.   Earth-waves and earth-pulsations.   List of earthquakes recorded in Japan 1893 February.   Overturning and fracturing of masonry and other columns.   Publication of a seismological journal.*   **Ipswich** 1895 pp 81-112   *Records from the Gray-Milne seismograph of earthquakes.   Observations with horizontal pendulums, the instrument, observation at Kamakura, movement of pendulums.   Sensitiveness of the horizontal pendulum.   Daily tilting and wandering of pendulums.   Movements of water in a well.   Observations at Yokohama and Kanagawa.*   pp 113-183   *Records from the Gray-Milne seismograph.   Observations with horizontal pendulums: Daily wave records.   Tremors, microseismic disturbances and earth-pulsations.   Relationship of tremors to time and location.   Records of earthquakes recorded by horizontal pendulums.   Description of catalogue of 8,331 earthquakes 1885-1892.   On the velocity of waves on the surface and through the earth.   The paths of earthquake motion.   Large earthquakes.   Apparatus and instruments at Shide.*

REPORTS OF THE BRITISH ASSOCIATION FOR THE ADVANCEMENT OF SCIENCE SUB-COMMITTEE FOR SEISMOLOGICAL INVESTIGATION

Liverpool 1896 pp 180-230 Dr C. Davidson and Prof. J. Milne Joint Secretaries   *Instruments which will record earthquakes of feeble intensity.   Observations with Milne's Pendulums T and U 1895-1896.   Changes in vertical observed in Tokyo 1894 to March 1896.   Notes on special earthquakes.*   **Toronto** 1897 pp 129-206 Dr C. Davidson and Prof. J. Milne Joint Secretaries   *Work done for establishment of a seismic survey of the world.   Records of the Gray-Milne seismograph.   The installation and working of the Milne horizontal pendulum.   Observations at Carisbrooke Castle and Shide.   Earthquake records from Japan and other places.   The highest apparent velocity at which earth-waves are propagated.   Diurnal waves.   The Perry tromometer.   Sub-oceanic changes.*   **Bristol** 1898 pp 179-276 Dr C. Davidson and Prof. J. Milne Joint Secrataries   *Progress to the establishment of earthquake observing stations round the world.   Notes on special earthquakes.   Earthquakes at Tokyo 1896 December 17 to 1897 December 16.   Earthquakes recorded at Shide, Edinburgh, Bidston, Europe.   On certain characteristics of earthquake motion.   Magnetometer disturbances and earthquakes.   Sub-oceanic changes in relation to earthquakes.   A time indicator.   On civil time employed throughout the world.   Great circle distances and chords of the earth.   Earthquake observations in Italy and Europe.*   **Dover** 1899 pp 161-238   *On seismological stations already established.   Notes respecting observing stations and their registers.   Discussion on the preceding registers.   Varieties of earthquakes and their respective durations.   Earthquake echoes.   Earthquake precursors.   On certain disturbances in the records of magnetometers and the occurrence of earthquakes.   Forms of reports.*   **Bradford** 1900 pp 59-120   *Analysis of earthquake records record in 1899.   Earthquakes and timekeepers at observatories.   Earthquakes and rain.   Earthquakes and changes in latitude.*   **Glasgow** 1901 pp 40-54   *Analysis of records for 1900.   Approximate frequency of earthquakes at different stations.   Experiments upon piers.   Comparison of earthquake registers.   Movements of horizontal pendulums in relation to barometric pressure.*   **Belfast** 1902 pp 59-75   *Seismological stations at home and abroad.   Instruments in use at Shide.   Origin of earthquakes recorded in 1899, 1900 and 1901.   Direction of the first preliminary tremors.   Time curves for earthquakes.   Comparison of the records obtained from three horizontal pendulums at Shide.   Clinometric experiments.   Experiments on vertical spring seismographs.   On the nature of earthquake movement.   The relationship between rockfolding, seismic and volcanic activities.   Comparison of the registers of Shide, Kew, Bidston and Edinburgh.*   **Southport** 1903 pp 77-85   *General notes on stations and registers.   The origins of large earthquakes recorded 1902 and since 1899.   Earthquake changes in latitude.   Comparison of records from three Milne pendulums at Shide.   Comparison of registers from Shide, Kew, Bidston and Edinburgh.   Earthquake commencements as recorded at Strasburg and in Britain.   The velocity of propagation of earthquake vibrations.*   **Cambridge** 1904 pp 41-55   *General notes on stations and registers.   The comparison of records from three Milne pendulums.   An improved record receiver.   The origins of large earthquakes in 1903.   On international co-operation for seismological work.   Seismic work now in progress.   Directions in which seismological work may be extended.   Experiments at the Ridgeway Fault.*   **South Africa** 1905 pp 83-94   *General notes on stations and registers.   The situation of stations.   The origins of large earthquakes in 1904.   On international co-operation for seismological work.*   **York** 1906 pp 92-103   *General notes on* *stations and registers. The situation of stations. The origins of large earthquakes in 1905. Large earthquakes in relation to time and space. The relationship of large earthquakes to each other and to volcanic eruptions. Earthquakes and changes in latitude. On the change of level on two sides of a valley. Antarctic earthquakes.*   **Leicester** 1907 pp 83-93   *General notes on stations and registers. The situation of stations. Photographic record receivers. Origins and relationships of large earthquakes in 1906. On the apparently luminous effects from certain rocks.*   **Dublin** 1908 pp 60-112   *General notes. Sites of stations. On the orientation of an instrument with regard to the building in which it is placed. The large earthquakes of 1907. After-shocks of the Jamaica earthquake, 1907 January 14. On the dissipation of earthquake motion as measured by amplitude and duration. On the direction in which earthquake motion is most freely propagated. A catalogue of destructive earthquakes. On a seismogram obtained in London, 1907 Oct 16.*   **Winnipeg** 1909 pp 48-65   *General notes. Sites of stations, Eskdalemuir, Agincourt, Porto Rico, Stonyhurst. The large earthquakes of 1908. The records of the small earthquakes from Jamaica. Quick vibrations as applied to seismology. On the possible synchronism between seismic activity in different districts. The time of maximum motion as indicated by three different horizontal pendulums. The number of earthquake records obtained at British Stations. Luminous effects obtained from rock surfaces. A catalogue of destructive earthquakes. Developing, fixing and copying a film.*   **Sheffield** 1910 pp 44-71   *General notes. New stations. Distribution of earthquakes 1909. A new departure in seismology. Changes in level accompanying earthquakes. Changes in level due to tidal influence. Megaseismic activity and rest. A catalogue of large earthquakes. A catalogue of destructive earthquakes in the Russian Empire, Iceland and the Western part of South America.*   **Portsmouth** 1911 pp 30-67   *General notes. Double and multiple earthquakes. Seismic activity in Japan, Italy and America 1700-1900. Synchronism of seismic activity in different districts. Megaseismic frequency. Tidal load observation at Ryde. Tidal load experiments in Pensylvanian Railway tunnels. Experiments in pits in the Midlands. List of strong shocks in the United States. Destructive earthquakes in Peru and North Chile. Unpublished notes relating to destructive earthquakes. Seismic activity 1899-1903 inclusive. Sensibility of seismographs recording on smoked surfaces.*   **Dundee** 1912 pp 69-103   *General notes. Seismic activity 1904-1910. Relation of amplitude in second of arc to distance of an origin. Direction of earthquake motion. Relative duration of two components of earth movement at a given station. Megaseismic activity and periods of quiescence. Megaseismic frequency in different seasons. Earthquake periodicity. Intervals in days from the commencement of one group to the commencement of another. Intervals and days between successive megaseismic activity in particular districts. Geographical distribution of megaseisms and thermometric gradients. A possible cause of megaseismic activity. Seismic and volcanic activity. On the mitigation of air tremors at Cardiff.*   **Birmingham** 1913 pp 45-86   *General notes, registers and visitors. Seismic activity in 1910. On the 443 or 452 day period. On the determinations of the positions of epicentres. On the variation of earthquake speed with the variation in the direction of propagation. Comparison of the amplitude of the east-west and the north-south motion at a given point. On the direction in which earthquake motion is most easily propagated. On the times of occurrence of maximum motion on pendulums differently orientated. Disturbances only recorded at two or three widely separated stations. Recurrence of megaseismic groups. Frequency of earthquake followers. Large earthquakes recorded at different observatories 1910 January to June. Seismic and volcanic activity. Report on an improved seismograph. Material published by the British Association and the Seismological Society of Japan relating to geophysics.*   Obituary notice for Shinoba Hirota.

OTHER WORKS BY MILNE IN THE REPORTS OF THE BRITISH ASSOCIATION FOR THE ADVANCEMENT OF SCIENCE

1881 pp 646-7 (with T. Gray) *A contribution to seismology.*   1895 p 691   *On earth movement observed in Japan.*   1897 p 716 *On certain submarine geological changes.*   1905 pp 340-1 *Recent advances in seismology.*   1908 p 701 *Duration and direction of large earthquakes.*   1911 pp 649-740 *A Catalogue of destructive earthquakes.*

CONTRIBUTIONS TO 'NATURE'

Vol. 21 1880   *Methods of detecting seismic trembling* p 382.   **Vol. 24** 1881   *Earthquakes in Japan* pp 64, 388, 462.   **Vol. 25** 1881-82   *Earthquakes in*

Japan p 126. *Volcanoes of Japan* p 420. *On the Koro-Pokrom Guru* p 470. **Vol. 26** 1882 *Earth Tremors in Japan* p 125 *Seismology in Japan* p 627. **Vol. 27** 1882-83 *Proposed study of earthquakes in Japan* p 463. **Vol. 29** 1883-84 *Earthquakes and buildings* p 290. *Establishment of underground observatory* p 413. *Earth Tremors* p 456. **Vol. 30** 1884 *Diffusion of scientific memoirs* p 267. *Earth tremors* p 614. **Vol. 31** 1885 *Tokyo earthquake of 15th October 1884* p 150. **Vol. 32** 1885 *Notes on Kurile Isles* p135 *Observation of earth-tips and earth-tremors* p 259. *An earthquake invention* p 573 **Vol. 33** 1886 *An earthquake invention* p 438. *Seismology in Japan* p 465. **Vol. 34** *The geology of Japan* p 59. *The Crater of Asamayama* p 130. *Prize essays on earthquakes* p 153. *An earthquake invention* p 193. **Vol. 35** *Volcanoes of Japan* p 19. *Seismometry in Japan* p 36. **Vol. 35** 1887 *History of earthquake investigation in Japan* p 559. **Vol. 36** *Protection of buildings from earthquakes* p 89 *Effects of earthquakes upon lower animals* p 350. **Vol. 37** *Earth tremors and the wind* p 214. *Tremors in Central Japan* p 399. *Earth sounds* p 543. *Pendulum seismometers* p 570. **Vol. 38** 1888 *Time distribution of Japanese earthquakes* p 597. **Vol. 40** 1889 *Earthquake and volcanic phenomena of Japan* p 608. *Seismological work in Japan* p 656. **Vol. 42** 1890 *System of building to withstand earthquake shocks* p 36. **Vol. 43** 1891 *Vibration recorders* p 154. **Vol. 45** 1892 *Seismology and engineering in relation to the recent earthquakes in Japan* p 127.

Vol. 46 *A dust storm at sea* p 128. **Vol. 47** 1893 *The volcanoes of Japan* (Fujisan) p 178. *Yezo and the Ainu* p 330. *Chicago exhibition earthquake laboratory instruments* p 356. **Vol. 50** 1894 *Seismic, magnetic and electric phenomena* p 145. **Vol. 51** 1895 *The observation of earth waves and vibrations* p 548. **Vol. 53** *The movements of horizontal pendulums* p 180. **Vol. 55** 1897 *Two unfelt earthquakes* p 390. **Vol. 57** 1898 *Recent seismology — earth movements* p 246. *Recent seismology — unfelt movements of the earth's crust* p 272. **Vol. 58** *Letter recording large earthquake* p 228. **Vol. 59** 1899 *Earthquake echoes* p 368. *Earthquake precursors* p 414. *A seismological observatory and its objects* p 489. **Vol. 60** *Review of Charles Davison's The Hereford Earthquake 1896* p 194. *The Darjeeling disaster* p 545. **Vol. 63** 1901 *The publications of the Earthquake Investigation Committee in foreign languages* p 588. **Vol. 65** *Meteorological phenomena and changes in the vertical* p 118. **Vol. 65** 1902 *What are seismometers indicatng* p 203. *Earthquake observations in Strasburg* p 438. **Vol. 66** *Recent volcanic eruptions in the West Indies* pp 56,107, 151, 370. *The West Indian Eruptions — B.A. report* p 619. *Review of Seismological Journal of Japan* p 702. **Vol. 67** *West Indian eruptions* p 91. **Vol. 67** 1903 *Earthquake observations in Galicia* p 235. *Recent earthquakes* p 348. *Earthquakes in the Midlands* p 491. *Seismometry and géite* p 538. **Vol. 68** *Further letter seismometry and géite* p 127. **Vol. 69** 1904 *Review of The evolution of the Earth Structure* by T. Mellard Reade p 251. **Vol. 70** *Nature and origin of earth movements* p 519. **Vol. 73** 1905 *Call for international meeting or convention* p 77. *Observations with horizontal pendulum in Antarctic regions* p 210. **Vol. 74** 1906 *Abridged Bakerian lecture* p 42. *Radioactivity and the interior structure of the earth* p 454. *Horizontal pendulums and earthquake echoes* p 515. **Vol. 76** 1907 *Note on Catalogue of Destructive Earthquakes* p 484. **Vol. 77** 1908 *Reply to criticism of his seismometer* p 198. *Recent earthquakes* p 592. **Vol. 78** *Review of Californian Earthquake* by D. Starr Jordan · p 27. *Shide seismographs* p 61. *Report on a seismic storm* p 374. *Duration and direction of large earthquakes* p 591. **Vol. 79** 1909 *Need for accurate time signals* p 23. *Earthquake records* p 321. *Automatic recording of vernier readings* p 329. **Vol. 81** *A new departure in seismology* p 38. *Earthquake 22nd October* p 524. **Vol. 82** 1910 *Surface deformation and the tides* p 427. **Vol. 83** *Review of Les Tremblements de Terre* Abbe Moreux p 5. **Vol. 84** *Review of The Californian Earthquake 1906 The Mechanics of the Earthquake* p 165. **Vol. 85** 1911 *Criticism of reviewer* p 511. *The observatory at Messina* p 515. **Vol. 86** *The National Physical Laboratory* p 123. *Velocity of earth movements caused by the Messina earthquake* p 125. *Daylight saving bill* p 183. *The penny — a suggestion* p 216. **Vol. 88** *Irregular long period changes of level* p 6. *The Taal volcano* p 12. *The propagation of earthquake waves* p 47. *Seismology at the British Association* p

124. *The Central Europe earthquake 1911* p 146.   **Vol. 90** 1912   *'Snowy' Shinobu Hirota* p 435.   **Vol. 91** 1913   *The new seismology* p 190.

REFERENCES TO MILNE IN 'NATURE'

Vol. 20 1879 Review of *Crystallography* p 73.   **Vol. 29** 1884 Notes on Milne papers p 584.   **Vol. 30** Notes on seismographs p 276.   **Vol.32** 1885 An earthquake invention criticism of Milne by D.A. Stevenson p 213 and **Vol. 33** p 7.   **Vol. 34** 1886 Review of *Earthquakes* p 141.   **Vol. 38** 1888 Order of the Rising Sun bestowed on Milne p 302.   **Vol. 45** 1892 Review of *Great Earthquakes of Japan* p 145.   **Vol 50** 1894 Review of the *Miners Hand Book* p 145.   **Vol. 52** 1895 Letter from E. von Rebeur-Paschwitz p 55. Report of British Association meeting p 533. Report on Vol. 4 Seis Journal of Japan p 304.   **Vol. 54** 1896 Recording of earthquake at Carisbrooke Castle p 229. H.H. Turner — *An earth-bending experiment* p 257. Earth disturbances in Cyprus p 352. Siesmological observation during year in I.O.W. p 587.   **Vol. 56** 1897 B.A. Seismological Committee report p 461. Notes on two earthquakes recorded at Shide p 523.   **Vol. 58** 1898 B.A. report p 532.   **Vol. 59** Review of *Seismology* p 97. 1899 Notes on G.M.T. — Civil Time tables p 349.   **Vol. 62** 1900 Report of B.A. meeting p 587.   **Vol. 66** 1902 Report on volcanic eruptions in the West Indies p 642.   **Vol. 67** Report on paper to Geographical Society *World-shaking earthquakes* p 69. 1903 Paper by Dr Farr to Physical Society *Interpretation of Milne seismograms* p 501.   **Vol. 82** 1910 Report of records by Kew seismograph p 398.   **Vol. 85** Extract from *Times* interview — *Pacific 'quakes* p 115.   **Vol. 89** 1912 Notes on *Catalogue of Destructive Earthquakes* p 109.   **Vol. 91** 1913 Comment on *Earthquakes and other Earth Movements* p 371. Obituary by J.W. Judd p 587 Continuation of Milne's work in seismology p 610.   **Vol. 92** Milne's bequest of books and scientific instruments p 48.

ENTRIES CONCERNING MILNE IN THE GEOLOGICAL MAGAZINE

2 Vol. 1 1874 Notes from the neighbourhood of Cairo pp 353-62.   **2 Vol. 3** 1876 *Ice and Ice-work in Newfoundland pp 303-8, 345-50, 403-10.*   **2 Vol. 4** 1877 *Considerations on the flotation of Ice-bergs* pp 65-71. *On the Rocks of Newfoundland* pp 251-262. *A visit to the volcanoes of Oshima* pp 193-199, 289-297, 337-346, 389-406, 511-518, 557-568.   **2 Vol. 5** *Across Europe and Asia* pp 29-37, 62-73.   **2 Vol. 5** 1878 *On the form of volcanoes* pp 337-345. Letter on glaciers p 93. Letter on coast ice p 425.   **2 Vol. 6** 1879 *A cruise among the volcanoes of the Kuril Island* pp 337-348. *Further notes upon the form of volcanoes* pp 506-514. Review of *Crystallography* p 373.   **2 Vol. 7** 1880 *Geographical distribution of volcanoes* pp 166-170. *Notes on the cooling of the earth* pp 99-102.   **3 Vol. 9** 1892 Milne's report to the B.A. p 465.   **4 Vol. 1** 1894 Review of *Seismic Journal of Japan* p 178, p 471.   **4 Vol. 2** 1895 Review of earthquake and volcanic phenomena Japan p 84.   **4 Vol. 9** 1902 B.A. report reviewed p 514.   **5 Vol. 5** 1908 *Duration of a large earthquake* p 467. Milne's Royal Medal p 576.   **5 Vol. 9** 1912 *Eminent Living Geologists* pp 337-346.   **5 Vol. 10** 1913 Obituary p 432.

FURTHER ARTICLES BY MILNE OR REFERENCES TO HIM

Quart Jr Geol Soc **Vol. 30** 1874 pp 722-745   *Notes on the physical features and mineralogy of Newfoundland.*   The Field **Vol. 45** 1875 p 296, p 370   *Relics of the Great Auk.*   Philosophical Mag. 1875 p 327 *Newfoundland Mineralogy.*   Quart Jr Geol Soc **Vol. 31** 1875 pp 1-28   *Peninsular and North-Western Arabia.*   Quart Jr Geol Soc **Vol. 33** 1877 pp 929, p 931   *The action of coast-ice on an oscillating area.*   *Sinai in Arabia* Beke C. Appendix (Trubner & Co. 1878).   Imperial College of Engineering, Tokyo   *Phenomena connected with Mineral deposits.*   Trans Asiatic Soc Japan **Vol. 7** 1879 pp 1-72   *Journey across Europe and Asia.*   Imperial College of Engineering,

Tokyo, 1879   *Notes on the ventilation of mines.*   Imperial College of Engineering,
Tokyo, 1880   *Catalogue of rocks, fossils, shells and cast in museum.*   Japan Gazette 24
February 1880   *The earthquake in Japan Feb 22, 1880.*   Min. Mag **Vol. 3** 1880 pp
178-185   *Experiments in the elasticity of crystals.*   Min. Mag **Vol. 3** 1880 pp 96-
100   *List of Japanese minerals.*   Popular Science Review **Vol. 19** 1880 pp 336-
345   *A large crater — Asosan in Kiushi, Japan.*   Trans Asiatic Soc 1880 pp 61-
91   *Stone implements from Otaru and Hakodate, prehistoric remains.*   Japan Gazette May
1880   *Seismic science in Japan.*   Jr Anthorp Inst **Vol.10** 1881 pp 389-423   *The
stone age in Japan and geological changes.*   Trans Asiatic Soc Japan 1881 *Evidence of glacial
period in Japan.*   Phil Mag **Vol. 12** 1881 pp 356-377   *Earthquake observations and
experiments in Japan.*   The Chrysanthemum, Yokohama 1881   *The earthquake of
December 23, 1880.*   Japan Gazette 1881, 1882   Papers on Japanese
earthquakes.   Proc Roy Soc **Vol. 33** 1882 pp 139-140   *On seismic
experiments.*   The Times 1 Oct 1882   *Earth movements.*   The
Chrysanthemum 1882 p 289-297   *Earthquake motion.*   Japan
Gazette 1882   *Earthquake distribution in Japan.*   Quar Jr Geol Soc **Vol. 39** 1883 pp
139-140   *Elasticity and strength constants of Japanese rocks.*   Phil Trans **Vol
173** 1883 pp 863-883   *On seismic experiments.*   Lit and Sc Soc, Rochdale 5 Dec
1884   Paper on Milne by James Ogden.   Yokohama 1884   *Recherches sur les
tremblements de terre.*   Proc Inst Civil Eng **Vol. 83** 1885   *Construction in earthquake
countries.*   Japan Mail 16 Oct 1886   Lecture on the causes of earthquakes.   Journal
of Engineering, Japan 1886   *Relation Earthquakes and Industry.*   Japan Education Mag
57 1887   *Human senses of earthquakes.*   Proc Inst Civil Eng **Vol.
100** 1889   *Building in earthquake countries*   Geogr Jr **Vol. 7** 1896 p
229   *Movement of the earth's crust.*   Engineering **Vol. 61** 1896 p 337, p 675, p
721   *Vibrations and engineering.*   Proc R Inst Gt Brit **Vol. 15** 1898 pp 326-336 Rev
Sci Paris **Ser 4 Vol. 9** 1898 pp 357-364   *Recent advances in seismology.*   Pearson's
Mag **Vol. 5** 1898 pp 483-495   *The man who measures earthquakes* — Moffett.   Geogr
Jr **Vol. 13** 1899 pp 173-194   *Civil time.*   Geogr Jr **Vol. 21** 1903 pp1-
22   *Seismological observations and earth physics.*   Phil Mag **Vol. 6** 1903 p 401   *On
the interpretation of seismograms* — C. Coleridge Farr.   Geogr Jr **Vol. 25** 1905 pp
531-533   *A new island in the Pacific.*   Proc Roy Soc **Ser A Vol. 76** 1905 pp
284-295   *Observations with horizontal pendulum in the Antarctic.*   Proc Roy Soc Ser
A **Vol. 77** 1906 pp 365-376   Bakerian lecture — *Recent advances in seismology.*   Bul
Seis Soc America **Vol. 2** 1912 pp 2-7   *John Milne seismologist* — L.H.
Hoover.   Engineering **Vol. 93** 1912 p 867   *The Milne
seismograph.*   Engineering **Vol. 96** 1913 p 164, p 200, p 453   *The late Prof. Milne.*
An improved seismograph.   Fore, I. W Golf Magazine **Vol 1** 1913   *Biographical Sketch of
Prof. Milne* — F.M. Walker.   Gatugizashi, Tokyo 1913   *Biographical Sketch of Prof
Milne* — Prof. Omori.   Proc Roy Soc **Vol. 89** 1914 pp 21-25   Obituary — J.
Perry.   Bul Seis Soc America **Vol 4** 1914   *Works of John Milne* — Comte de
Montessus de Ballore.   Science Progress April 1914   *Works of Milne* — C.
Davidson.   Pamphlet Hakodate Library 1926   *Prof. and Mrs Milne.*   The Found-
ers of Seismology, Cambridge 1927 pp 177-202   *Survey of Milne's work* — C.
Davidson.   *Earthquakes* (7th ed 1959) re-written A.W. Lee.   Science Museum
H.M.S.O. 1957   *Seismology* J. Wartnaby.   M.Sc Dissertation, University of
London 1967   *Early Scientific Works of John Milne* — J. Wartnaby.   Japanese Studies in
the History of Science No 8 Hist Sc Soc Japan 1969   *Early Scientific Works of John Milne* — J.
Wartnaby.   Ph.D Thesis, University of London 1972   *Nineteenth Century Seismology*
— J. Wartnaby.

NEWSPAPERS

Daily Mail, London 1900-13 Many articles, letters and references to Milne's work.
1 August 1913   Obituary notices in most leading national newspapers.

ARTICLES BY THE AUTHORS

Herbert-Gustar A.L. and Nott P.A. *Earthquake Milne and the Isle of Wight* (Vectis Biographies, pamphlet, 1974) (Rochdale Observer, England: 26 July to 16 August 1975) *The Lady from Hakodate* (Hokkaido Shinbum, 27 July 1977) in Japanese.   *Two Islands linked by love* (Kaihatsu Koho, February 1978) in Japanese.   *John Milne — A Teacher in the Meiji Period* (London: Japan Education Journal, February 1979).   *Building Construction in Meiji Japan* (Kaihatsu Koho, February 1979) in Japanese

The John Milne slide collection

Notes to plates featured between pages 104 and 105
by Susumu Takiguchi

1. Sumo wrestlers practising

Sumo was made a national sport of Japan towards the end of the Meiji period. Yet the history of *sumo* goes back to earliest times. For example, it is said that Buddha was rewarded with a princess for winning a *sumo* championship when he was young. The sanskrit word *godabara*, meaning wrestling, was translated by an Indian translator into Chinese which was then introduced to Japan via China.

The two Chinese characters used to describe wrestling and pronounced *sumo* in Japan was readily connected with a Japanese native word *sumau* which means to struggle or quarrel. However, the kind of wrestling associated with *sumo* had been practised in Japan from ancient times. In the *Kojiki* it is recorded that two deities, Take-mikazuchi-no-mikoto and Take-minakata-no-kami challenged each other to a *sumo* wrestling match to determine which of the two should rule Japan.

The first historical record of *sumo* appears in 642 when the Japanese court entertained Korean diplomats by showing them *sumo* wrestling performed by the *Kondei* (guards) of the court. At one point the Meiji Government virtually banned *sumo* on account of what they thought to be the barbaric nature of the sport, but after the victory of Japan in the Sino-Japanese and Russo-Japanese wars *sumo* started to be strongly encouraged to enhance national prestige and patriotism.

2. A scene in Asakusa, Tokyo

Asakusa is a region in the south-east of Tokyo along the Sumida River. It was one of 35 wards of old Tokyo city until it was amalgamated with Shitaya to form the present Taito-ku in 1947. In the eastern part runs the Sumida River featuring such famous bridges as Kototoi, Azuma, Komagata and Kuramae Bashi, while in the western part it is connected with Ueno region. After the great fire of 1657, Yoshiwara, the famous entertainment district, was moved from Nihonbashi Ningyo-cho to Asakusa, bringing prosperity as well as gaiety. Senso-ji, a well-known temple, is situated in the heart of Asakusa (burnt down in 1945) and around it are places of interest, theatres of Edo-shibai, comedies, strip-tease and a whole variety of entertainment.

The picture seems to be Asakusa-koen (park). The attractive banners are advertising various actors and plays of the time. There is also a tower in the distance that is called Ryounkaku, a twelve-storey brick building about 50 metres high. The crowd wear traditional Japanese kimono and sport western umbrellas, showing the quickening pace of westernisation — even in areas such as this bastion of traditionalism.

3. Street scene with carts and rickshaws

One might have thought this is a photograph of Nihon-bashi, had the bridge been slightly arched instead of straight. The onion-shaped *Giboshu* (the knobs on top of the bridge posts) are typical of old bridges in Japan.

The first rickshaw business was started in Meiji 2, or 1869, in the Nihonbashi district of Tokyo. This mode of travel caught people's imagination and flourished to such an extent that within two years the number of rickshaws in operation in Tokyo alone reached 25,000. From about 1874 Japan exported rickshaws to Shanghai, Hong Kong, Singapore, India and elsewhere. In Japan today they have been completely superseded by tramcars and cars. In 1875 the number of rickshaws in the whole of Japan reached 110,000 and the traditional transport method, *Kago* (palanquins), had vanished from Japanese streets.

4. Carpenters at work

Japanese carpentry is not so different from the English counterpart in principle, except for things like saws which should be pulled to saw rather than pushed, and planes which should be drawn towards the worker rather than pushed away. An admirer of Hokusai's prints will recognise the tool which the man on the right is using to hack a piece of timber. The meticulous nature of the Japanese is suited to fine cabinet-making and carpentry — fully exploiting the timber which is one of Japan's few natural resources.

5. Early Meiji railway station

This is an extraordinary mixed scene of the old and new in modern Japan. Against the background of what to most Japanese then must have been a majestic western-style station building can be seen a rickshaw (leaving the station without his passenger seems to indicate that he was paid to do so by the photographer), then a man carrying two buckets (possibily of human manure) and a gentleman traveller wearing white summer kimono and straw hat and carrying a *Yagagi-goori* (wickerwork basket), plus a number of people with umbrellas — the symbol of civilisation.

The first train in Japan was called Benkei-go, which started its service between Shinbashi and Yokohama in Meiji 5, or 1872. Two years later the line between Osaka and Kobe was opened. The station building in the picture may well be that of Yokohama Station, although it looks very much like Shinbashi Station which has three storeys instead of the two in the picture.

Trains and railway systems had become known to the Japanese before this date through John Manjiro, who disseminated the idea of railways for the first time in Japan, an.¹ tʰᵣough the writings of Fukuzawa Yukichi in his popular book *Seiyo-jijo* ('Things Western'). The fund to construct the first Japanese railway was raised through bonds floated in the United Kingdom, and the actual construction was supervised by British engineers using British machinery and materials.

6. Terraced dwellings

Eighty per cent of the Japanese land mass is mountainous which means that the majority of the population is confined to the remaining 20 per cent of the land including hilly slopes such as the one shown in this photograph. Horses and donkeys had long been the only means of transportation except of course on foot. Since John Milne spent so much of his time in Hokkaido, it is quite probably from that region — the deep gulleys running along the sides of the houses being designed to cope with heavy snowfalls.

7. Ainu village scene

Thought to be members of an aboriginal race of northern Japan, Ainu still pose a number of important questions to be solved for anthropologists and archaeologists, such as how widespread they originally were in the early centuries of Japanese history, how and when they were driven towards the northern regions of Japan, and what race they are ethnically connected with.

Ainu means 'man' in their language which has no writing system. During the Meiji period the Japanese language with its writing system was introduced to the Ainu, which ultimately led to the extinction of the Ainu language.

Not only their language but their existence itself has been at peril in modern times. In the early nineteenth century the Ainu population was about 21,000 which was reduced to about 16,000 in the following fifty years, mainly because of epidemic diseases brought to them by the Japanese. Inter-marriage with the Japanese has drastically decreased the number of Ainu who retain ethnic purity, and it is said that today only a small number of 'pure' Ainu live in a protected area of Hokkaido.

Before Meiji, the Ainu were constantly attacked by the Japanese and gradually driven to the north. They were called *emishi* or *ezo* (northern barbarians) and treated as such until the Meiji Government began to protect them, treating them as *heimin*, or commoners. They were given land and education, and intermarriage with the Japanese was strongly encouraged. During this period of assimilation Ainu began to develop agriculture and leave aside their traditional activities of hunting and gathering. This is reflected even in their attire in that they had given up the traditional clothing made of fur and materials derived from birds and fish which made them look very distinct. Instead they began to wear cotton clothing. Embroidery, symbolic of the Ainu, can be seen on the garments worn by the two women in the picture. The picture also shows the kind of change that was taking place in Ainu life during this period. Compare the features of the traditional Ainu thatched roofs, in the foreground, to the single large rectangular room which was the entire house — an import from the south — in the middle of the picture.